RURAL DEVELOPMENT IN IRELAND

# Rural Development in Ireland

## A challenge for the 1990s



*Edited by*

MICHAEL MURRAY
*Department of Applied Economics and Human Resource Management*
*University of Ulster at Jordanstown*

JOHN GREER
*Department of Architecture and Planning*
*The Queen's University of Belfast*

Avebury

Aldershot · Brookfield USA · Hong Kong · Singapore · Sydney

Published by
Avebury
Ashgate Publishing Limited
Gower House
Croft Road
Aldershot
Hants GU11 3HR
England

Ashgate Publishing Company
Old Post Road
Brookfield
Vermont 05036
USA

**British Library Cataloguing in Publication Data**

Rural Development in Ireland: Challenge for the 1990s
I. Murray, Michael R. II. Greer, John V.
307.7209415

ISBN 1 85628 408 5

Typeset by
Ronan Press
William Street
Lurgan BT66 6JA
Co. Armagh
Northern Ireland

Printed and Bound in Great Britain by
Athenaeum Press Ltd, Newcastle upon Tyne.

# Contents

# Contributors

Leslie Caul is Principal Lecturer in Education, Stranmillis College, Belfast, Northern Ireland.

Susan Chilton is Research Associate, Department of Agriculture and Food Economics, The Queeen's University of Belfast, Northern Ireland.

Patrick Commins is Acting Head, Rural Economy Research Centre, Agriculture and Food Development Authority (Teagasc), Dublin, Ireland.

Mark Conway is Business Manager, Area Mental Health Unit, Western Health and Social Services Board, Northern Ireland and Chairman of Rural Community Network (Northern Ireland).

Nigel Curry is Professor of Countryside Planning, Cheltenham and Gloucester College of Higher Education, England.

John Greer is Senior Lecturer, Department of Architecture and Planning, The Queen's University of Belfast, Northern Ireland.

Mark Hart is Senior Lecturer, Department of Applied Economics and Human Resource Management, University of Ulster at Jordanstown, Northern Ireland.

Michael Keane is College Lecturer, Department of Economics, University College Galway, Ireland.

Aideen McGinley is Director of Development, Fermanagh District Council, Northern Ireland.

John McPeake is Head of the Northern Ireland Housing Executive's Research Unit and is Visiting Research Fellow in housing at the University of Ulster, Northern Ireland.

Kay Milton is Lecturer, Department of Social Anthropology, The Queen's University of Belfast, Northern Ireland.

Joan Moss is Senior Agricultural Economist, Department of Agriculture and Food Economics, The Queen's University of Belfast, Northern Ireland.

Michael Murray is Lecturer, Department of Applied Economics and Human Resource Management, University of Ulster at Jordanstown, Northern Ireland.

Brendan Murtagh works in the Public Sector Divison of Price Waterhouse, Belfast. He was formerly Lecturer in the Department of Public Administration and Legal Studies, University of Ulster at Jordanstown, Northern Ireland.

Áine Ní Dhubháin is Research Associate, Department of Agribusiness, Extension and Rural Development, University College Dublin, Ireland.

Eoin O'Malley is Senior Research Officer, The Economic and Social Research Institute, Dublin, Ireland.

Vincent Reynolds is Cavan County Development Officer, Ireland.

# Preface

This book reports on rural development matters in both Northern Ireland and the Republic of Ireland. A number of chapters derive from presentations made to the Annual Conference of the Irish Planning Institute in 1992. These have been revised for publication and have been augmented by a suite of specially commissioned papers. Our thanks are extended to all contributors for their willing participation in this venture. We are grateful to Josephine Gooderham of Avebury for her interest in this book. Our special thanks go to Elizabeth Jess for her efficient word processing and to Ian Alexander for his cartography. We also wish to acknowledge the support of the Department of Architecture and Planning, Queen's University, Belfast and the Department of Applied Economics and Human Resource Management, University of Ulster at Jordanstown in producing this edited book.

# Section 1
# POLICY OVERVIEW

# 1 Rural Ireland - Personality and policy context

*John Greer and Michael Murray*

## Introduction

The personality of rural Ireland has generated an extensive literature drawn from an amalgam of specializations which as Boylan (1991) notes includes rural geography, rural sociology and rural economics. In Ireland the tradition of the base-line rural survey (Mogey 1947, Newman 1964) has commanded reverence. However, such surveys have almost invariably remained as isolated icons, giving insights into rural life at a particular point in time but without follow up so as to explore the dynamics of change or, more importantly, the causes of such change as informed by a wider socio-political analysis. The quality of individual contributions to the understanding of rural society in Ireland (Evans 1957, 1981, Arensberg and Kimball 1940, Hannon 1970, Brody 1970) has been such that their pre-occupation with description rather than prescription tends to be overlooked. As a result an idealised view of rural Ireland was created, very much in accord with that as summarized in the case of Britain by Palmer et al (1977) as:

> a place to preserve rather than to change, a place to visit rather than to live, a place of sentiment rather than a place of work (p.739).

These are precisely the views which have dominated economic and physical pla nning in Ireland; the rural areas are perceived largely as scenic backdrops to the drama of urban based investment in infrastructure, industry and services. This approach was massively reinforced until recently by the overriding pre-occupation with agricultural issues within the rural realm, and their isolation from non-agricultural concerns. The correlation of the "rural" with agriculture, specifically agricultural production and allied factors such as chemical/mechanical advances in the pursuit of efficiency, relegated other dimensions of the wider rural economy to the sidelines of inquiry and policy formation. Today rural industrialisation struggles to shed its craft image, rural tourism remains folksy in appeal, while housing and service provision, together with infrastructure have yet to overcome many of the more abrasive interpretations of the friction of distance.

An increasing volume of writing, primarily from the Republic of Ireland, has assisted with the challenge of changing these perceptions of the rural condition (e.g. Commins et al 1978, Bohan 1979, Armstrong et al 1980, McDyer 1982, Caldwell and Greer 1984, Breathnach and Cawley 1986, Healy 1988, Varley et al 1991). A common feature of all these contributions is recognition of the crucial importance of rural development to the future wellbeing of rural life in Ireland. This book seeks to reinforce that view.

The purpose of this chapter is to provide an overall context for the papers which follow. Accordingly the next section considers some of the important changes that have taken place over the past 30 years in Ireland, and the implications for rural areas are identified. One response to the ongoing transformation of rural society in advanced capitalist economies is the support now given to rural development measures. Hence, the chapter goes on to trace the emergence of the rural development approach and its transference from Third World countries to Western Europe by the European Commission. The thrust of rural development in Ireland is then introduced and the content of other chapters briefly reviewed by way of conclusion.

## Changing Ireland

The European Commission (1991) has reconfirmed that on a range of economic indices both the Republic of Ireland and Northern Ireland remain most seriously disadvantaged. An analysis of 171 Level 2 regions within the Community found them respectively to have the 14th and 16th highest unemployment rates for the period 1988-1990. In both territories per capita GDP remains significantly less than the Community average. A growing labour force in a combined population of just over 5 million continues to depend on emigration for job opportunity. The the island of Ireland is located not only on the economic periphery of Europe but also on the geographical margin. It suffers from the double disadvantage of distance from major markets and isolation by sea, the associated effects of which can be expressed in terms of higher transport costs for local business, additional organisational and administrative costs and potential production dislocation (Keeble et al 1982, 1988, Peida 1984). Yet it is the European dimension which increasingly shapes the economic environment of Ireland. The passage of the

Single European Act in 1986 and the adoption of measures towards closer market integration have added to the urgency of structural adjustment. In this context Ireland as a whole enjoys Objective One status for the reformed operation of the Community Structural Funds, while the Maastricht Treaty holds out the promise of additional transfers to the Republic of Ireland from a newly established Cohesion Fund. But the extent to which this intervention is capable of countering any tendency towards over-concentration of capital in the core regions of Europe remains uncertain.

The context of change in Ireland may be more closely considered under 3 broad themes: agricultural restructuring, industrialisation, economic development and physical planning.

*(1) Agricultural restructuring*

A basic division of problem regions within the European Community into agricultural and industrial has placed the Republic of Ireland and Northern Ireland in the former category (Klein 1981). The prosperity of the agricultural sector has long had a major bearing on the prosperity of the economies of Ireland, not least because of the role of agriculture related industries. Thus within Northern Ireland primary agriculture production accounts for 4 per cent of GDP and 7 per cent of civil employment making the industry three times as important as in the United Kingdom overall. When the agri-business sector is viewed as a whole the estimated shares of GDP and employment rise to 7 per cent and 10 per cent respectively (Department of Agriculture for Northern Ireland 1992). Within the Republic of Ireland the economic contribution of agriculture is even more marked; during the 1980s it was accounting for some 11 per cent of GDP and 15 per cent of total employment (Brunt 1988). In both jurisdictions production agriculture is essentially similar, comprising livestock husbandry in medium and small owner occupied farms in the main. As noted by Gillmor (1989) this resemblance is to be expected given a shared island location, a largely common land heritage and similar physical conditions.

During recent decades the restructuring of agriculture is evident in increased use of technology, the replacement of labour by capital, specialisation in production, the enlargement of the scale of production units, and the concentration of production on larger farms and in particular regions (Walsh 1991, 1992). With the long term tendency for the cost of purchased inputs to rise more rapidly than product prices there has been a sustained downward pressure on farm incomes. Significant inequalities have emerged between farmers and farming regions so that many farm households have become marginalised rather than modernised (Kelleher and O'Mahony 1984, Walsh 1986). The behaviourial responses of farmers in Ireland have varied from becoming even more commercialised in conventional agriculture to opting for part-time farming. Thus in Northern Ireland some 17 per cent of farmers under the age of 65 are engaged in other gainful activity (Moss et al 1991); in the Republic of Ireland income from farming is not the main source of livelihood in 42 per cent of households where the head of household has farming as a principal occupation. Latterly farmers under pressure from reform of the Common Agricultural Policy have been urged to diversify into non conventional forms of production, though research in Northern Ireland (Magee 1990) points to little enthusiasm for this option; only 8 per cent of farms are engaged in some form of alternative enterprise. In short the agricultural imperative is becoming that of sustaining incomes and retaining a presence on the land. The difficulties created by these restructuring tendencies are most directly experienced in the less favoured areas of Ireland which extend over more than 60 per cent of the land area.

At a wider level farming has increasingly become incorporated into transnational food chains through the globalisation of agribusiness both in sourcing inputs and marketing outputs. A much greater emphasis on quality food production has put pressure on farmers to invest in upgraded production facilities. The net result of this change has been keenly felt in the food and drink industries within which employment has fallen markedly in an effort to facilitate competitive processing in an international market. In the Republic of Ireland the number of dairy cooperatives, for example, declined over the period 1973-1990 as small farmer owned enterprises were absorbed by large integrated companies (Agriculture and Food Policy Review Group 1990). In Northern Ireland about a quarter of total milk output is now under the control of one operator. It may well be the case that even greater increases in scale are necessary to maintain European competitiveness in milk assembly and processing costs (Northern Ireland Economic Council 1992a).

### *(2) Industrialisation*

The dominant agricultural personality of Ireland serves to mask other significant internal characteristics. Industrialisation has long been a feature of economic development policy and over the period since the 1960s state sponsored multinational investment has formed an important element of government economic strategy in both Northern Ireland and the Republic. Research by Harrison (1986) has demonstrated that between 1946 and 1970 over 110,000 manufacturing jobs were promoted in Northern Ireland with just over 50 per cent of these falling into the category of new inward investment. But problems of large scale labour shedding in the traditional industries of shipbuilding, engineering and textiles did considerably offset this success. By 1960 in the Republic of Ireland new outward-oriented policies of attracting foreign enterprise and producing for the export market had replaced an earlier preference for trade protection and a dependency on indigenous industry. This resulted in an immediate improvement in economic performance with GDP increasing at an annual rate of 4.4 per cent over the period 1960-1973 (Kennedy et al 1988). The effect on the labour force was dramatic in that the decline of some 200,000 in the number at work in the previous decade was replaced by an increase of just over 30,000 between 1961 and 1971.

During the late 1970s and 1980s high rates of new inward investment proved difficult to maintain though there was some difference in the experience of Northern Ireland and the Republic of Ireland in this regard. Over the period 1973 - 1990 there was an increase from 31 per cent to 45 per cent in the proportion of industrial employment accounted for by externally owned companies in the Republic of Ireland. As noted by the Northern Ireland Economic Council (1992b) this contrasts with a falling dependence on employment in externally owned plants in Northern Ireland from 53 per cent in 1973 to 39 per cent by 1990. The international impact of the "Troubles" in Northern Ireland would seem to account for this poor performance. But also significant has been global economic stagnation and the restructuring of the capitalist space economy. Previously dominant industries, technologies, production methods and skills were being increasingly superseded by alternative systems (Martin 1989). These new arrangements involved greater mobility of different components of capital in search of more profitable sites and inevitably in Ireland the implications of these restructuring processes lay in the vulnerability of a small island economy to international movements of investment. In Ireland throughout most of the 1980s there were significant losses in overseas industry employment as some plants were either closed as part of international rationalisation programmes by their parent corporations or subjected to automation. In this context, for example, it would now be difficult for the Republic of Ireland to replicate its policy from the early 1970s of rural industrialisation on a comparable scale.

Government has responded to these shifts with reviews of industrial policy. In the Republic of Ireland several weaknesses were identified including the degree of dependence on foreign controlled firms, the low skill content of much of the employment, the high cost and short duration of much of the assisted employment, the low level of commitment to research and development, the very limited amount of independent marketing capacity, the poor performance of the indigenous sector and the limited linkages with the rest of the economy (National Economic and Social Council 1982). A corresponding assessment of the need for structural change was undertaken within Northern Ireland (Department of Economic Development 1987). The key problems in the face of the difficulties of maintaining an inward investment strategy were identified as the lack of an entrepreneurial culture, an overdependence on external funds, the predominance of service sector activity and in particular a disproportionately large public sector based service economy. Key proposals included the stimulation of a more positive local attitude to enterprise, changing attitudes to competitiveness, encouraging export activity, exploiting the strengths of the public sector and the better targeting of public funds. While the Pathfinder process, as it was known, generated a measure of debate on its vision and prescription (see for example Teague 1989a, 1989b, Hitchins and Birnie 1989), the fact remains that with the unemployment rate at that time running at about 18 per cent (comparable with the Republic of Ireland) it represented an important milestone in establishing the direction of economic development policy for the 1990s. Indigenous enterprise creation in rural areas now commands a high profile as part of this policy restructuring process.

### *(3) Economic development and physical planning*

The outward oriented economic policies pursued in Ireland during the 1960s were paralleled by an intense interest in the contribution which physical planning could make to modernisation. Within Northern Ireland the Belfast Regional Survey and Plan in 1963 advanced a strategy of demagnetizing the Belfast Urban Area while simultaneously expanding several of the larger towns within the immediate sphere of influence of the city. These de facto growth centres were not only to receive population from Belfast but also to act as holding points for people migrating from the rural heartland of Northern Ireland in search of jobs and houses. The distinct urban bias of physical and economic planning at that time was echoed in the Republic of Ireland with the preparation of a national/regional planning strategy by Colin Buchanan and Partners. This report, published in 1968, proposed that regional planning policy should be based on a hierarchy of growth centres involving, in addition to Dublin, two national and six regional centres. Essentially this prescription sought to inform local physical planning, while at the same time matching efficiency with equity in the distribution of economic opportunity.

However, political considerations played a major part in modifying these blueprints. In Northern Ireland the number of selected growth centres was repeatedly increased by the 1970-1975 Development Programme and the 1975-1995 Regional Physical Development Strategy. This reflected a somewhat belated recognition of the important economic and social role played by more peripheral parts of the region. Within the Republic of Ireland the abandonment of the concept of promoting growth in a small number of centres was underscored by manufacturing employment targets set in 1972 by the Industrial Development Authority for some 137 towns. This action effectively sounded the deathknell for the Government's brief flirtation with regionalism (Breathnach 1982). The mid 1970s recession further diverted interest from regional issues to national concerns, while membership of the European Community created the imperative of having the Republic of Ireland declared a single region for drawing down resources from the European Regional Development Fund. As noted by Bannon (1989) the emphasis was to shift from internal regional disparities to a priority on bringing the Republic of Ireland as a whole into line with the rest of Europe.

The 1980s, in contrast, have evidenced a profound change of emphasis to more local levels of concern. Ireland is marked by highly centralized public administration systems and under their auspices initiatives have been promulgated by each government, occasionally in partnership with the European Commission, which can appropriately be dubbed central government localism (after Martin 1989). In Northern Ireland the implementation of an Integrated Operations Programme for the Belfast Urban Area, a Making Belfast Work Programme, the designation of Enterprise Zones, and the regeneration of Belfast's waterfront by Laganside Development Corporation have been matched by a number of Designated Area revitalization schemes in key cities and towns within the Republic of Ireland. The operational hallmarks of this planning style are marketing, negotiation and leverage in order to capture ever greater private sector investment within these urban cores. This mode of intervention on a local scale continues to embed itself ever more deeply in urban and rural Ireland during the 1990s and is helping to forge new relationships between place, society and economy whose characteristics include forceful expressions of rooted identify, self help, voluntarism, networking and partnership.

To conclude this review of some regional and local dimensions of economic restructuring during the past three decades in Ireland, it would seem that the dominant large scale development paradigm conceived and directed by central government has begun to break down. A great diversity of macro and micro level factors has successively adjusted this top down focus. In so far as the future of rural areas is concerned it is Integrated Rural Development that is increasingly being looked to by policy makers and local communities as a vital way of responding to change.

## The emergence of Integrated Rural Development

Integrated Rural Development is a phrase of powerful currency which trips easily off the tongues of politicians, policy makers and academics alike. The term originates in Third World countries (Greer 1984), where an earlier emphasis on comprehensive agricultural reform was replaced during the 1970s by a much broader suite of policies. These were designed to address problems of unemployment and underemployment, lack of productivity in the agricultural sector, high levels of rural to urban migration, a constricted internal market, high population growth rates, large foreign trade deficits and shortages of staple foodstuffs (Grindle 1981). Integrated Rural Development lays claim to a plethora of characteristics and objectives (cf. e.g. Khan 1977, Leupolt 1977, Dawson 1978, Wulf 1978, Basler 1979, Ruthenberg 1981) but experience within developing countries would suggest the following main tenets:

(1) a multi-sectoral approach to development. While improvements in agricultural performance and structures are crucial elements in addressing the problems of disadvantaged rural communities, measures to promote other sectors of the economy to supplement or to provide alternatives to incomes from farming are fundamental to the process of improving the standards of living in such areas;

(2) economic measures to be parallelled by initiatives in education, training and physical infrastructure investment;

(3) an attempt to concentrate effort on aiding poor areas and more specifically poor people living in such areas. As a corollary development inputs have to be matched with the specific needs and aspirations of the target groups to which Integrated Rural Development programmes are addressed;

(4) a requirement that local people become actively involved, not only in identifying needs and opportunities for development, but also in the implementation of projects;

(5) a demand for institutional reform, expressed mainly as the devolution of powers from the national to regional and local levels of administration.

These policy goals represent a major challenge to the longstanding orthodoxy of single sector strategies for economic growth. As Basler (1979) has succinctly suggested, Integrated Rural Development is a new approach which is unmistakably targeted on regional development, a view echoed by the President of the European Commission:

> Rural development is a collective good which is fundamentally linked to regional planning. It requires a new approach, a departure from present-day thinking. In clear terms, rural development cannot be left solely to market forces because the market is incapable of providing the requisite guidance (Delors 1990, p.7).

Integrated Rural Development is interventionist and seeks to bring benefits to rural areas by placing emphasis on assisting low income groups or those who have been passed by in the growth process (Yudelman 1979). "Integrated" is the potent adjective in this search for change. Thus agricultural development is to be integrated with other sectors to increase incomes and create employment opportunities. Social development is to be integrated with economic development to increase the attraction of rural areas and to lessen out-migration. Policies are to be integrated to realise the aspirations of local communities and finally the local scale or bottom-up approach to development is to be integrated with the national level or top-down perspective (McNab 1984).

## Rural development and the European Community

The adoption of the term "integrated development" into the vocabulary of the European Commission may be traced to the late 1970s and has been attributed by Van Der Plas (1985) to the influence of expatriate experts returning from working on large scale development projects in the Third World. The concept was taken up jointly by the directorate-general dealing with agriculture (DGVI) and the directorate-general responsible for regional policy (DGXVI) with each launching its own set of initiatives. In the case of DGVI these included the commencing in 1981 of integrated development programmes for the Western Isles of Scotland, the Department of Lozere in France, and South East Belgium. At the same time twelve major research studies were commissioned into aspects of Integrated Rural Development.

However the contribution made by external influences to the adoption of the integrated approach to rural development has been questioned. Boylan (1988), for example, places more weight on practical organisational problems and issues of political expediency within the European Commission. Three main and related matters are cited:

(1) considerable overlap and duplication in the financing of projects under the European Agricultural Guidance and Guarantee Fund and the European Regional Development Fund;

(2) less than perfect visibility in regard to the impact of Community funds in the less developed regions;

(3) dissatisfaction with the operation of the Common Agricultural Policy and the imperative of reorganising its funding in order to achieve progress in the less developed regions of the Community.

The emergence of a rural development emphasis ought to be located therefore within this much wider context of the need for structural change. Indeed in its evaluation of the integrated approach to Community financing of measures related *inter alia* to the development programmes for the Western Isles, Lozere and South East Belgium the Court of Auditors (1988) reported a series of disappointing conclusions in regard to administrative and financial management procedures. These early initiatives were of course experimental and during the interim rural development has become a priority policy area within the Commission (MacSharry 1990). A number of reasons can be identified:

(1) the enlargement of the Community has contributed to greater disparities in income and employment opportunities between regions (Kowalski 1989);

(2) the passage of the Single European Act in 1986 and the adoption of measures towards closer market integration have added impetus to the urgency of structural adjustment in peripheral rural areas;

(3) the search for a fundamental reform of the Common Agricultural Policy linked to the future of trading relationships within the General Agreement on Tariffs and Trade has endorsed the need for a broader rural policy;

(4) a growing environmental consciousness and concern about the appearance and ecological quality of the countryside in the Community have made necessary management alliances between conservation and development.

Thus in 1988 the Commission published its document *The future of rural society* and agreed to reform the operation of its structural funds comprising the European Regional Development Fund (ERDF), the European Social Fund (ESF), and the guidance section of the European Agricultural Guidance and Guarantee Fund (EAGGF). Total resources have been increased from 7.7bn. ECUs in 1988 to 14.5bn. ECUs in 1993. Their allocation has been accompanied by a promise of much greater co-ordination than previously and a greater regional concentration with some 60 per cent being targeted on Objective 1 regions whose development is lagging behind. These cover 38 per cent of the Community, account for some 21 per cent of its population and are primarily rural in character. The areas comprise Greece, Portugal, a large part of Spain, Southern Italy, Corsica, the French Overseas Departments, the Republic of Ireland and Northern Ireland (Fig.1.1). The development of other rural areas in the Community amounting to a further 17 per cent of its territory and some 5 per cent of its population is also provided for under Objective 5b. In both types of region the envisaged financing of rural development programmes relates to:

(1) diversification of agricultural activity and the promotion of local products;

(2) encouragement of small and medium sized enterprises and the development of rural tourism;

(3) labour force training;

(4) infrastructure improvement;

(5) conservation of natural resources and the environment.

While the structural funds may well make a significant contribution to enhancing the economic competitiveness of peripheral rural regions, the modest percentage of Community gross domestic product which they account for has drawn criticism. Cuddy (1989) suggests that funds have only increased from 0.2 per cent of GDP in 1988 to 0.33 per cent of GDP in 1993 and that, if regional

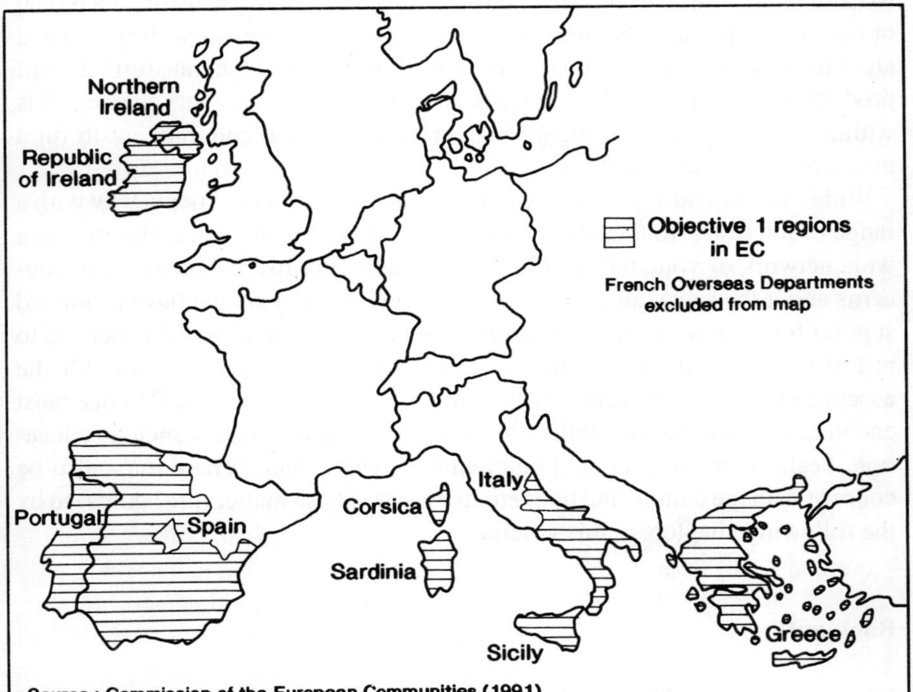


**Figure 1.1 Objective One regions in the European Community**

convergence is a real objective, the structural funds should be at least between two and four times what is presently planned. However, as further evidence of its declared commitment to Integrated Rural Development the Commission has launched a series of additional initiatives. These include programmes for transfrontier co-operation (INTERREG), community based economic development (LEADER), a network of rural information centres (MIRIAM), and the application of information and communication technology in rural areas (ORA). Again these hold out promise for enhanced development opportunity in peripheral rural regions in Ireland.

## Rural development and Ireland

Economic and social change within rural areas of Ireland may be viewed as but one element of a much wider process of restructuring within the island as a whole which in turn is conditioned by changing relationships in the international economy. Commins (1991) has cogently argued that many rural socioeconomic issues can no longer be usefully analysed separately from mainstream national or regional trends and that there are common sets of forces impacting on local areas in modern advanced economies. Key dimensions of the transformation of production, capital and labour have been identified earlier in this chapter. It is within this complexity of organising forces that a new commitment to rural development has emerged.

Within Ireland rural matters are enjoying an unprecedented popularity with a range of interests, from central government agencies and local authorities to a wide network of voluntary and local community groups. Contemporary concerns about the social and economic wellbeing of rural people have prompted support for a range of rural development initiatives. The aim of this book is to reflect the diversity of the rural development challenge and to argue for the acceptance of rural development as a policy area in its own right. Practice must encompass economic diversification and socio-cultural issues such as education, health care, housing and community involvement. There must also be concern with the natural and built environment. These matters are addressed by the following chapters in this volume.

## Book outline

Curry explores in Chapter 2 the historical context for rural planning and development within the British policy arena. The orthodoxies of policy are questioned and matters relevant for the future of rural society are identified. His analysis is profoundly important to the current debate about rural issues not just in Ireland but elsewhere in Europe. Particularly important are the themes of policy interdependence through multiple objectives, integration and community participation. These are developed in more detail by other contributors to this book and as such represent a recurrent benchmark for policy prescription. Chapter 3 by Commins and Chapter 4 by Murray and Greer offer an overview of rural development in the Republic of Ireland and Northern Ireland respectively. Each chapter traces the emergence of policy initiatives out of a mosaic of macro and local economic circumstances impacting on rural areas. An interesting contrast is that it is Northern Ireland with its urban policy tradition, and not the Republic of Ireland with its longstanding association with rural development, which has established an apparatus for rural policy delivery based on a partnership between public, private and voluntary interests.

Section Two of the book concerns itself with a review of sectoral issues related to the rural economy. In Chapter 5 Moss and Chilton report on the distinguishing characteristics of participating and non participating landholders in Northern Ireland's first Environmentally Sensitive Area Scheme. The discussion is timely given the importance now attached to sustainable agriculture by the European Commission and the imperative of bringing concern for the environment back into the rural development process. Chapter 6 by Ní Dhubháin examines the prospects for rural employment from forestry. Traditionally a state activity, forestry is now attracting a greater number of private landowners on either an individual or a co-operative basis. In Chapter 7 Hart considers the prospects for rural revitalisation as a result of enterprise creation. His overview of the United Kingdom situation as a whole concludes that rural industry has expanded and will continue to expand faster than the national average. But in Northern Ireland it is clear that some evidence of potential enterprise growth is more than offset by the enormity of the unemployment challenge and the low employment base upon which that limited growth is occurring. The discussion of community business, in particular, provides a useful insight into the relevance of process related policy considerations in devising a response to the rural development challenge. Keane concludes this section in Chapter 8 by examining the proposition that rural tourism can act as a passport to development. It is argued that a community based framework comprising local co-ordination and participation offers the best prospect for tourism development in rural areas.

Section Three deals with a number of key social issues facing rural areas in Ireland and seeks to demonstrate that the rural development challenge is much more than solely the need for economic diversification. In Chapter 9 Milton traces the evolution and impact of physical planning policies in the Northern Ireland countryside. The tensions between landscape protection and development in the countryside are identified and the scope for future policy succession is considered. Chapter 10 by McPeake and Murtagh discusses the emergence of a public sector led housing policy for disadvantaged rural areas. The authors stress the need for an integrated approach by all those who have a role to play in rural society. This requires a working partnership between the statutory and voluntary sectors, the tailoring of housing provision to local needs and the participation of rural communities. The viability of the rural primary school is discussed by Caul in Chapter 11. At a time when governments in both Northern Ireland and the Republic of Ireland are driving forward with education reform, his analysis of spatial distribution, costs and curriculum offers an important contribution to this often emotive debate. Chapter 12 by Conway considers some of the main issues involved in developing a model for rural health care. The discussion is located within the wider restructuring of the National Health Service and by using a local case study related to mental health provision the author identifies a critical path for the delivery of rural specific health care.

The theme running through Section Four of the book is action and change. The particular focus is on the capacity of rural communities to engage with government at local, national and EC levels. The agenda, however, goes further than simply obtaining funds for rural development; a key goal is to establish a long term rural understanding and policy receptiveness. In Chapter 13 McGinley examines the supportive role of local government in meeting these challenges. Her analysis of the contribution of Fermanagh District Council provides a useful illustration of how to foster community involvement in strategic policy making. In Chapter 14 Reynolds describes the functions and impact of County Development Teams established in the more peripheral rural regions of the Republic of Ireland by central government. State intervention remains a pre-requisite for rural regeneration and in this chapter the author clearly demonstrates the value of an agency based approach which is both resourced for and resourceful in helping local people. Chapter 15 by O'Malley reports on the Pilot Programme for Integrated Rural Development which operated in the Republic of Ireland over the period 1988 to 1990. It attempted to mobilise local people to work for the economic, social and cultural betterment of their own area. The discussion sets out the approach taken by the programme to building community capacity for action and offers a preliminary assessment of outcomes. Finally, in Chapter 16 Murray and Greer review the prominent features of this contemporary phase of rural development in Ireland. Insights obtained from previous chapters are explicated and an agenda for the rural policy community is generated by way of conclusion.

**Acknowledgement**

The section in this chapter on Changing Ireland draws upon insights from P. Commins and J. Walsh.

**References**

Agriculture and Food Policy Review Group (1990) *Agriculture and food policy review*. Dublin.

Arensberg, C.M. and Kimball, S.T. (1940) *Family and community in Ireland*. Peter Smith, London.

Armstrong, J., McClelland, D. and O'Brien, T. (1980) *A policy for rural problem areas in Northern Ireland*. Working Research Paper Series, Volume V, No. 1, School of Applied Economics, Ulster Polytechnic.

Bannon, M. (1989) Development planning and the neglect of the critical regional dimension, in Bannon, M. (ed) *Planning - The Irish experience 1920 -1988*. Ch. 5, pp. 122-157, Wolfhound Press, Dublin.

Basler, A. (1979) The concept of Integrated Rural Development. *Intereconomics*, July/August, pp. 190-195.

Bohan, H. (1979) *Ireland green: social planning and rural development*. Veritas Publications, Dublin.

Boylan, T. (1988) *Integrated economic development: a critical perspective*. Paper presented at the Conference on Integrated Economic Development in the Border Areas of the North West, Regional Studies Association and Co-operation North, Enniskillen.

Boylan, T. (1991) *Paradigms in rural development: from critique to coherence?* Paper presented at the First International School of Rural Development, Galway.

Breathnach, P. (1982) The demise of growth-centre policy: the case of the Republic of Ireland, in Hudson, R. and Lewis, J. (eds) *Regional planning in Europe*, pp. 33-56, Pion, London.

Breathnach, P. and Cawley, M. (eds) (1986) *Change and development in rural Ireland*. Geographical Society of Ireland Special Publications No. 1, Maynooth.

Brody, J. (1974) *Inishkillane: change and decline in the West of Ireland*. Penguin, Hamondsworth.

Brunt, B. (1988) *The Republic of Ireland*. Paul Chapman Publishing Ltd., London.

Caldwell, J.H. and Greer, J.V. (1984) *Physical planning in rural areas of Northern Ireland*. Occasional papers in Planning No. 5, The Queen's University of Belfast.

Commins, P., Cox, P.G. and Curry, J. (1978) *Rural areas: change and development*. National Economic and Social Council No. 41, The Stationery Office, Dublin.
Commins, P. (1991) *Rural change and development in the Republic of Ireland: global forces and local responses.* Paper presented at the Annual Conference of the Sociological Association of Ireland, Termonfeckin.
Commission of the European Communities (1988) *The future of rural society.* Office for Official Publications of the EC, Luxembourg.
Commission of the European Communities (1991) *The regions in the 1990s.* Office for Official Publications of the EC, Luxembourg.
Court of Auditors (1988) *Special Report No. 2/88 on the integrated approach to Community financing of structural measures together with the Commission's replies.* Official Journal of the European Communities, No. C 188/1-21.
Cuddy, M. (1989) Irish economic development and the structural funds. *Pleanail*, Vol. 9, pp. 9-34.
Dawson, A. (1978) Suggestions for an approach to rural development by foreign aid programmes. *International Labour Review*, Vol. 117, No.4, pp. 391-404.
Delors, J. (1990) *Rural development and the Common Agricultural Policy.* Paper presented at the European Conference on Rural Society 5-7 November, Economic and Social Committee, Brussels.
Department of Agriculture for Northern Ireland (1992) *Annual report 1991/1992*. Belfast.
Department of Economic Development (1987) *The Pathfinder Initiative: an interim report*. HMSO, Belfast.
Evans, E.E. (1957) *Irish folk ways*. Routledge and Keegan Paul, London.
Evans, E.E. (1981) *The personality of Ireland: habitat, heritage and history.* Blackstaff Press, Belfast.
Gillmor, D. (1989) Agricultural development, in Carter, R.W.G. and Parker, A.J. (eds) *Ireland: contemporary perspectives on a land and its people*. Ch. 8, pp. 171-200, Routledge, London.
Greer, J.V. (1984) Integrated Rural Development: reflections on a magic phrase. *Pleanail*, Vol.1, No.4, pp. 10-15.
Grindle, M.S. (1981) Anticipating failure: the implementation of rural development programs. *Public Policy,* Vol. 29, No. 1, pp. 51-74.
Hannan, D. (1970) *Rural exodus*. Chapman, London.
Harrison, R.T. (1986). Industrial development policy and the restructuring of the Northern Ireland economy. *Environment and Planning*, Vol. 4, pp. 53-70.
Healy, J. (1988) *No one shouted stop!* The House of Healy, Achill.
Hitchins, D. and Birnie, J.E. (1989) Economic development in Northern Ireland: has Pathfinder lost its way? A reply. *Regional Studies*, Vol. 23, No. 5, pp. 477-483.

Keeble, D., Offord, J. and Walker, S. (1988) *Peripheral regions in a Community of twelve member states*. Commission of the European Communities, Brussels.

Keeble, D., Owens, P. and Thompson, C. (1982) *Centrality, peripherality and EEC regional development*. HMSO, London.

Kelleher, C. and O'Mahony, A. (1984) *Marginalisation in Irish agriculture*. An Foras Taluntais, Dublin.

Kennedy, K.A., Giblin, T. and McHugh, D. (1988) *The economic development of Ireland in the twentieth century.* Routledge, London.

Khan, A. (1977) Integrated Rural Development. *Philippine Journal of Public Administration*, Vol. 21, No. 1, pp. 20-34.

Klein, L. (1981) The European Community's regional policy. *Built Environment*, Vol. 7, Nos. 3/4.

Kowalski, L. (1989) Major current and future regional issues in the enlarged Community. In Albrechts, L. et al. (eds) *Regional policy at the crossroads - European perspectives*, Ch.6, pp. 90-106, Jessica Kingsley, London.

Leupolt, M. (1977) Integrated Rural Development: key elements of an integrated rural development strategy. *Sociologia Ruralis*, Vol.17, pp. 7-28.

MacSharry, R. (1990) Rural development: the challenge of the 1990s. *Business Outlook and Economic Review*, Vol. 5, No.2. pp. 10-15.

Magee, S.A.E. (1990) *Diversification in Northern Ireland farms 1989*. Studies in Agricultural and Food Economics, Department of Agriculture for Northern Ireland, Belfast.

Martin, R. (1989) The new economics and politics of regional restructuring: the British experience, in Albrechts, L. et al (eds) *op. cit.* Ch. 3, pp. 27-51, Jessica Kingsley Publishers, London.

McDyer, J. (1982) *Fr. McDyer of Glencolumbkille*. Brandon Book Publishers, Dingle.

McNab, A. (1984) *Integrated rural development in Britain*. Gloucester Papers in Local and Rural Planning, Issue No. 22, Cheltenham.

Mogey, J. (1947) *Rural life in Northern Ireland*. Oxford University Press, London.

Moss, J., McHenry, H., Cuskie, D.P., Markey, A.P., and Phelan, J.F. (1991) *Study of farm incomes in Northern Ireland and the Republic of Ireland*. Third Study Series: Report No. 1, Co-operation North, Belfast.

National Economic and Social Council (1982) *A review of industrial policy.* No. 64, Stationery Office, Dublin.

Newman, J.J. (1964) *The Limerick rural survey 1958-1964*. Muintir na Tire, Tipperary.

Northern Ireland Economic Council (1992a) *The food processing industry in Northern Ireland*. Report 92, Belfast.

Northern Ireland Economic Council (1992b) *Inward investment in Northern Ireland.* Report 99, Belfast.

Palmer, C.J., Robinson, M.E. and Thomas, R.W. (1977) The countryside image -an investigation of structure and meaning. *Environment and Planning A*, Vol. 9, pp. 739-750.

Peida (1984) *Transport costs in peripheral regions.* Report to the European Commission, Industry Department for Scotland and Department of Economic Development for Northern Ireland.

Ruthenberg, H. (1981) Is integrated rural development a suitable approach to attack rural poverty? *Quarterly Journal of International Agriculture*, Vol. 20, No.1, pp. 6-14.

Teague, P. (1989a) Economic development in Northern Ireland: has Pathfinder lost its way? *Regional Studies*, Vol. 23, No. 1, pp. 63-69.

Teague, P. (1989b) Pathfinder: a reply to Hitchins and Birnie. *Regional Studies*, Vol. 23, No. 5, pp. 483-485.

Van Der Plas, L. (1985) *Rural development and conservation: new approaches.* Seminar Report, Peak Park Study Centre, Rosehill.

Varley, T., Boylan, R. and Cuddy, M. (1991) *Rural crisis: perspectives on Irish rural development.* Centre for Development Studies, University College Galway.

Walsh, J.A. (1986) Uneven development of agriculture in Ireland. *Geographical Viewpoint*, Vol. 14, pp. 37-65.

Walsh, J.A. (1991) A regional analysis of enterprise substitution in Irish agriculture in the context of a changing Common Agriculture Policy. *Irish Geography*, Vol. 24, No. 1, pp 10-23.

Walsh, J.A. (1992) Adoption and diffusion processes in the mechanisation of Irish agriculture. *Irish Geography*, Vol. 25, No. 1, pp. 33-53.

Wulf, R. (1978) On the concept of integrated rural development. *Economics*, Vol.17, pp. 63-80.

Yudelman, M. (1976) *Integrated Rural Development projects: the Bank's experience.* XVI International Conference of Agricultural Economists, Vol. 26, No. 7, Nairobi.

# 2 Rural development in the 1990s - Does prospect lie in retrospect?

*Nigel Curry*

## Current policy problems for rural development

It is a commonly held view that the origin of rural development problems today can be traced back, in England and Wales at least, to the wartime reports of Scott (*Land utilisation in rural areas* - Ministry of Works and Planning, 1942) and Barlow (*Distribution of the industrial population, 1940*). In fact, their philosophies have become pervasive across Europe including Ireland, not least because of the sentiments of Scott being encapsulated in the Common Agricultural Policy.

In essence, Barlow called for comprehensive town and country planning controls in urban areas to steer development effectively, but because development should not be encouraged in rural areas, thought such controls were not necessary in the countryside. Scott complemented this view by proposing autonomous agriculture and forestry sectors in rural areas, where "every agricultural acre counts" and therefore a clear national need would have to be proven for any other form of development in the countryside. Because of their strategic importance, agriculture and forestry should be exempt from planning controls and should be developed through what have turned out to be much more powerful government economic incentives to ensure expansive and prosperous agriculture and forestry.

These sentiments were embodied in the 1947 Town and Country Planning Act, the 1947 Agriculture Act and the 1947 and 1949 Forestry Acts. The Acts provided the framework for the planning of rural development that still pertains today and introduced a number of characteristics that have burdened rural areas ever since. This overall framework comprised two almost entirely independent planning systems - for resources on the one hand and for town and country on the other - and the lack of any real relationship between the two lies at the centre of current rural development problems. Such a system was termed by Green in 1972 "twenty years of wasted opportunity in rural planning". In the 1990s this can safely be extended to over 40 years. Policy has been marked by four characteristics.

*(1) Town and country are seen as opposites*

The first characteristic of this overall planning framework that has burdened rural development for the past 40 years is that town and country planning are seen as opposites. Rural areas are to be conserved and urban areas exploited for development. The enduring effect of this has been that the "no development" ethic in the countryside has sustained a duality of rural poverty and urban affluence that remains a principal problem in the 1990s. Even in the early 1980s this was still the establishment view. The then Director of the Countryside Commission for England and Wales writing in the late 1970s (Hookway 1978) stated:

> planning the countryside is a matter of the conservation of natural resources. Planning our towns on the other hand is a matter of the development of land.

Ironically in the 1990s, the "no development" ethic in the countryside is actually thwarting the resource policy of farm diversification. Farmers seeking to develop new non-agricultural enterprises are invariably frustrated by restrictive planning policies all but prohibiting any industrial development outside of agriculture.

*(2) Resource planning is largely exempt from planning controls*

The second characteristic is that resource planning is largely exempt from planning controls. This has contributed as much as anything else to the despoilation of the environment of the countryside not only in respect of aggressively productive agriculture and forestry sectors that have mangled the open landscape through the removal of field boundaries and linear coniferous planting, but also in respect of the erection of large industrial farm and forestry buildings that show little regard to their setting in terms of either size or materials. Even with the passing of the 1968 Town and Country Planning Act in which structure and local plans were to cover the whole of the countryside and planning was to become less physically deterministic, the opportunity to extend planning controls over agriculture and forestry was ignored.

### *(3) Economic incentives are separated from physical controls*

The third characteristic is that resources have been planned with economic incentives, but development has been restricted by physical controls. Forty years of this duality now make it virtually impossible to rescind the lucrative economic incentives to agriculture and forestry even when environmental considerations form part of the resource planning agenda. Thus environmental planning in agriculture, for example through management agreements, Environmentally Sensitive Areas, Nitrate Sensitive Areas, Setaside and the Countryside Stewardship Scheme still takes place on the basis of economic incentives. For nearly all other sectors environmental considerations are controlled through regulatory mechanisms such as planning permissions, prohibitions and conditions invariably without compensation. Worse still, attempts to control the agricultural environment through economic means have met with limited success because overriding economic production incentives remain in place. Farmers rationally remain driven by production goals.

In the sphere of town and country planning, however, attempts by planners to grapple with control through economic mechanisms - such as obligations and agreements under the 1991 Planning and Compensation Act - have met with a barrage of criticism on such grounds as morality and accountability (Curry and Edwards 1991). This has ensured that planning developments determined through economic negotiation comprise less than 1 per cent of all planning applications (Roger Tym and Partners 1989).

This duality between economic and physical planning has led to a deep-seated antipathy between resource economists and planners which is difficult, but nevertheless essential, to overcome. Resource economists claim that planners have tended to consider economics outside their jurisdiction - "an anti-economic cult is worshipped with almost innate depravity by the planning profession" (Whitby and Willis 1978) and therefore the dominance of economically-determined policies in the countryside means that planners have little role to play in the totality of countryside planning. On the other hand, planners have suggested that economists have little concern for the objectives-based approach of planning evaluation and have little understanding of the spatial and aesthetic nature of planning (Healey 1990). As a consequence, she maintains, the economic basis of countryside planning has led to a situation little short of an environmental disaster in the countryside. This scepticism of one profession about the other has compounded the duality between resource economics and physical planning.

### *(4) Organisational structure and public accountability*

The final characteristic that has burdened rural development over the previous 40 years is the almost complete lack of co-ordination in the organisational structure of both resource planning and town and country planning and significant differences in public accountability. The resource sectors have been planned through a number of independent sectoral agencies organised horizontally with little publicly available strategic planning and certainly no public participation in the resource planning process. Town and country planning, on the other hand, has a more comprehensive framework, implemented through a vertical structure from Ministry through tiered local authorities to the parish. Development plans are subject to public consultation and development decisions are made by publicly elected representatives.

The lack of collaboration both within and between sectors has led to the development of policies with overlapping and often conflicting objectives. Further, it has led to not inconsiderable confusion over different responsibilities, at the margin, of different agencies. Thus, responsibility for the Farm Woodland Scheme rests with the Ministry of Agriculture and not the Forestry Commission. Despite English Nature and the Countryside Commission in England having the remits for nature and landscape conservation respectively, 60 per cent of all conservation expenditure in rural areas comes from the Forestry Commission and the Ministry of Agriculture (Hill et al 1989). Recreation, particularly walking in the countryside, is seen by the Countryside Commission as one of its principal responsibilities and yet the Sports Council claims that walking in the countryside is the most popular sport of all. Clearly this structure breeds organisational inefficiency as well as policy ineffectiveness.

## The need for rural policy reform

To compound these characteristics that have inhibited rural development over the past 40 years, as Newby (1991) notes, the 1947 legislation is now effectively redundant since not only have the 1947 Agriculture and Town and Country Planning Acts achieved their objectives in their own terms, but changes in the countryside of the 1990s are now rendering them counterproductive. The objective of the 1947 Agriculture Act was the production of more and cheaper food. This has now been achieved, but the policies that achieved it have overrun into the production of food surpluses, environmental deterioration and detrimental impacts on Third World economies. Clearly the purpose of this Act, which has remained the central thrust of all agriculture Acts since 1947, has run its course.

The planning legislation, too, has been remarkably successful at resisting development in the countryside - one of its principal purposes - to allow the countryside to remain unequivocally rural. In large part because of the success of this policy the countryside has remained an idyllic image for most people, causing it to be at a premium as a place to live or, where beyond commuting distance, to have a second home. As a result, most people now living in the countryside do not derive their living from agriculture, forestry or the other resource sectors. Thus, despite the undeniable success of planning policies in resisting development in the countryside it has become, by dint of social and economic aspiration, undeniably urban.

The inevitable conclusion from these characteristics and developments is that extant policies and legislation for rural development no longer have a relevant role in the future of the countryside, and a reformulation of policy processes, objectives and legislation is imperative. In looking towards the development of a new rural policy for the 1990s it is useful to consider a number of policy attributes. The first of these is a cautionary note on how policies might be developed - there are policy fallacies that should be avoided. Secondly, it is important to articulate the underlying objectives of any rural policy. Thirdly, the principal structural characteristics of any future rural policy should be summarised. Finally, it will be instructive to speculate on the central issues of concern for a rural policy for the 1990s.

## Three popular policy fallacies

### *(1) The fallacy of reversibility*

This fallacy states that if a policy is having a particularly adverse impact, then the opposite policy will have the opposite impact. This was a notorious mistake on the part of the Scott Committee (Ministry of Works and Planning 1942) which noted that a depressed agriculture of the 1920s and 1930s was leading to significant environmental deterioration in the countryside. This is well expressed in the preface to Thomas Sharp's (1931) book, *Town and countryside*:

> During the last 10 years many hundreds of angry letters relating the "desecration of the countryside" have appeared in various sections of the Press. One or two angry books and pamphlets also have been written. It is a question which causes anger - at times of a despairing kind - to all who have any feeling for the beauty of rural England.

Scott fell prey to the fallacy of reversibility by stating that if a depressed agriculture led to environmental deterioration (loss of amenity in his terms), then a prosperous agriculture would automatically lead to environmental enhancement. The environmental ravages of his post-war prosperous agriculture do not need to be articulated here. In parallel with Thomas Sharp, Marion Shoard (1980), writing at the peak of agricultural expansion, stated (in somewhat allegorical terms) in her preface to *The theft of the countryside*:

> The English landscape is a symphony whose unique sound depends on the harmonious orchestration of a wide range of instruments. It is the overall balance of features in our countryside that matters. But the best way of appreciating how agricultural change is turning harmony into discord is to anatomise its impact on each of the instruments which contribute to our rural symphony.

Clearly, agriculture was having a similar impact on the environment of the countryside in 1980 as it was in 1930 for precisely the opposite reasons.

*(2) The fallacy of creeping incrementalism*

This fallacy states that if a policy is apparently not achieving its objectives then adjusting it incrementally, rather than fundamentally reappraising its premise, will lead to the fulfilment of its objectives. Creeping incrementalism of this nature may be simply pushing the policy further down the wrong path. Setaside provides a good example of this.

Setaside was introduced in England and Wales in 1988, to encourage farmers, through financial incentives, to take arable land out of production. At the time it was estimated that somewhere in the region of 3 million hectares of land would have to be taken out of production to bring the supply of and demand for arable crops into balance (Blunden and Curry 1988). The terms of the scheme were complex, but in 1988 farmers were offered up to £200 per hectare to take a minimum of 20 per cent of their land out of production. By 1990, it was clear that nowhere nearly enough land was being taken out of production to fulfil the objective of significant reductions in arable output. Indeed many farmers were taking the least productive 20 per cent of their land out of production and increasing output on the remaining 80 per cent, leading to no overall output reductions at all on certain individual farms. In response, the 1990 Setaside scheme offered greater financial incentives (up to £222 per hectare) and greater flexibility (again within a complex set of arrangements) in the hope of encouraging greater take-up. At the same time, one of the unintended side effects of the 1988 scheme was the appearance of tracts of derelict scrubland-type farmland, and to address this problem, the Countryside Commission introduced a pilot

Setaside Top-up Scheme in East Anglia, to offer farmers a further £80 per hectare for undertaking positive conservation and recreation management within an agreed farm plan. Good money, perhaps, was beginning to chase bad.

By 1991, the Commission's Countryside Stewardship Scheme was introduced in parallel with Setaside, offering farmers £120 per hectare in exchange for farm plans that had clear conservation objectives for certain valued landscape types -a scheme which parallelled and perhaps had a confused relationship with Environmentally Sensitive Areas. By 1992, the Setaside scheme still had not made a significant dent in arable overproduction, and yet, it had become an integral part of the McSharry proposals for the reform of the Common Agricultural Policy. Fundamental to the lack of success of this policy is that its overall objectives have not been questioned seriously by the Ministry of Agriculture. Simply put, arable overproduction has been caused, not only by price supports but also by 40 years of the subsidisation of capital inputs to agriculture (for example through farm modernisation directives providing subsidies to machines, fertilisers and pesticides which has led to an industry that is vastly overcapitalised (Bowers and Cheshire 1983). It logically follows, therefore, that if arable output is to be significantly reduced it is capital and not land that should be taken out of agriculture. Setaside is attempting to remove precisely the wrong factor of production (Curry 1988).

### *(3) The fallacy that rural means agricultural*

This fallacy simply assumes that agricultural is synonymous with rural. It is encapsulated well in the Less Favoured Areas (LFA) Policy which is an agricultural policy that has as one of its principal objectives the stemming of rural depopulation. A study of the LFA in the Radnor district in Wales by Hearne (1985) identified a stable population and increasing employment opportunities, but these were attributable to a growth in manufacturing in the district and not due to LFA policy. He maintains that although LFA policy is intended to stem rural depopulation, the fact that it subsidises livestock (through headage payments) and not people means that LFA subsidies are very different in different LFAs, according to stocking densities. The less disadvantaged the area, the higher the stocking densities and therefore the greater the level of subsidy. Perversely, therefore, the policy is less likely to achieve its retaining the rural population objective, the less favoured the area it is applied to.

Further, despite the fact that on-farm employment made a very limited contribution to employment opportunities and therefore population retention in Radnor, agriculture was by far the main recipient of public funds. During 1981, 80 per cent of public expenditure in the district went to agriculture and only 14 per cent to manufacturing, 3 per cent to services, 2 per cent to social development and 1 per cent to environmental enhancement. From this study, Hearne was able to make a number of comments about the nature of policies for rural areas, and the relationship between their objectives:

> Neither their objectives nor their results are integrated into an overall package designed to achieve rural development. Such integration is vital if only to ensure cost effective expenditure between sectors in the rural economy. Yet whilst this study was in progress the Government was depriving Radnor of Assisted Area status whilst, at the same time through the marginal lands survey, seeking to expand the boundaries of the Less Favoured Area.

The fallacy informing the LFA policy is therefore clear - that supporting agricultural populations will not necessarily support rural populations. Indeed agricultural support through the LFA Directive can actually be damaging to rural populations as a second example illustrates when the rural policy objective of efficiency is considered below.

**Underlying objectives of rural policy for the 1990s**

A cautionary note having been expressed in general terms about how policies should not be developed, it is now useful to turn to the issue of what the generic objectives of a rural policy for the 1990s might be. It is proposed here that all rural policy developments into the 1990s should be measured against four principal criteria: equity, efficiency, environment and culture. These are in no particular order of importance although equity might be considered the most crucial.

*(1) Equity*

To include equity in policy objectives is an attempt to ensure a fair distribution of resources across the whole of the rural population. Currently in comprehensive rural development terms, this is not the case. A recent study by Hill et al (1989) clearly illustrates this. This project, funded, significantly, by both the Ministry of Agriculture (MAFF) and the Department of the Environment, examined the pattern of direct public support into rural areas and developed a framework for assessing its ability to meet the objectives set for it. Particular focus was placed on both policy efficiency and the conflict of objectives, together with gaps in current policy provision, and the assessment of alternative policies to deliver policy objectives more effectively.

The study developed a comprehensive taxonomy of support to embrace payments to producers, tax concessions, income transfers, payments to households, payments to public institutions for the provision of goods and services, payments to public institutions for the provision of advice and payments to public institutions for the provision of marketing. The activities of local government, and policies which were not specifically rural were excluded from the analysis, but despite this over 178 discrete policy programmes that targeted funds specifically for rural areas were identified and evaluated. A database of such support was developed and set against declared objectives. Significantly in the case of many areas of support, objectives were not clearly stated and therefore had to be interpreted by the research team. These objectives were found to bear little relation one with the other, a product of the lack of an integrated rural development policy in England and Wales.

The analysis of these support measures revealed that 70 per cent of total support for rural areas went into supporting agricultural prices. Farmers were the main intended beneficiaries of total support, absorbing 92 per cent of it. The objective of farm income support accounted for 80 per cent of all spending. Despite these intentions, 60 per cent of funds aimed at direct income support for farmers went to traders and processors and farmers received only 27 per cent directly. Of resources intended to improve business efficiency, 94 per cent went to farmers, coming mainly from MAFF and the Forestry Commission. Some 80 per cent of a much smaller sum aimed at employment creation came from the Rural Development Commission. Of conservation expenditure, the Countryside Commission and the Nature Conservancy Council together accounted for only 40 per cent, the majority again coming from MAFF and the forestry agencies. Farmers again received 56 per cent of the sums of money disposed to this objective.

Overall, the inventory indicated a dominant disposal of public funds to agriculture, despite the fact that this sector is not the prime mover in the achievement of public expenditure objectives, particularly in relation to employment, conservation and recreation goals. This supports Hearne's (1985) conclusions for Radnor. The study found that although 3.6 million people live in rural areas, fewer than 20 per cent of them work in agriculture even in a part-time capacity. Further, agriculture accounts for only 1.7 per cent of economic activity in rural areas across England and Wales and where regionally at its highest, in East Anglia, this is still only 6.3 per cent. With these small contributions of agriculture to economic activity in rural areas, the case for 92 per cent of all public support in rural areas going to farmers appears untenable on equity grounds. Clearly, the need to redress this kind of distributional imbalance of resources must be a cornerstone of rural policy for the 1990s.

### (2) *Efficiency*

The objective of efficiency can be a confusing one. Agriculture ministers claim their industries to be technically efficient in terms of outputs per unit of labour or outputs per hectare. In Britain and Europe, these are some of the highest in the world. But this hides a huge economic inefficiency where agriculture is producing way beyond optimum output levels in terms of total factor inputs, made possible only through huge levels of public subsidy. Clearly it is economic rather than technical efficiency that should be a policy objective for rural policy into the 1990s. Such an objective is not just pertinent to single sectors of the economy such as agriculture. The crucial challenge is to ensure economic efficiency across sectors since all too often individual sectoral policies pull in different directions. Indeed in Hill et al's (1989) study of alternative rural support systems, many instances of rural policy objectives either overlapping or working in diametric opposition were found. For the economically efficient allocation of resources across all rural sectors, policy objectives and expenditure must act in concert.

The economic inefficiency of overlapping and conflicting policy objectives is well illustrated by a study conducted by Slee (1981) which was concerned with an evaluation of agricultural policies on the one hand and planning policies on the other at both regional and local levels and to examine the compatibility of their impacts on the local economy. This was done for the county of Orkney in Scotland. As with Hearne's (1985) study, Slee initially concentrated on assessing the Less Favoured Areas Directive. He noted that, of itself, this policy was somewhat schizophrenic. On the one hand it had the objective of giving out social subsidies to farmers, through headage payments, to keep rural populations at socially desirable levels. On the other, its objectives embraced farm modernisation grants at higher levels than elsewhere which, because they chiefly subsidised capital inputs, were causing capital substitution and thus labour shedding, in the farm production process. Overarching this economic agricultural policy were the planning policies of the Highlands and Islands Development Board, the broad objectives of which were akin to the social goals of the LFA Directive. They were principally concerned with arresting rural depopulation. At the more local level, the Orkney structure plan saw the counteracting of population drift as one of its principal objectives.

Slee's evidence found that, on balance, expenditure on the LFA Directive (in excess of £3m in the county over a four year period) was leading to mechanisation of a small number of farms and a net effect of labour shedding rather than population retention across the whole of the agricultural labour force. At the same time as this element of public expenditure was causing the shedding of labour, the Highlands and Islands Development Board was providing loan finance, information, advisory services, and the Island Council infrastructure, with the essential purpose of creating employment. It was estimated that expenditure on these initiatives was to be in the region of £31m over a five year period, £700,000 of which was to be on one industrial estate. This expenditure was, of course, further exacerbating the labour shedding in agriculture, attracting workers out of this sector. Thus, one element of public expenditure, in agriculture, was actually creating a problem that another element, in factory and infrastructure provision, was trying to solve.

The Slee study points to the importance, then, of not only measuring policies against their objectives and assessing their internal efficiency, but also looking at the interaction of one set of policy objectives and actions with others, to evaluate the extent to which policies may be at cross purposes. A rural policy for the 1990s must seek to ensure the economic efficiency of public expenditure across the full range of policy objectives and instruments.

### *(3) Environment*

In addition to the social and economic objective of distributional equity, and the economic objective of efficiency, a third generic objective of rural policy in the 1990s must be to embrace environmental considerations. The assembly of a series of international conferences during the 1980s and 1990s leading to policy statements on global environmentalism such as the Montreal protocol on CFCs, the *World conservation strategy* (1980), the World Commission on Environment and Development (1987) report *Our common future* (the Bruntland Report), and the 1992 *Bio-diversity treaty* at the Earth Summit in Rio de Janeiro, together with domestic policies such as the United Kingdom Government's White Paper *This common inheritance* (Department of the Environment, 1990), is causing global environmental issues to become part of all public policy objectives. They too should be central to rural policies for both the physical and business environment.

As Turner (1988), cited in Gilg (1991), notes, these global considerations need not be part of a radical deep ecology but for operational policy purposes could simply comprise three conservation rules for sustainable growth:

(1) maintain the regenerative capacity of renewable resources and avoid excessive pollution;

(2) encourage technological research allowing a move from non-renewable to renewable resources;

(3) switch wherever possible in a phased way from non-renewable to renewable resources.

The preoccupation with global or sustainable environmental objectives for rural policy must, however, not be allowed to occlude environmental objectives closer to home. These used to be referred to as amenity objectives and are concerned with the maintenance of the countryside in terms of both its ecology and its landscape. It is the incorporation of these objectives into the reformulation of agricultural objectives that is likely to have just as significant an impact on the countryside as global objectives, into the 1990s.

*(4) Culture*

The final generic objective - preservation of culture - is one that is more commonly overlooked in rural development, particularly in Northern European countries. In the European Commission Integrated Rural Development Experiments of the early 1980s, funded by the Agriculture Directorate, there was an interesting dichotomy in the perception of culture between the northern and southern countries. Northern countries by and large saw, as a result of these experiments, Integrated Rural Development (IRD) essentially as a means of stimulating economic development. Southern countries on the other hand interpreted IRD as a means of cultural revival. It was a mechanism through which heritage (in terms of local buildings in their historic setting, customs and traditions) could be reinforced and the unique identity of localities (through the development of local products and the uniqueness of place) could be developed. The fact that the only clear policy to emerge from these experiments was the Integrated Mediterranean Programmes indicates the neglect of cultural preservation as a generic objective for rural development while in fact it should become a central plank of any rural policy for the 1990s.

## Principal structural characteristics of rural policy for the 1990s

If these generic objectives for rural policy for the 1990s can, in part at least, be accepted, then three structural characteristics of such a policy logically follow. The first of these, not surprisingly, is integration. The researches by Hill et al (1989), illustrative of inequity in rural policy, and Slee (1981), exemplifying inefficiency, both state that the core of the problems that they have uncovered is the failure to integrate sectoral policies in terms either of objectives or of public expenditure. Integration, too, will become central in overcoming the fallacy that rural means agricultural as the quotation from Hearne (1985) above, clearly illustrates. It is essential here not only to integrate policy objectives and expenditures but to begin to take down the dividing wall between resource economists and planners. The very systems of rural development that have been pervasive for the past 40 years must address this issue of integration.

The second characteristic is policy interdependence through multiple objectives. Since each of the generic objectives of a rural policy for the 1990s has a significance for all rural policy components it follows that policies should move away from singular objectives and embrace a wider range of considerations.

The final characteristic of a rural policy for the 1990s is that of community participation. Policies that are sensitive to local circumstances will not only be more effective in taking the uniqueness of local social structure, economy, environment and culture into account, but also, through the involvement of the local community, will be likely to be more successful in their implementation. Communities that have a say in the development of policies for their locality are much more likely to be enthusiastic about their implementation. Such participation will also do much to enhance the public accountability of policy implementation, the lack of which, particularly in the resource sectors, has become a hallmark of rural policies over the past 40 years.

In this respect, village appraisals as a policy tool have a useful role to play. They provide an opportunity for the community itself to select the issues that are locally important and to formulate proposals for change. Problems relating to the poor design and execution of appraisals have been ameliorated by the production of the *Village appraisals software* pack (Countryside and Community Research Unit 1991) which makes appraisals easier to execute, more effective and quicker (a very important characteristic in the light of many appraisals unfinished owing to dwindling community enthusiasm and stamina). In the piloting of the software in 30 parishes in Gloucestershire, response rates to village appraisals questionnaires ranged between 80 per cent and 95 per cent providing an unprecedentedly representative sample of views that would be impossible to achieve through district or county authority surveys. Such successes can only be beneficial to the pursuance of community participation.

## Central issues of rural policies for the 1990s

In some ways it is difficult to zero in on the central issues of concern for rural policies of the 1990s in the face of so many publications and ideas that have been generated in the late 1980s and early 1990s. Indeed as Gilg (1991) has shown, it would take a whole book to review them fully. In the final part of this chapter, therefore, two themes are presented. Firstly, the principal issues articulated by Newby (1991) are summarised as being representative of much of the current thinking about rural policy reform. Secondly, and possibly more significantly, these issues for the 1990s are compared with those articulated by Professor Dennison in his minority report to the Scott Committee on Land Utilisation in

Rural Areas (Ministry of Works and Planning, 1942) of August 1942. In undertaking this comparison, it is fascinating to speculate on what the state of rural development might be if Dennison's views had held sway, against the prevailing agricultural fundamentalism of Scott that was instrumental, as has been noted, in creating many of the principal problems of rural development that exist today. It is also important to note that the increasing consensus about what constitutes issues of central concern for rural policy in the 1990s is not new. It is a tribute to Dennison's vision that contemporary views are broadly identical to his perceptions of 50 years ago. It has taken 50 years of agricultural autonomy, and all of the problems that this has sustained, for their force to be realised.

Newby begins by stressing the multi-functional nature of rural areas and calls for a balance between competing uses, adapted to local circumstances. The basic tenet of Dennison's report was that the countryside must be multi-functional to have a sound economic base but that the balance of activities should be different in different areas. On this premise, Newby articulates five central areas of policy concern - so did Dennison, and broadly, these areas are the same:

| Newby (1991) | Dennison (1942) |
|---|---|
| Agricultural Adjustment | The Maintenance of Agriculture |
| Human Capital and Enterprise | The Location of Industry |
| Environmental Sustainability | The Preservation of Amenities |
| Balanced Communities | The Well-being of Rural Communities |
| Planning Policy | The Control of Land Use |

*(1) Agriculture*

Central to Newby's approach to agriculture is that it must now become less ubiquitously production orientated and must fully embrace policies for diversification. Dennison (paras 39 and 55) claimed that diversification in the rural economy was essential since the dependence on a single sector economy in decline could be devastating to communities. He cited the social and economic devastation of certain coal mining communities in the inter-war years as evidence of this. In the general context of diversification, Newby considers that agriculture should now pursue three objectives in different parts of the countryside. Firstly, food should be produced cheaply and efficiently, principally by a minority of large agribusiness farmers concentrated in specific areas and encouraged by government production incentives. Dennison (paras 3 - 21) argued strongly and persuasively that an efficient agriculture was not the largest agriculture in terms of acres, men and machines because this led to low returns for agricultural factors of production. Comprehensive government support

would stop these factors from leaving the industry ensuring a low
for them and therefore an inefficient industry. A smaller product
would be a more prosperous agriculture. As a second agricult
Newby maintains that the social fabric of the countryside, particul
rural areas, should be maintained by supporting the rural populat
(para 38) argued that alternative employment opportunities in rur... would provide higher standards of living for the rural population, improved physical and social services, and as a result population retention. Newby's third objective for agriculture is that public policy should seek to support farmers in order to maintain an attractive, diverse and ecologically rich rural environment. Dennison considered that if agriculture was to be considered the guardian of amenity this should not be left to chance, but rather:

> the farmer should be paid by the state in respect of his function as a landscape gardener, rather than an agriculturalist. (para 42).

*(2) Industry and enterprise*

In terms of industry and enterprise, Newby maintains that a growth in rural employment will not now come from agriculture or indeed from forestry, but from manufacturing and services. Dennison was vociferous on this point. He argued that industry must be allowed into the countryside if the perpetuation of the rural/urban duality between poverty and affluence was to be avoided (para 38). There was no reason why the lower living standards in the countryside, brought about by an inefficient agriculture, should be protected from higher ones (para 36). In developing industry in rural areas Newby sees a great spur coming from improved technologies and telecommunications which make many rural areas positively advantageous particularly for the service industries. Prophetically, Dennison's view concurs since he noted that:

> much of the isolation of rural communities has been overcome by the advent of the motor car, the wireless and the telephone and these will act as great facilitators to economic progress in the countryside. (para 38).

Finally in respect of industry and enterprise, Newby stresses the importance of investing in human capital and of developing enterprise in rural areas, but outside of agriculture. Dennison (para 58) noted that diversifying employment opportunities in the countryside would allow the labour factor of production new opportunities, through reskilling, for employment outside of agriculture. This would be particularly beneficial for rural women.

*Environment and amenity*

n respect of the environment, Newby suggests that agriculture will have to become, and is indeed becoming, much more accountable in line with the Brundtland Report and the UK Government's environmental 1990 White Paper. It will have to carry the burden of the polluter pays principle and will have to develop cleaner technologies. Dennison's ends were the same, but his means were different. Rather than using market mechanisms for controlling the agricultural impact on the environment, he felt that the solution to the preservation of amenity lay in the comprehensive extension of planning controls over agriculture (paras 50 and 75 (1)).

*(4) Rural communities*

The crux of the development of rural communities for Newby is rural housing. Current rural housing policies have impaired the social fabric of rural areas more than anything. In his opinion, there is a need for more local authority housing, but this can be provided in innovative ways, and not just for rent. The cornerstone of the well-being of rural communities for Dennison was rural housing. Because of the inherently low wages in rural areas, the need for adequate housing would never be met in the countryside through market forces. The priority here was for coherent and comprehensive public policies for rural housing (paras 25 - 29).

*(5) Planning and land use*

Newby outlines five main themes for the development of planning policy into the 1990s. The first of these is that planners can no longer leave the rural economy or the environment to agriculture. Dennison foreshadowed this sentiment exactly. In his concluding comments (para 71) he stated in respect of the rural economy and amenity:

> my colleagues (members of the Scott Committee) place chief reliance on the maintenance of a traditional agriculture; I prefer to rely on the maintenance of better standards of Town and Country Planning.

He felt that good quality agricultural land must not be immune to development because it might have a greater economic or amenity use. There was no place for agricultural land having privileges over other uses (para 60).

Secondly, Newby feels that planners have to overcome the popular belief that the countryside is under constant threat, because this leads to the "no development" ethic that is so damaging to rural economies and rural societies. Dennison similarly felt that preventing development in the countryside did not equate to the preservation of amenity (para 41); indeed strong planning controls were likely to enhance amenity (para 44) and certainly should be used to prevent the avoidable destruction of amenity and not to prevent reasonable development (para 56). He considered that the most significant rural planning problems were not to be found in areas where development was likely to occur but where employment and economic activity remained static (para 40).

Thirdly, Newby argues for a broader interpretation of what constitutes appropriate industrial development in the countryside. It is certainly no longer just blacksmithing and basket weaving on the one hand, nor on the other hand telecommuting, pluriactive farm households and the electronic cottage which are rather elitist and socially narrow. As well as calling for a broad industrial base for the countryside Dennison claims that it is essential to get away from the notion that rural crafts are the only acceptable industries for rural areas (para 55).

Fourthly, Newby calls for some adaptations to the planning process itself. There should be less "planning" and more "strategy", fewer "blueprints" and more "guidelines". Further, strategic planning should perhaps be coupled with more environmental and social impact analysis and less development control. Dennison did not depart strongly from this view. Whilst he felt that industrial development must be well designed, well sited and well laid out rather than prohibited (paras 37 and 41) he did stress that care should be taken not to create too rigorous standards of design (para 75(6)). On the matter of impact assessments, he stated that in determining development technical analyses should be undertaken of the economic, social and amenity consequences of development (paras 62 and 65).

Finally, Newby calls for a move away from food overproduction and a preoccupation with conservation in the 1990s and a move towards sensitive economic development, housing and public services. Again, Dennison considered that the major social need for land in rural areas was for housing and not for agriculture (para 65) and argued:

> I can conceive of no more proper way to use land in the national interest than that it should be used for the new construction necessary to provide better living conditions for the people - and their children after them - now living in our congested towns (para 49).

## Conclusion

Thus, the central rural development issues articulated by Newby, which are representative of an increasing number of policy proposals from non-governmental organisations, professional bodies and pressure groups alike, not only provide an agenda for the future, but also a lesson in history. The views of Dennison, propounded 50 years ago are every bit as relevant to the countryside of the 1990s as they were to the countryside of the 1940s. He was clearly a person before his time. And it is ironic indeed that his views were expressed within the same covers of the Scott report which was central in contributing to the principal rural problems that remain to be solved today.

**References**


Blunden, J. and Curry, N.R. (1985) *The changing countryside.* Croom Helm, Birkhamstead.

Blunden, J. and Curry, N.R. (1988) *A future for our countryside.* Basil Blackwell, Oxford.

Bowers, J.K. and Cheshire, P.C. (1983) *Agriculture, the countryside and land use*. Methuen, London.

Countryside and Community Research Unit (1991) *The village appraisals software*. Countryside and Community Research Unit, Cheltenham and Gloucester College, Cheltenham.

Curry, N.R. (1988) Countryside capital conspiracy. *Town and Country Planning*, Vol. 57, No.1, January.

Curry, N.R. and Edwards, D. (1991) *The planning policy context for planning agreements*. Working Paper 4, Planning gain, a strategy for conservation? project, University of Bristol, Department of Geography, April.

Department of the Environment and others (1990) *This common inheritance*. CM1200, HMSO, London

Gilg, A. (1991) *Countryside planning for the 1990s.* CAB International, Wallingford.

Green, R.J. (1972) *Country planning: the future of rural regions*. Manchester University Press, Manchester.

Healey, P. (1990) *Beyond the post-modern city and countryside.* Conference paper, Urban growth and the British countryside, St. Catherine's Conference, Northumberland Lodge, Windsor, November.

Hearne, A. (1985) Integrated Rural Development in Less Favoured Areas, in Rural development symposium, *Journal of Agricultural Economics*, Vol. 56, No. 1, January.

Hill, B., Young, N. and Brookes, G. (1989) *Alternative support systems for rural areas.* Wye College, University of London, Ashford, Kent.

Hookway, R. (1978) National Park plans. *The Planner*, Vol. 64 No. 1, January.

International Union for Conservation of Nature and Natural Resources (1980) *World Conservation Strategy.* IUCN, Gland, Switzerland.
Ministry of Works and Planning (1942) *Report of the committee on land utilisation in rural areas (the Scott report).* Cmd 6378, HMSO, London.
Newby, H.(1991) The future of rural society: strategic planning or muddling through? The Dartington Lecture, cited in *The Planner*, November, Vol. 77, No.36.
Roger Tym and Partners (1989) *The incidence and effects of planning conditions.* HMSO, London.
Sharp, T. (1931) *Town and countryside: some aspects of urban and rural development.* Oxford University Press, Oxford.
Shoard, M. (1980) *The theft of the countryside.* Temple Smith, London.
Slee, R.W. (1981) Agricultural policy in remote rural areas. *Journal of Agricultural Economics*, Vol. 32, No. 2, May.
Turner, K. (ed) (1988) *Sustainable environmental management: principles and practice.* Belhaven Press, London.
Whitby, M.C. and Willis, K. (1978) *Rural resource development: an economic approach.* Methuen, London.
World Commission on Environment and Development (1987) *Our common future (the Bruntland report).* Oxford University Press, Oxford.

# 3 Rural development in the Republic of Ireland

*Patrick Commins*

## Introduction

In one guise or another rural development in the Republic of Ireland has a long lineage. At times broad aspirational aims have been expressed for rural development policy even if concrete operational objectives were not so clearly stated. On other occasions policy aims were not explicitly formulated but could be inferred from the way particular policy measures - such as industrialisation -were pursued. Rural development has been linked very much with remedial approaches to the problems of particular regions. Just over one hundred years ago the Congested Districts Board was established to improve the condition of small-holders in the western counties by relieving land congestion, improving local infrastructures and promoting supplementary sources of income to small-scale farming. On the abolition of the Board in 1923 much of its work was continued by the Irish Land Commission and various Gaeltacht development agencies. Almost 90 years ago Horace Plunkett enunciated a concept that was later to become known as "integrated rural development". He argued that "not by agriculture alone is Ireland to be saved" and called for the development of industries subsidiary to agriculture in the countryside (Plunkett 1904). However, Plunkett's early influence did not prevail and the co-operative movement which he pioneered went in a direction different from his vision of rural revitalisation. However, his viewpoint foreshadowed the Industrial Development Authority's (IDA) programme of rural industrialisation in the 1970s.

From the late 1930s to the 1970s Muintir na Tire advocated and practised the "community development approach" to deal with rural problems before this term came to be commonly used in the lexicon of development. In more recent times, Muintir's strength as a national non-government organisation has been failing while, ironically, its philosophy has become assumed into the rhetoric of government statements. In the current wave of enthusiasm for "integrated rural development" (IRD) it may be sobering to note that the concept was used in the 1960s. *The Second Programme for Economic Expansion* (Agriculture in the Second Programme 1964), in particular, saw part of the solution to the problems of low income farming in the development of industry, forestry and tourism, even then including the idea of package farmhouse holiday schemes. The government at the time considered that IRD, in practice, involved closer collaboration among public service agencies and closer linkages between these agencies and non-statutory organisations. It was in this context that County Development Teams were established in the mid-1960s (see Reynolds in this volume).

With the Republic's impending entry into the European Community in the early 1970s much of the impetus for IRD was displaced by a widespread but simplistic faith in the EC's Common Agricultural Policy (CAP) and Regional Fund as providing the answer to the country's farm incomes problem. Besides, the IDA's programme of rural industrialisation became the main public policy prescription for rural development, and this had a creditable degree of success until overtaken by the world-wide recession at the end of the decade. Nevertheless, during the 1970s and 1980s there was a wide range of state-sponsored and community-instigated initiatives in the course of implementation i.e community development activities, community co-operative ventures, community enterprise developments and the EC anti-poverty projects. By the mid-1980s rural development as a policy issue had come back on the agenda, not because of any unilateral action on the part of the Irish Government but as a response to the prominence being given to this theme in EC policy.

The main purpose of this chapter is to provide an overview of current rural development measures in the Republic. However, it will be useful to place these in the context of the evolution of policy and policy perspectives through the 1960s and 1970s.

## The rural problem in pre-EC years

It is of interest to note the striking similarities between the situation in the Republic's rural economy of the 1960s and the current difficulties facing the agricultural sector in the EC. In the 1960s there was growing concern about the difficulties of disposing of agricultural produce due to the limited home market and adverse conditions in foreign markets. The UK imposed quotas on butter imports from the Republic. Commodity surpluses in other agricultural exporting countries meant limited opportunities in wider world markets. While governments of the time accepted that a measure of price support was necessary to maintain some degree of stability in returns to producers, they also warned that the capacity of the Irish exchequer to support farm prices was not unlimited. Accordingly, it was pointed out in the First Programme for Economic Expansion that state expenditure on agriculture would be concentrated more on measures to improve agricultural productivity and competitiveness than on additional price supports. Government programme statements also pointed out that agricultural development alone would not solve such rural problems as outmigration and rural depopulation.

These Irish problems and the policy responses they evoked foretold much of the current debate about the dilemmas facing rural areas in the contemporary EC context. Indeed in terms of policy ideas - if not in actual operational measures -Dublin's official thinking was almost as advanced as that now emanating from Brussels. The Second Programme for Economic Expansion, for example, contained a separate chapter on rural development and recognised the need for an integrated or multi-sectoral approach to the task of revitalising the rural economy.

Five sub-themes can be discerned under the rubric of rural development in policy documents for the years immediately preceding EC membership. First, there was an emphasis on maintaining - even strengthening - the upward trend in agricultural output but recognising the necessity for competitiveness by reducing costs per unit of output and intensifying land use within the limits set by market possibilities. Second, legislation sought to intensify progress on land structures through granting the Land Commission greater powers of land acquisition (in the 1965 Land Act), controlling access to land by non-nationals and introducing a pension scheme to induce elderly or incapacitated farmers to retire and offer their lands to the Commission for the improvement of farm structures. Third, the need to diversify the rural economy, highlighted in the report of the Interdepartmental Committee on the Problems of Small Western Farms (in 1961), was reiterated in subsequent programmes for economic expansion. What is now referred to as "agri-tourism" was envisaged as having much expansionary potential with the growth in private transport. Promotion of amenity and recreational facilities was seen as complementary to the development of forestry and fishing. Fourth, while in early policy documents rural development was considered as a means of solving the adjustment problems of the agricultural sector - and especially the small-farm problem - it later became fused with the ideas about regionalism and regional development. Thus, for example, the Third Programme (in 1969) stated that progress in dealing with agricultural problems would depend on the full development of the non-agricultural sectors; this in turn would require comprehensive policies for the regional economies and "synchronised programmes of development". Fifth, in the context of the current emphasis on partnerships in rural development it is of interest to note that pre-EC policy discussions were concerned with devising institutional arrangements to support regional and local development. The 1960s saw the establishment of County Development Teams, the Regional Development Organisations, Regional Technical Colleges and regional boards for health and tourism.

**1970s to mid-1980s: eclipse**

From the early 1970s to the mid-1980s, rural development receded from the national policy agenda - apart from some exceptional measures to be noted presently. One reason for this was the pragmatic consideration that, as it made tactical sense to secure the maximum flow of funds from the EC, the emphasis had to be on the CAP. The CAP dominated the EC budget and price and market policy dominated the CAP. There was, however, an underlying and unwarranted optimism about the efficacy of the CAP to deal with the endemic problems of the Republic's agriculture - the low incomes on a substantial proportion of farms and poor farm structure in the western region. As is now well known the impact of the CAP price policy was to widen the farm income gap between the larger and smaller producers. While CAP structures (non-price) policies were made more regionally specific (e.g. through the Programme for Western Development), and thus helped to lessen the disparity trends, their ameliorating effects were not pronounced.

There was also an expectation on EC entry that rural Ireland would, in time, benefit substantially from the Regional Fund (ERDF). In the event, however, these hopes were not realised; they were hardly justified in the first place. Of the IR£7000m worth of grants and subsidies provided to Ireland during 1973-86 the Regional Fund accounted for only 7.1 per cent, as compared to 73.6 per cent in the case of farm price guarantees, and 5.5 per cent for structural (non-price) measures in agriculture. As Lee (1989) states, Irish governments had effective tactics for negotiations in Brussels but not strategies for agriculture beyond making the biggest possible short-term gains. Still less was there any strategy for rural development. Furthermore, as the government decided that all of the Republic was to be eligible for ERDF support (again to maximise the receipts), the Fund was not used to improve any particular region but to help finance the public capital programme. The regional planning activity of the 1960s faded out of existence. Rural development, in the comprehensive sense envisaged in policy statements in the 1960s, was also displaced in the 1970s and early 1980s by the emerging problems of national budgetary management.

*Rural development through rural industrialisation*

However, one notable exception to the eclipse of rural development in the period was the IDA's programme of industrialisation. This provided for the distribution of new employment so as to moderate the growth of the eastern metropolitan region and to encourage industrial activity in other main urban and smaller population centres. The IDA's plans of the later 1970s continued to give recognition to the concept of dispersed development although these were less detailed on the matter of regional and sub-regional job targets.

Until overtaken by the world-wide recession of the 1980s, the IDA's programmes had a commendable degree of achievement, as evidenced by the general reversal of rural population trends during the 1970s. Employment in agriculture, forestry and fishing continued to decline (from 273,000 in 1971 to 168,000 in 1986) but rural population recovery was widespread, being evident in all of the provinces. Nor was rural population growth confined to the towns; it also took place in open country districts. The only censal areas failing to achieve population turnaround were 27 Rural Districts (out of 158), most of which were in north-east Connacht and in the peninsular areas of west Munster.

*Community-based development*

As noted at the outset, there survived from the 1960s a fairly vibrant non-governmental sector, though with various degrees of public sector support. This included the voluntary community council movement, community co-operatives, various types of local development associations, and local projects sponsored by EC poverty programmes but managed by local groups. The general picture these present is one of enormous citizen commitment but of unremitting struggle. In the main their activities have been confined to improving local infrastructures and services. They have made little impact on the critical rural problems of unemployment and low incomes.

## The re-emergence of rural development

Following the Republic's entry into the EC governments had, in general, lapsed into a pattern of reacting to policy initiatives and viewpoints originating from Brussels. Similarly, since the mid-1980s policy discourse and action in regard to rural development have been mostly in response to the thinking in Brussels, or have been implemented as a result of Commission requirements. To provide a context for describing rural development actions it is necessary to refer briefly to EC perspectives.

The crisis in the CAP - its generation of surpluses, high cost, its skewed distribution of benefits, and the negative impacts on the environment - impelled the Commission to identify other ways of supporting the incomes of farming households and stabilising the economies of rural areas. The Commission's report *The Future of Rural Society* was essentially a manifesto for rural development. One of its points had particular relevance for the Republic, namely, that as rural areas could not depend on external investment to the same extent as in the past the emphasis would have to be on the development of indigenous resources (CEC 1988). This view had effect in a context where industrial employment had been based on imported enterprise and branch-plant factories had been severely hit by the recession.

The other major impetus for rural development in the Republic came from the intention to establish the Single European Market (SEM). To lessen the contradiction between the threat posed to lagging regions by the SEM and the need to foster social and economic cohesion in an enlarged Community the Commission reformed its Structural Funds (Social Fund, ERDF and the structures element of the Agricultural Fund). Apart from doubling, in real terms, the amounts available the reform meant: (1) a funding emphasis on certain priority regions (one entity being the whole of the Republic of Ireland); (2) an emphasis on organisational arrangements which would represent a move away from single actors (e.g. public agency or local community) and towards formalised institutional partnerships to combine several sets of resources in mutually agreed plans; and (3) a change from annual financing of individual projects to multi-annual funding of operational programmes which would include a diverse but coherent set of interventions. A number of operational programmes (e.g. for rural development) were agreed with the Commission under a Community Support Framework.

As might be inferred from what has been said the Republic does not have a coherent strategy for rural development, even granting the point that as a set of problem issues and policy dimensions rural development is not a clearly demarcated area of action. Nevertheless, there is increasing recognition of the need for multisectoral action, for locally-based or bottom-up initiatives, for participation in planning for development, and for partnerships between agencies (statutory and non-governmental) in implementing development.

The *National Development Plan 1989-93* (NDP 1989) and the *Programme for Economic and Social Progress* (PESP 1991), taken in combination, set out the aim of rural development. This, in summary form, is the stabilisation of the rural population through the promotion of the viability of the maximum number of farms, and through the diversification of the rural economy. The National Development Plan, in particular, includes a wide range of measures under "agriculture and rural development", including increasing efficiency on farms;

supporting farm incomes through animal headage payments; promoting forestry, fishing and farm tourism; investing in human resources; and developing infrastructure and communications. Operational programmes for other sectors, e.g. tourism, would also contribute to rural development. Space does not permit examination of the full spectrum of measures under these various headings so it is appropriate to confine discussion to the more "rural", as distinct from "agricultural" programmes, under the three points of origin noted in Fig 3.1 below.

ORIGIN OF PROGRAMMES

| National (autonomous) Measures | National Programmes under Community Support Framework | EC Initiatives |
|---|---|---|
| TYPES OF PROGRAMMES | | |
| (1) IRD Pilot Programme | (3) Operational Programme for Rural Development | (4) LEADER |
| (2) Area-based Response to Unemployment | | (5) Model Action Project |

**Figure 3.1 Rural development programmes in the Republic of Ireland**

*(1) IRD pilot programme*

A pilot programme for Integrated Rural Development was the first significant attempt at a revival of 1960s' concepts of rural development (for a fuller account see O'Malley in this volume). The programme was based on the idea of extending advisory and other interventions beyond agriculture, and on establishing linkages between local voluntarism and statutory action within an area-based development strategy. It was administered by the Department of Agriculture and Food and put into operation in 12 sub-county areas over the period 1988-1990. A rural development co-ordinator was appointed to each area which had mostly between 6,000 and 15,000 persons. The task of the co-ordinator was to organise a core group of local leaders who would decide on local development priorities and ensure their implementation. The co-ordinator effectively acted as a facilitator to this group by co-ordinating their activities, building-up links among various agencies, and by networking with other pilot area groups. Apart from a small amount of money for technical assistance no new funding was provided for the programme. The National Development Plan 1989-93 envisaged the results of the programme as assisting in directing policy and resources towards local community development in a more broadly-based programme.

In 1991, it was announced that the programme would be extended to the entire country. However, the significance of this announcement could be questioned because the organisational arrangements were not replicated. Instead, the extended programme would draw on funds available for small and community enterprise under the Operational Programme for Rural Development (see below). In the 13 western counties the County Development Officers (working with the County Development Teams) act as coordinators in addition to carrying out their other functions. For the remaining counties the plan is to have rural development co-ordinators based in strategically located centres. This means a much lower intensity of staffing than what obtained under the pilot programme and a more extensive coverage of rural areas. Extension of the pilot scheme thus seems a misnomer in describing its follow-up.

*(2) Area-based response to long-term unemployment*

This is part of the 1991 Programme for Economic and Social Progress and includes 12 pilot projects, of which four are in rural areas. Companies limited by guarantee have been established in the selected areas to reproduce at the local level the social partnership approach adopted at national level. Each rural-based company is a partnership between local community interests, social partners (i.e. employers, farmers and trade unions), and state agencies. Administered by the Central Review Committee of the Department of the Taoiseach the scheme has little funding beyond the specific budgets prepared by the relevant public authorities and the other partners for each participating local area. Partnerships operate as self-managing units of their own local action plans within the broad guidelines established. These plans are expected to encompass two modules of activity: one based on achieving more effective operation of education, training and social welfare provisions and the other based on enterprise creation.

*(3) Operational programme for rural development*

Under the EC Structural Funds the Republic's operational programme for rural development was approved for the years 1991 to 1993. This allows for a total expenditure of IR£104m, of which the EC contributes IR£60m. The programme includes measures for the diversification of the rural economy (e.g. alternative farm enterprises, horticulture, agri-tourism, forestry, services to farmers), and for small and community enterprises, rural infrastructure, research and development in the food industry, and training. Noticeably, only 7 per cent of expenditure in the programme will go to small and community enterprise and as already stated this will be used to fund the extension of the pilot programme. Also, compared to the other initiatives listed here the operational programme is weak in terms of an area-based focus.

*(4) LEADER programme*

Through this programme the EC seeks to pursue initiatives of its own in rural development. Monies are made available to local development groups which must include the major agencies within an area of up to 100,000 persons. Of some 200 LEADER groups selected throughout the Community by the Commission, 17 were chosen in the Republic from 34 projects submitted. Selections were made on the basis of the business plans proposed by the groups. These plans include rural tourism, the development of small firms and craft enterprises, vocational training and marketing of local produce. The total financial outlay over 1992-93 will be IR£70m, of which IR£21m comes from the EC and IR£14m from the national exchequer. The remaining IR£35m must be provided from local sources. This has raised the question as to whether the benefits of the LEADER programme will accrue to those areas or beneficiaries which are already sufficiently well circumstanced to provide the matching capital. However, this is an issue that must await full evaluation of the programme. It also remains to be seen how much each project constitutes a managed programme of coherent actions, or becomes a mere conduit for funds going to a variety of groups dispersed around the project areas.

*(5) Model Action Project of the Third EC Anti-Poverty Programme*

There is one Irish rural project (north-west Connemara) in the Third EC Anti-Poverty Programme. This is of interest in a rural context because the design of the programme and of the individual projects incorporates a considerable amount of learning from earlier anti-poverty programmes. First, being a Community initiative it is part-funded by the EC; the remainder is provided by a national co-funder (the Combat Poverty Agency in the Republic). Second, whereas earlier poverty programmes either sent in development workers from a central ad hoc committee to a local area, or funded local groups to manage their own projects, the Poverty 3 Programme requires that the local project be implemented by a formally constituted partnership made up of such public agencies as the local authority, health boards, FAS (the manpower and training agency) and the vocational education committee - as well as representatives of the local community or other non-government organisations. Third, the local model action programme must be based on a strategic plan, and must be multi-sectoral but integrated into a coherent set of operations. (The North-West Connemara project incorporates a number of local economic developments, health and other support services for the elderly and training and other programmes for youth and for women). Fourth, it must provide - through its structures - for the participation of disadvantaged groups (the target groups) in project planning and operation. Fifth, there is an emphasis on networking or on shared learning with similar projects. Sixth, the project must provide for self-evaluation as an aid to project management and as a contribution to the assessment of the overall performance of the Poverty 3 Programme. Seventh, in each Member State the Programme is supported by a small research and development unit which provides technical assistance to projects and helps to evaluate the whole Programme for future policy-making. Finally, the projects in the Poverty 3 Programme are much larger in scale (geographical area, resources and staffing) than earlier anti-poverty projects. Taken together with the multi-agency partnership this implies a belief that to make an impact on rural poverty the scale of organisation must go beyond funding local voluntary action, and must draw on the resources of public sector authorities. Thus, compared to the LEADER initiative, which seemingly leaves projects with a high degree of operational autonomy, the Model Action Project is expected to conform to several principles in a centrally designed programme.

**Institutional arrangements**

In the Republic shifts in policy orientation and the increasing variety of programmes relating to rural development have not been accompanied by any substantial re-organisation of institutional structures for steering rural development. In this regard the Republic would seem to lag behind changes made in Northern Ireland as described in the next chapter. When operational programmes were being prepared for inclusion in the Community Support Framework, the EC made known its wish to have local and regional involvement in this process. However, the Republic did not have the ready-made regional structures for this purpose, as the Regional Development Organisations had been abolished. In the event, seven new regions were designated and ad hoc Steering Committees set up to activate the planning process in them. These comprised representatives of local authorities, government departments and state agencies, as well as representatives of the private sector. Provision was made for Advisory Groups as a means of giving a voice to non-statutory organisations. There were many criticisms of this arrangement - especially when the overall national plans appeared - to the effect that it was a token gesture to the notion of participation and specifically cut out participation by locally-based or community groups.

At present administrative responsibility for rural development rests with a very small group of overworked officials at the Department of Agriculture and Food. The Department's Policy Review Committee (1990) acknowledged this weakness and recommended that structures be clarified and strengthened. A Ministerial announcement has, however, stated that a consultative committee would be established to advise in regard to progress on rural development. To date there has been no follow-up to this statement, although a junior Minister was appointed to the Department of Agriculture and Food, with responsibility for both rural enterprise and horticulture.

## Conclusion

*Rural development and regional development*

While the context and the operational measures of rural development in the Republic have varied over time there has tended to be one constant underlying aim, namely that of maintaining the rural population. This has been couched not just in terms of retaining an aggregate number of people in rural areas but also in maintaining the existing spatial distribution. Viewed in this light the challenge has now intensified. While in the mid-1980s rural development emerged as a policy issue in the context of dealing with the adjustment problems of production agriculture it cannot be considered any longer as an appendage to agricultural policy. In fact it overlaps greatly with the national problem of widespread unemployment and emigration in the regions. This is evident from the preliminary returns for the 1991 Census of Population. These show that during 1986-91 rural depopulation has been quite extensive outside of the Dublin metropolitan perimeter and some of the major provincial centres. These declines cannot be accounted for by the problems of agriculture (which employs only one-third of rural labour) but are the result of the general debilitation of the Republic's regional economies. Consequently, rural development should be addressed as an issue of regional and sub-regional development on a comprehensive basis - as was intended in the 1960s.

*Need for rural policy*

The Republic now has a wide range of measures that could be considered as a response to its rural problems. But it would be difficult to argue that these add up to a coherent rural policy. They do not reveal a guiding vision or set of values about the future of different kinds of rural areas (e.g. the remote, sparsely populated districts). There is no clearly formulated set of reference criteria against which decisions by various arms of the public sector can be judged desirable or otherwise. It is highly unlikely that all rural areas can hope to maintain existing levels of population and services (such as post offices) but decline may be publicly and politically acceptable if planned for strategically at sub-regional or sub-county level.

*What concept of rural development?*

The question of the form and content of rural development needs to be clarified. A multi-sectoral but integrated approach on the lines pursued by the Poverty 3 Model Action Project seems an effective way of maximising the synergy that could be derived from various EC funds and national measures. But whereas the Model Action project is based on a partnership at sub-county level, rural development may be more sustainable by having a reformulated and strengthened County Development Team, with provision for local popular participation. This of course would mean a rejuvenated system of local government in the Republic.

*Co-ordination at the centre*

An integrated team approach at county or sub-regional level would have to be complemented at central level by appropriate inter-departmental structures. A main function of these would be to sort out quickly any inter-agency matter not capable of resolution by the discretionary powers available to officials at local level.

*Human resources*

Another requirement would seem to be training in the area of development planning and project management. Investment to date in this sphere bears little relationship to the amount of other funding being provided for projects and programmes. Similarly, the development activities referred to earlier seem to be under way with limited institutional and financial provision for feasibility studies, research and evaluation, the structured sharing of experiences, and the development of training inputs. Rural development in the Republic needs supportive investments in human capital as well as funding for development projects.

## References


Agriculture and Food Policy Review Group (1990) *Agriculture and food policy.* The Stationery Office, Dublin.

*Agriculture in the Second Programme* (1964) The Stationery Office, Dublin.

CEC (Commission of the European Community) (1988) *The future of rural society.* Brussels.

Lee, J.J. (1989) *Ireland 1912-1985.* Cambridge University Press, Cambridge.

NDP *(National Development Plan 1989-1993)* (1989) The Stationery Office, Dublin.

PESP *(Programme for Economic and Social Progress)* (1991) The Stationery Office, Dublin.

Plunkett, H. (1904) *Ireland in the new century.* Reprinted by Irish Academic Press, 1982.

# 4 Rural development in Northern Ireland

*Michael Murray and John Greer*

## Introduction

Northern Ireland has been described by Hoare (1982) as a problem region with a regional problem. An important dimension of this condition is located in rural areas where changes associated with agricultural restructuring and Province-wide deindustrialization continue to have a deep impact on rural society. In drawing attention to the distribution of rural problem areas in the region (Fig. 4.1) and the need to develop a strategy to meet these problems, research published in 1980 (Armstrong et al) has been of seminal significance. Using data from the 1971 census some two thirds of the land area of Northern Ireland were classified as disadvantaged on the basis of a high dependence on agriculture, high rates of unemployment and underemployment, low population density, and imbalances in the demographic structure. But it has taken a further decade for government to engage more fully in the formulation and implementation of policies aimed at the rural economy and society. This chapter traces the emergence of a rural development policy response in Northern Ireland, describes the institutional structures set in place and examines the contribution to date of community-led rural development.

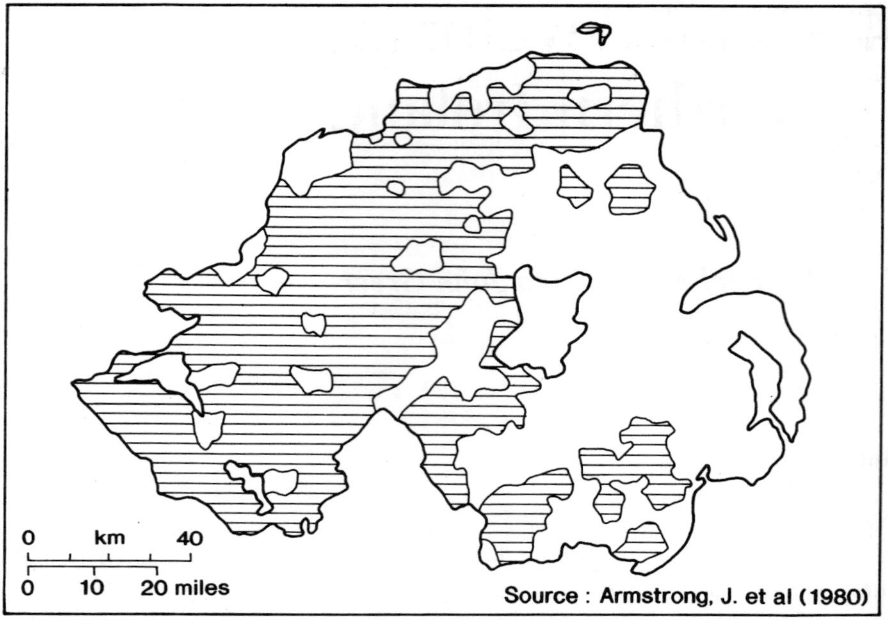


**Figure 4.1 Rural problem areas in Northern Ireland**

## The emergence of rural development in Northern Ireland

In contrast to other peripheral rural regions within the United Kingdom where the contribution of rural development initiatives to economic and social regeneration is longstanding, Northern Ireland is marked by the absence of any comprehensive response by government. However, during the latter part of the 1980s public policy interest in rural development has been stimulated by a number of interlinked factors comprising the Maher Report, the Rural Action Project, the International Fund for Ireland and the European Commission. Each may be briefly considered.

### *(1) The Maher Report*

Such consciousness as exists in Northern Ireland in regard to rural development policy owes much to the initial prodding by the Maher Report prepared on behalf of the European Parliament. A resolution calling for the preparation of an integrated rural development programme for the less favoured areas of the region was tabled in October 1984 and following its completion was adopted unanimously by the European Parliament in September 1986. The Maher Report provides a comprehensive description of the multifaceted disadvantage faced by rural Ulster and the case for urgent intervention by all participants in the development process is well articulated. The recommendations which flow from consultation and analysis embrace an essentially multisectoral approach to problem solving and include agricultural diversification, the processing of agricultural goods, exploitation of peat resources, biomass, fisheries development, craft industry, infrastructure investment and a central co-ordinating body to oversee implementation. While the report provides little detailed examination of these opportunities which has generated criticism from sections of the rural community, it still stands as an important attempt to encapsulate and publicise the disadvantaged condition of Northern Ireland's rural periphery.

*(2) Rural Action Project*

The Rural Action Project (RAP) emerged from concern by local voluntary organisations about the lack of emphasis on and knowledge of conditions in rural Northern Ireland. Under its auspices funding for a series of action-research initiatives, set at the community scale of involvement, was secured from the local Department of Health and Social Services and the European Community Second Combat Poverty Programme for a four year period ending in 1989. In the main RAP's work was targeted on four pilot areas within the more remote periphery of the Province and as noted by the UK evaluator (Rural Action Project 1989) was locally rooted, well researched, and carefully developed in partnership with local community organisations and district councils. More particularly it began to develop and test practical projects and programmes as prototypes for larger scale solutions to rural poverty and contributed to the policy debate at both national and European levels. It is, however, worth noting that the initial sponsorship of this rural development project in Northern Ireland by a social services agency throws into sharp focus the perceived residual nature of rural disadvantage from the standpoint of those government departments with responsibility for economic development at that time whose priority has long been the solution of the serious problems of Belfast and Derry. Yet through its dogged persistence within the crevices of government RAP succeeded in eventually prompting a wide-ranging scrutiny of rural affairs in the Province.

*(3) International Fund for Ireland*

The International Fund for Ireland was established by the Governments of the United Kingdom and Ireland in 1986 with the objectives of promoting economic and social advance in Northern Ireland and encouraging contact, dialogue and reconciliation between Nationalists and Unionists throughout Ireland as a whole. The Fund has drawn upon contributions from the United States, Canada, New Zealand and the European Community. Cumulative committed expenditure by 1992 reached some £224m and has been spread across a number of sectors including business enterprises, tourism, urban development, agriculture and fisheries, science and technology and vocational preparation and training. By the end of 1992 the total number of projects offered assistance amounted to 2,800 and they are expected to generate some 18,700 new full time jobs. Early criticisms that the Fund was not sufficiently targeting resources on areas of greatest need (OhAdhmaill 1991) have resulted in the introduction of a Disadvantaged Areas Initiative which in its coverage closely relates not only to areas of urban deprivation but also to the earlier identified problem rural areas (Armstrong et al 1980). Development projects in small towns, villages and rural communities lacking any nucleated settlement are now eligible for financial assistance. But by seeking to target a greater proportion of its resources on disadvantaged rural communities, the Fund has reinforced the need for a corresponding policy response from government.

*(4) European Commission*

During 1989 the 12 member states of the Community submitted development plans in accordance with arrangements introduced by the reform of the structural funds (cf. Commission of the European Communities 1989). A regional development plan[1] for Northern Ireland, the only Objective 1 region in the United Kingdom was submitted by government to the European Commission. Image enhancement, infrastructure, expertise, enterprise and exports were identified as key areas requiring measures adding up to a strategy for "strengthening the economy". Envisaged Community assistance, inclusive of existing programmes, was put at some £1,069m, of which 51 per cent related to ERDF finance, 39 per cent to ESF and 10 per cent to EAGGF (Guidance Section). The Northern Ireland bid thus fitted well with the more general observations made subsequently by the European Commission (1990) that the volume of funds requested by member states was very large, far exceeding the amount available and that stated needs all too often reflected a conception of regional policy based on the importance of infrastructure. The Commission concluded that this approach was not in itself sufficient to solve problems of economic development. The negotiated Community Support Framework[2] for Northern Ireland ultimately secured some £610m for the five year period 1989-1993. Close reading of both the regional development plan and the Community Support Framework for Northern Ireland points to scant appreciation of the need for and scope of rural development as a substantive policy area for economic development. Indeed the less than satisfactory response by the Northern Ireland authorities to this matter has prompted Commissioner MacSharry to remark that progress locally on the rural development front has been slow (MacSharry 1990). The agriculture and rural development component of the Community Support Framework is mainly a continuation of existing measures and programmes. The subsequent Operational Programme[3] for this sector makes little advance in this regard and even makes explicit reference to the absence of any rural development dimension outwith the suite of agricultural measures.

## New structures for rural development

In response to these pressures the Secretary of State for Northern Ireland appointed an Inter-Departmental Committee on Rural Development in October 1989 to advise him on "the best way of carrying forward action to tackle the social and economic problems in the most deprived rural areas of Northern Ireland".[4] The Committee was chaired by the Permanent Secretary of the Department of Agriculture for Northern Ireland and its members were drawn from all the Northern Ireland departments and non-departmental statutory bodies with an involvement in rural matters. The Committee reported to ministers in December 1990 and the broad thrust of its recommendations was accepted. In summary these were:

(1) the establishment of a formal hierarchy of responsibility for integrated rural development within government. The Minister of Agriculture has been designated as Minister for Rural Development and departmental responsibility for rural development lies with the Department of Agriculture. These arrangements mirror the structures within the European Commission and, if nothing else, formally locate rural development in a particular department whereas previously it tended to float between departments. Within the Department of Agriculture a Rural Development Division has been established comprising a central policy unit. It administers EC rural development initiatives, promotes awareness throughout other departments and agencies of the needs of rural areas, and liaises with counterparts from the Republic of Ireland on cross-border initiatives.

(2) the establishment of an advisory body and resource centre, outside government, and under the management of a broad spectrum of rural interests, to act both as a channel of local views on rural development to ministers and as a source of expert advice and assistance, financial and otherwise, to local groups engaged in the regeneration of rural areas. This body, the Rural Development Council, is located in County Tyrone, the location being

important in that it is central to the areas of rural disadvantage. The Council comprises a management panel of 16 members representative of rural interests and employs a director and a support staff of 17. Its development officers and field staff are located in five centres within the rural periphery of Northern Ireland. Local networking activity is being assisted by Rural Community Network, an umbrella organisation for community groups in disadvantaged rural areas.

(3) the establishment, under the auspices of the Department of Agriculture, of a small team of 3 co-ordinators whose task is to ensure that public sector programmes are delivered in a way that is sensitive to local needs and, particularly, to co-ordinate the responses from statutory agencies to locally developed regeneration plans. In essence this has meant the drawing together of an interdisciplinary team of experts from other government departments into the Department of Agriculture, which is quite an innovation in terms of Civil Service practice to date.

It is clear from Fig. 4.2 that the interaction between the Rural Development Council and government is quite complex, involving a gamut of interests from government ministers, through district councils to local voluntary groups. Important questions remain as to the funding, powers and long term role of the Rural Development Council. Its budget for 1992-1993 was some £700,000. The

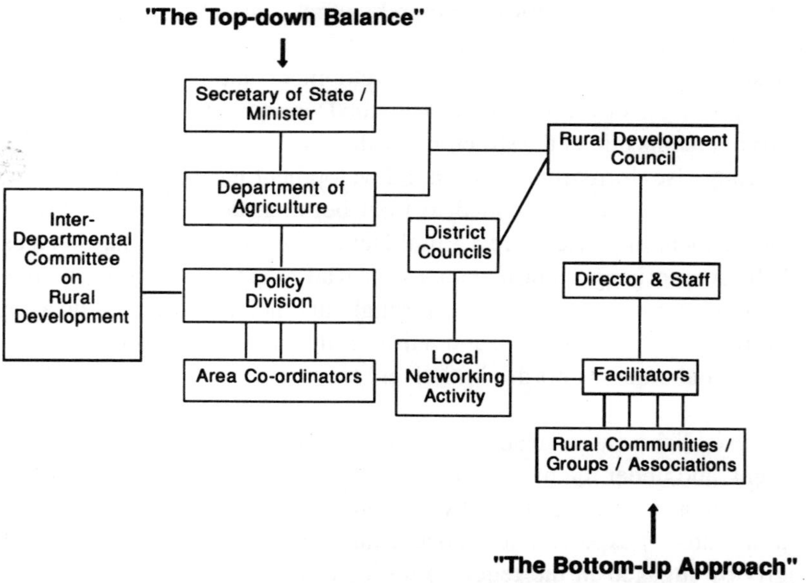


**Figure 4.2 Structures for rural development in Northern Ireland**

Council is also managing a farm diversification action research project for the International Fund for Ireland and is the Northern Ireland agent for the EC LEADER programme. The stimulation of community-led rural development is thus central to its brief.

## Community-led rural development

For operational purposes a simple model of stages of community action is being utilised in Northern Ireland whereby the preliminary phases of group formation, organisation and planning lead on to implementation through project funding and management. The remit of the Rural Development Council extends across all stages especially because of its role as agent for the European Commission in regard to the LEADER (links between actions for the development of the rural economy) special programme. This is designed to target project support at rural communities whose economic needs have been locally assessed and currently involves some 213 participating groups located in the Objective 1 (lagging) and Objective 5b (rural) priority regions of the European Community. The total EC commitment amounts to 439.397m ECUs of which 3.800m ECUs is allocated for Northern Ireland. When combined with domestic public expenditure (1.984m ECUs) and "private" contributions (5.506m ECUs) the Northern Ireland LEADER programme adds up to a total cost of 11.290m ECUs. Additional monies through other EC initiatives such as INTERREG (border areas special programme) are also available to local community groups.

It would seem, therefore, that government in Northern Ireland is intent on shifting community activity from the margins and turning it into the driving force for rural development. However, notwithstanding the availability of this capital for community based rural development, it remains the case that only a small number of local development organisations have reached that critical threshold between planning and implementation in Northern Ireland. Two groups which have arrived at that stage are the Seeconnell Initiative and the Ardboe Development Association. The next section of this chapter gives a brief account of each.

## Northern Ireland case studies

### *(1) Seeconnell Initiative*

Seeconnell is located in the northern uplands of the Mourne and Slieve Croob Area of Outstanding Natural Beauty in County Down. The small community of some 400 people is dispersed across three rural townlands of 20 square kilometres. The hill land supports sheep farming on a mainly part-time basis and given the relative scarcity of local employment opportunities the population has continued to decline in recent years. The legacy of disadvantage is well demonstrated by some 150 derelict houses scattered throughout the area. Inevitably there have been implications for the viability of local community services and in 1988 the closure of the local primary school was announced. The community responded by rejecting this decision and opting for independent status. Government funding was withdrawn but in the following academic year some £17,000 was raised locally to finance the school. This servicing commitment has continued and at present the enrolment of 30 pupils provides employment for 2 teachers.

This action has served to stimulate a wider commitment to rural regeneration. Pilot funding for rural development in Northern Ireland received from the European Commission was used to prepare a tourism development strategy (L and R Leisure 1990) for the Seeconnell area and assist with the appointment of a project co-ordinator and secretary. Further funding was secured to cover the costs of drawing up business plans for four key projects: a heritage and community centre; an equestrian centre; a bunkhouse barn and licensed restaurant; and self catering accommodation in refurbished derelict cottages. In March 1992 the Seeconnell Initiative was officially launched with a financial package of almost £1.8m assembled from the EC LEADER Programme, the International Fund for Ireland, the Department of Agriculture for Northern Ireland and the local community itself. The latter contribution amounts to some £234,000. However, by January 1993 formal letters of commencement were still awaited.

### *(2) Ardboe Development Association*

The Ardboe area is situated along the western shores of Lough Neagh in County Tyrone, extends to some 70 square kilometres and has a landscape marked by its flatness in the vicinity of the shoreline. A relatively large and growing population, estimated at just under 6000 people, the absence of any nucleated settlement of significant size and a mixed economic base of agriculture, fishing and industry combine to create a rural area which is quite distinctive in Northern Ireland. The current momentum for community based rural development can be traced back to the discovery by BP Coal of commercially viable deposits of lignite in the area. Concern about the adverse impact of future mining in the locality led to the formation of a Lignite Action Group in 1985. This campaigned successfully against mining in the area though ultimately the final decision in 1988 by government owed much to the preferred relationship between energy policy and privatisation plans in Northern Ireland at that time (see Baker 1990).

The activity of the Lignite Action Group was closely followed by the establishment of Loughshore Community Development Association whose brief extended to the provision of adult education, the production of a community magazine and the conducting of local historical and socio-economic research. Other interest groups to emerge within the area were concerned with the creation of local enterprises and with the securing of beneficial use of a disused airfield built during World War Two to train USAAF bomber crews. In 1989 these groups amalgamated to form Ardboe Development Association. Seed funding was secured for premises and the appointment of a project officer and secretary. Its initial tasks comprised the preparation of an economic development strategy (Greer and Murray 1991), the selection of key projects and the completion of business plans in respect of these. Present efforts are focused on winning grant support for a rural enterprise park comprising workspace premises, serviced industrial sites, a horticulture site and a cold store with blast freezing facilities. It is also proposed to develop an existing small harbour into a watersports activity centre complete with accommodation and elsewhere to build a cultural/interpretative centre. The estimated costs of these projects are in excess of £2.5m with funding being sought from the EC LEADER and INTERREG programmes, the Local Economic Development Unit, the International Fund for Ireland and the Department of Agriculture for Northern Ireland. A community contribution will be offered. But again, as with Seeconnell, approval of the development package was outstanding by January 1993, although the International Fund for Ireland has provided £90,000 for the cultural centre.

## Rural development tensions

It is clear from the discussion above that rural development in Northern Ireland is at an embryonic stage in its contribution to regeneration. Two of the leading groups in very different geographical circumstances have, as at January 1993, yet to commence projects on-site suggesting a gap between initial expectations of self help capacity and project completion which is the result of a series of tensions with wider applicability to understanding state-community relationships. Their willingness to become involved in community enterprise ventures is rooted in earlier crises which were perceived as threats on the very fabric of local rural society. As catalysts for community action these conflicts helped to mould local group formation, confidence and commitment. Thus at a time when government was itself examining the prospects for rural development in Northern Ireland, it would seem that both Seeconnell and Ardboe held comparative initial advantage over other rural development groups; they were in the right place at the right time. But their experience to date raises a number of matters relevant to those many other community groups which hope to follow this lead.

These comprise the need for strategy; the importance of partnership; and the search for success.

*The need for strategy*

A key feature of the rural development planning process in each area has been the preparation of a strategy by outside professionals. These strategies provide an information base of facts and forecasts and offer a framework, both spatial and sectoral, within which different policies might operate. They seek to raise awareness, to integrate state and community interests, to identify projects and to provide a device for winning funds. It is, however, questionable that these strategies truly articulate a shared local community vision. This philosophical tension relates on the one hand to building upon and extending community consensus through widely canvassed goals and objectives and on the other hand to reducing strategy preparation to a pragmatic technical appraisal of constraints and opportunities by consultants who report to a local steering committee. It would seem, moreover, that the perception of the planning stage as a mere technical element of the regeneration process has marginalised the scope for further developing local leadership and enhancing local decision making abilities. This matter is important since, in both Seeconnell and Ardboe, strategy completion was quickly followed by the preparation of detailed business plans for priority projects. This external testing of strategy and projects has helped shape the negotiating stances of state and community in regard to funding and has required a high level of expertise from rural development group representatives.

At a substantive level a further tension relates to strategy legitimacy especially when important aspects of public policy are perceived as being challenged. The workspace component of the Ardboe Development Association at one stage ran counter to the locational policy of the government agency responsible for small industry; the proposed equestrian centre in Seeconnell does not fit well with the broad presumption by the Department of the Environment against physical development in core areas of outstanding natural beauty. In short the implications of these strategies extend beyond the mere identification of investment proposals. They generate the requirement for wide-ranging mediation of a scale perhaps unappreciated at the outset by their local sponsors.

*The importance of partnership*

The launch of new structures for rural development in Northern Ireland has placed much emphasis on the concept of a working partnership between top-down and bottom-up perspectives on policy delivery. As suggested by Panet-

Raymond (1992) partnership must be distinguished from a paternalistic relationship between public institutions and voluntary organisations. Thus any notion of limiting the number of community groups which can meaningfully participate in rural regeneration would be unacceptable in this context and hint more at an attempt at social control than at any credible commitment to real partnership with the rural constituency. It is here that government in Northern Ireland walks the resource tightrope of encouraging community participation with a limited funding commitment. Partnership depends on trust and mutual understanding and accordingly it is interesting to note that both the Seeconnell and Ardboe communities have assiduously sought to win the confidence of civil service bureaucrats in order to advance their bids for funding. Frustrations with these officials because of imposed modifications to project briefs or delays in progressing project decisions have not provoked an alternative overtly political style of doing business. The community approach, while determined, has deliberately been low key in deference to the preferred style of the policy makers. But partnership also generates obligation and any easing of this tension will depend upon the ultimate content of government support.

*The search for success*

The economic problems of Northern Ireland have traditionally been described and addressed within an urban context. The rural development agenda is new and as with any process of paradigm change it is not without its critics. Much emphasis has, therefore, been placed by government on seeking out potentially successful prototypes for more extensive application while remaining mindful at the same time of the inherent dangers of promoting quick-fix solutions as a response to heightened public expectations. This local economic development emphasis is wedded to the concept of project sustainability as a key measure of success. No criticism is offered if this is defined as a reasonable expectation of a return on project investment. But any mention of possible project failure may be sufficient to damn a proposal while an explanation as to why rural development should be treated differently from other development initiatives is studiously avoided. The net result is that this almost absolute imperative to be successful may prove counterproductive. An element of risk-taking by government, closely linked to monitoring and evaluation, can advance understanding and in turn help formulate an informed longer term vision of rural society and economy. The extreme caution with which negotiations on the Seeconnell and Ardboe development programmes have progressed suggests that the minds of government officials may remain closed to this opportunity for shared learning by state and community. At a wider level it may well be the case that a continued emphasis on economic performance could result in the non-commercial aspects of community agendas being neglected.

## Conclusion

Within Northern Ireland much is expected by rural communities of the structures set in place by government for rural development. The experience of the two groups featured in this chapter would suggest that dependency relationships of community to state show little sign of weakening. Government has set an agenda on its terms and is operationalizing a process of change which may do little to advance the greater independence of rural communities. At this stage it is sufficient to suggest that a key element of the rural development paradigm will have reached maturity when communities have a greater capacity to guide their own futures and when the tensions identified above are replaced by shared confidence and enduring commitment.

## Notes

1. See, Regional Development Plan for Northern Ireland 1989-1993, European Community Structural Funds United Kingdom Regional Plans.
2. See, Commission of the European Communities, Community Support Framework 1989-1993 for the development and structural adjustment of the regions whose development is lagging behind (Objective 1), United Kingdom (Northern Ireland), Brussels, 1989.
3. See, European Community Structural Funds, Agricultural Development Operational Programme, Northern Ireland 1989-1993,Department of Agriculture for Northern Ireland, 1990, p.26.
4. See, Northern Ireland Information Service - New structures for rural development, 15 February 1991, 2pp.

## References

Armstrong, J., McClelland, D. and O'Brien, T. (1980) *A policy for rural problem areas in Northern Ireland*. Working Research Paper Series Volume V, No. 1, School of Applied Economics, Ulster Polytechnic, Jordanstown.

Baker, S. (1990) Privatisation policy in Northern Ireland, in Connolly, M. and Loughlin, S (eds) *Public policy in Northern Ireland: adoption or adaptation?* pp. 215-243. Policy Research Institute, Belfast.

Commission of the European Communities (1989) *Guide to the reform of the Community's structural funds.* Document, Brussels.

Department of Agriculture for Northern Ireland (1992) *Rural development - a government initiative.* Belfast.

Greer, J.V. and Murray, M.R. (1991) *A development strategy for Ardboe, Ballinderry and Moortown.* Ardboe Development Association, Ardboe.

Hoare, A. (1982) Problem region and regional problem, in Boal, F.W. and Douglas, J.H.N. (eds) *Integration and division.* Academic Press, London.

International Fund for Ireland (1992) *Annual Report.* Belfast and Dublin.

L. and R. Leisure (1990) *A study of the development potential of the Seeconnell area.* Seeconnell Initiative.

MacSharry, R. (1990) Rural development: the challenge of the 1990s. *Business Outlook and Economic Review*, Vol. 5, No.2, pp. 10-15.

OhAdhmaill, F. (1991) The IFI - how much hype, how much substance? *Scope*, April, pp. 14-17.

Panet-Raymond, J. (1992) Partnership: myth or reality? *Community Development Journal*, Vol. 27, No. 2, pp. 156-165.

Rural Action Project (1989) *Rural Development - a challenge for the 1990s.* Rural Action Project (N.I.), Londonderry.

# Section 2
# SECTORAL ISSUES

# 5 Agriculture and the Environmentally Sensitive Area scheme

*Joan Moss and Susan Chilton*

## Introduction

The Environmentally Sensitive Areas (ESA) programme in the United Kingdom dates from the mid 1980s and represents a significant departure from the longstanding productionist emphasis of agricultural policy. As noted by Blunden and Curry (1988) participating farmers are being paid by government to "produce" countryside in a manner which is compatible with environmental conservation. It was envisaged at the outset that the designations should apply to areas of prized environmental quality threatened by agricultural change but which could be conserved through the adoption or maintenance of a particular form of farming practice. By 1991 the United Kingdom Government had approved some 19 ESAs and were envisaging a further 12 over the period to 1993 (MAFF 1991). While the areas are very different in character it is the case that their rich habitats and landscape quality depend critically on the continuation of farming systems which in the main are extensive and livestock based.

The Mourne Mountains and Slieve Croob region was designated as the first Environmentally Sensitive Area in Northern Ireland and the Scheme came into operation on 1st May, 1988[1]. The Department of Agriculture (Northern Ireland) commissioned a socio-economic evaluation of the Scheme and this chapter arises from the baseline study for the evaluation. Its objective is to determine the existence, or non-existence, of any distinguishing characteristics between agricultural landholders participating in the Scheme (participants) and those not participating (non-participants). This should allow policy makers and field staff effectively to target the landholders most likely to join the Scheme or similar schemes in the future. It should also help indicate any appropriate tactics for carrying out the targeting, e.g. education/training of field staff or landholders, use of official advice sources, and aid in raising the level of environmental awareness of the general farming population.

## Characteristics of the designated area

The Mourne Mountains and Slieve Croob ESA encompasses the enclosed agricultural land on the foothills and lower slopes of the mountains -approximately 4 per cent of the total land and freshwater area of Northern Ireland (Fig. 5.1). Data from the Northern Ireland Agricultural Census reveal a farming region dominated by small farms with an average holding of 18 ha. These holdings tend to be family-owned and are usually farmed by a single person. In terms of land use/cover, grassland dominates the area (in 1988 over 90 per cent of the total utilized area of approximately 33,000 ha was under grass) with arable crops of minor importance. Woodland cover is minimal. Beef cattle and sheep are the major livestock enterprises, with sheep numbers increasing by 56 per cent between 1981 and 1988, which has significant implications for land use and environmental management.

## The ESA Scheme

The area currently enjoys a reputation for having one of the most beautiful

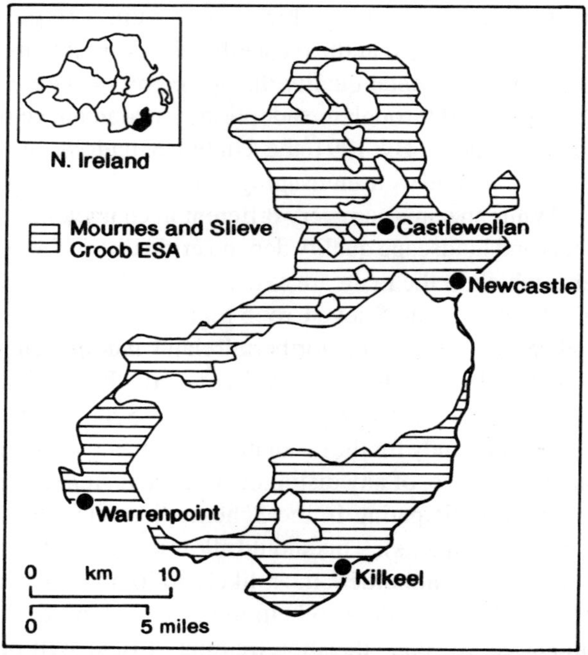


**Figure 5.1 Mourne Mountains and Slieve Croob Environmentally Sensitive Area**

landscapes in Northern Ireland and it is primarily this feature, but also its wildlife value, which led to its designation as the first ESA in Northern Ireland (DANI 1987). The quality of the landscape depends on the retention and maintenance of the traditional stone walls, hedges and other features which characterise the foothills surrounding the mountainous core. Agricultural landholders in the area are therefore offered incentive payments of £30/ha on an annual basis under the ESA Scheme in return for accepting five year management contracts which aim to integrate farming operations with sympathetic land management in terms of conservation and landscape maintenance. This is achieved in part by the five year work plan comprising various tasks such as wall maintenance, hedge/tree planting and painting/maintaining vernacular buildings and also by adherence to a number of defined agricultural practices such as selective use of pesticides/ herbicides and anti-pollution methods. Figs. 5.2 and 5.3 present the effects of current agricultural practices on the landscape, wildlife and archaelogical features in the designated area and the remedial measures of the ESA Scheme.

## Methodology

A random sample of 200 holdings (100 participants and 100 non-participants) plus replacements was selected from a total population of 1833 for the baseline study. The questionnaire was piloted prior to the main survey which was carried out through face-to-face interviews. The survey was so structured as to generate information on matters relating to the infrastructure and resources of each farm,

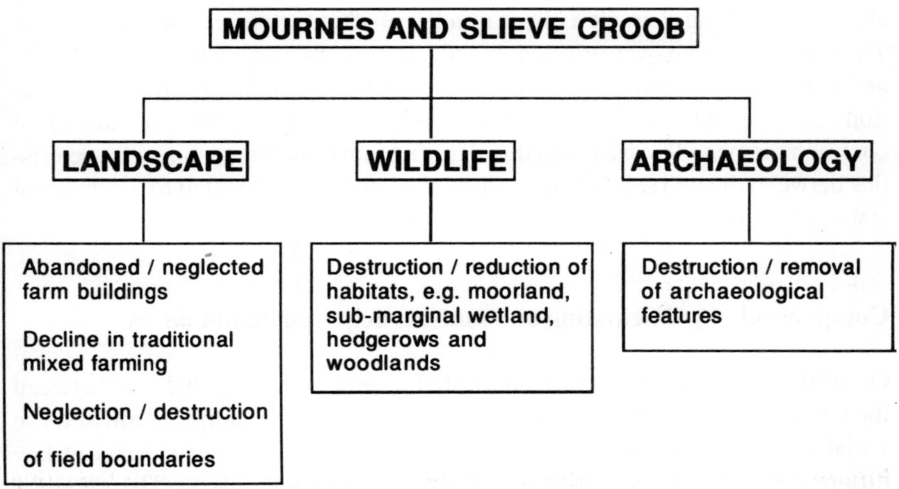


**Figure 5.2 The effects of agricultural practices on the area**

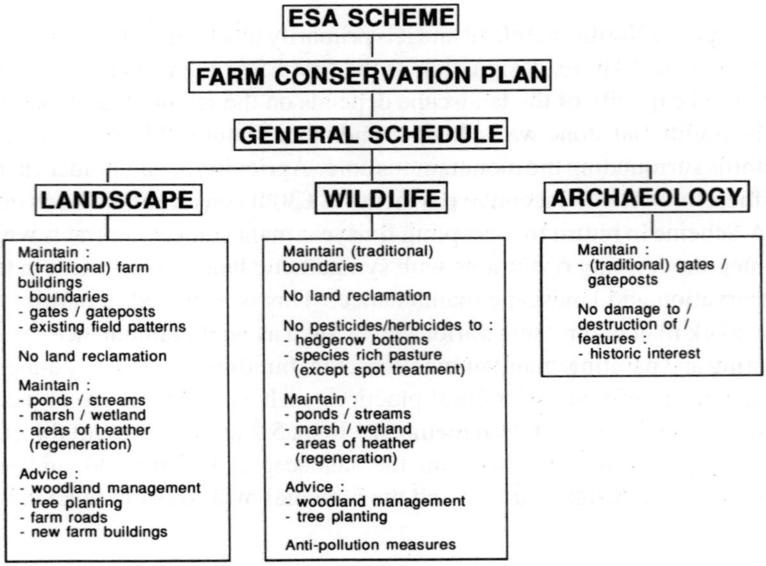


**Figure 5.3 Effects of the scheme on the environmental components of the area**

the various agricultural systems and husbandry techniques employed, the farm-family profile and off-farm income sources and also on issues such as attitudes towards the environment/conservation and the degree of business orientation. In order to take account of as many influences as possible affecting the landholders' likelihood of participating in the ESA Scheme and to further aid in identifying any distinguishing characteristics, a number of other factors were also examined. These arose from answers to open-ended questions pertaining to views/opinions and knowledge of issues, and anecdotal evidence from the informal conversations accompanying each interview, most of which contained a number of common themes. To assist with the identification of distinguishing characteristics between the two sets of landholders, the data were subjected to a number of statistical tests[2].

## Comparison of participating and non-participating landholders

Over 20 per cent of the 300 variables tested were significantly different between the two sub-samples at the level of 0.05 or higher. From interpretation of these variables there is strong evidence to suggest that there exists a number of key differences which characterise the two groups of landholders. These can be considered under the following headings:

*(1) Characteristics of participants and non-participants*

The participants tended to be younger (the average ages for participants and non-participants were 52 and 60 respectively), owned larger holdings and operated larger farm businesses (Table 5.1). For instance, the average holding size for the sample of participants was 23 ha, this being higher than the average of 18 ha for all holdings in the area (DANI, 1988), while non-participants had an average holding size of 17 ha (i.e. slightly below average). Over half of the participants farmed full-time as opposed to approximately one-third of non-participants, with the perceived hours per week of on-farm work for participants averaging about 61 hours compared to 48 hours for non-participants.

**Table 5.1**
**General characteristics of participating and non-participating landowners**

| | Average age (yrs) | Average Size of Holding (ha) | Farming Status F/T | P/T | Retired | Other |
|---|---|---|---|---|---|---|
| | | | (per cent) | | | |
| Participants | 52 | 23 | 58 | 31 | 9 | 2 |
| Non-Participants | 60 | 17 | 36 | 38 | 19 | 7 |

Source: Survey of Landholders - Mourne Mountains and Slieve Croob ESA.

*(2) Agricultural/farm management*

Considering the joint issues of farming techniques employed and the degree of progressiveness of the landholder, it was evident that the participants had, on the whole, a more active approach to land management and a more commercial approach to their farm business. Non-participants were more likely to let their land in conacre and less likely to have participated in one or more agricultural grant schemes in the past ten years or to grow crops. They were less likely to take advice from official sources - on average, the participants had four contacts in addition to ESA contacts with Department of Agriculture officials over the previous year, whereas the non-participants had two contacts. Participants displayed a stronger tendency to take up modern farming techniques such as silage-making and regular re-seeding of pasture. They were also more likely to have reclaimed land in the past ten years, to have put up more new buildings, to own more modern machinery and to have storage facilities for slurry on the farm. A higher percentage of participants also expressed a wish to expand their farms if the opportunity arose (Fig. 5.4).

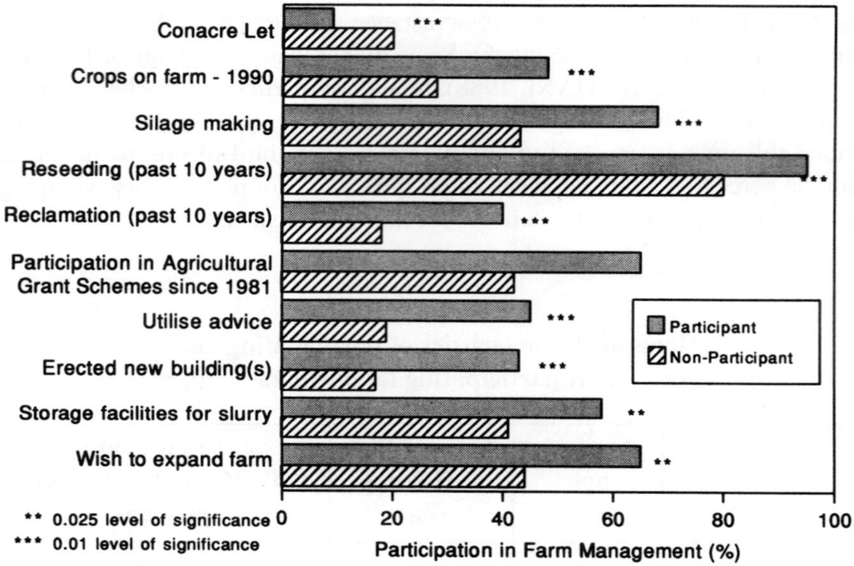


**Figure 5.4 Participation in farm management activities**

*(3) Environmental management*

It was evident from the survey results that participants had shown more propensity to undertake environmentally orientated work on their farms in the past. A larger number of participants carried out some form of active boundary maintenance or had created new boundary features (Fig. 5.5). Few non-participants anticipated planting trees in the future but the two groups showed little divergence concerning the actual rate of tree planting prior to the survey.

*(4) Clustering of key variables*

The cluster analysis lent support to the hypothesis of association between the variables highlighted in Fig. 5.3 and Table 5.1. At each stage of the clustering procedure the linkage among certain variables was revealed (Fig. 5.6). The first four stages identified a clustering of some land management techniques, with past reclamation and past building of new drystone walls having the strongest association, i.e. first in the hierarchy. The second cluster (i.e. second strongest level of association) was formed from the variables relating to the erection of new buildings in the past five years and the planting of hedges. A third cluster (reseeding and silage making) was formed before the two previous clusters

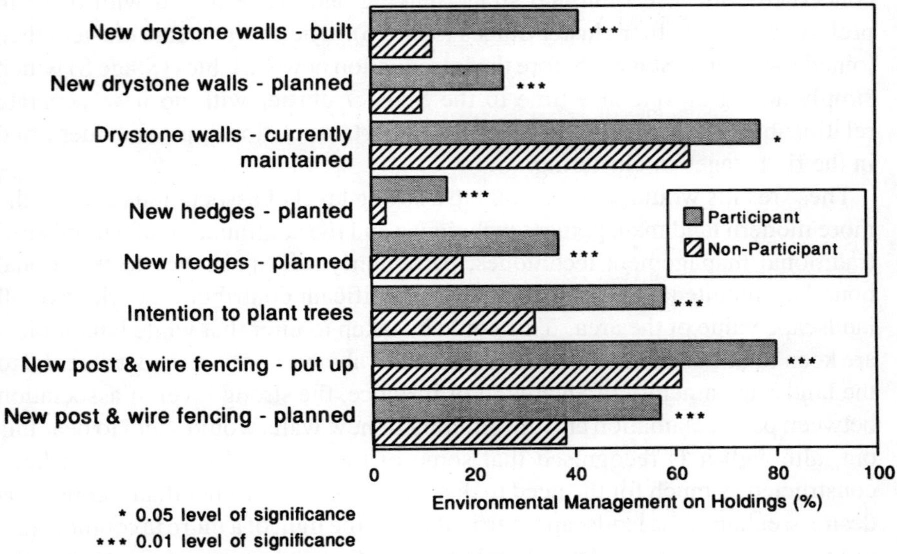


**Figure 5.5 Environmental management on holdings**

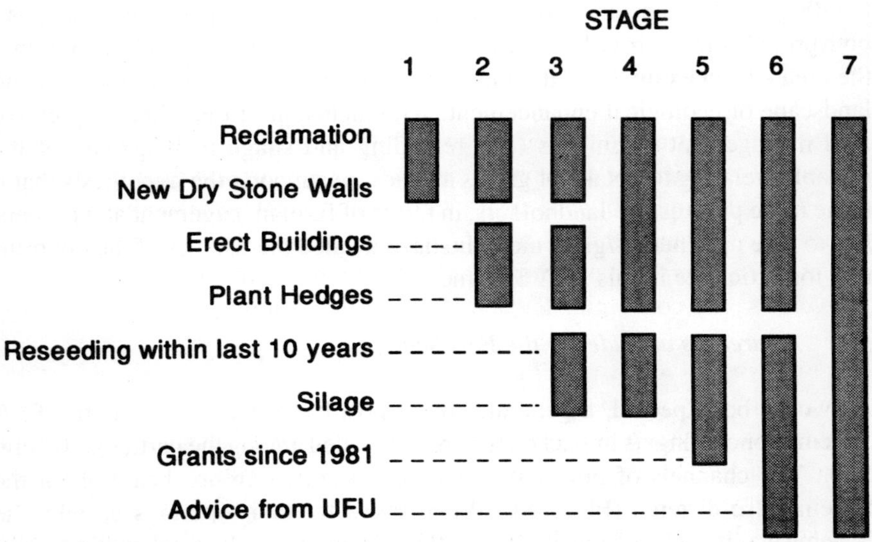


**Figure 5.6 Clustering of key variables**

merged (Stage 4) implying that the link between reseeding and silage making was stronger than that of the relationship between the two previously formed clusters. The variables relating to the uptake of grants and the taking of advice from the Ulster Farmers Union (UFU) more closely related to the cluster concerned with reseeding and silage making and hence joined with these in preference to the other cluster Stages (5 and 6). The two separate clusters then joined together at Stage 7 before the introduction new variables (Stage 8) which simply added on one at a time to the Stage 7 cluster with no new, separate relationships being identified. Thus the important relationships were identified in the first stages of clustering.

These results would seem to point to a strong level of association between the more modern land management techniques and the continuation of a number of traditional management techniques, particularly with reference to traditional boundary maintenance - which makes a significant contribution to the overall landscape value of the area. This could be taken to infer that while landholders are keen to utilize modern practices this is not always necessarily detrimental to the landscape amenity of an area. For instance, the strong level of association between past reclamation and the building of new walls would seem to bear this out, although it is recognised that some of the new walls would have been constructed as much for the need to dispose of the stone rather than a conscious desire to enhance the landscape, particularly in the light of a more favourable rate of grant aid for stone wall building in the past five or so years. Prior to this, the stone was often buried underground in a pit. Similarly, the linkage between new buildings (i.e. enhancement of the farm business) and the planting of hedges - both probably to improve livestock management, given the enterprise mix within the area - is an example of the integration of land management practices and landscape or ecological enhancement. The inclusion of the other progressive land management techniques (e.g. reseeding and silage making) and of the variables relating to uptake of grants and advice supports the hypothesis that it is the more progressive landholders, in terms of farm management and propensity to take up schemes/grant aid, who have availed themselves of the opportunity to participate in this ESA Scheme.

*(5) Awareness attitudes to the ESA Scheme*

As would be expected, a generally more positive attitude towards the ESA Scheme concerning its impact on the area prevailed among the participants (Fig. 5.7). The channels of information whereby the two groups heard about the Scheme also differed (Fig. 5.8). When asked for their opinions on why the Scheme was introduced into their area, the participants had a number of different perceptions. The most commonly expressed belief was that it was to benefit tourism in some way with over half the group mentioning improvement of the scenic value of the area for tourists as a reason. Approximately 30 per cent supposed it was to benefit the environment, while only 14 per cent perceived it

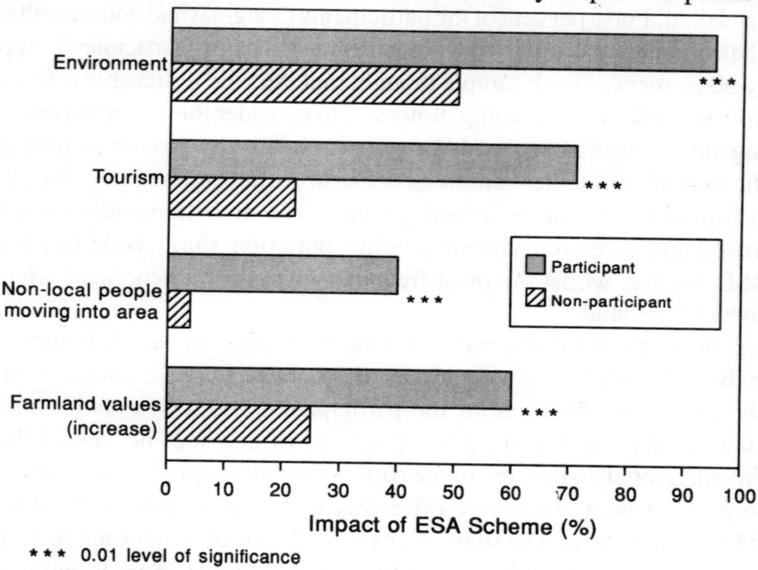


**Figure 5.7 Perceived impact of the scheme**

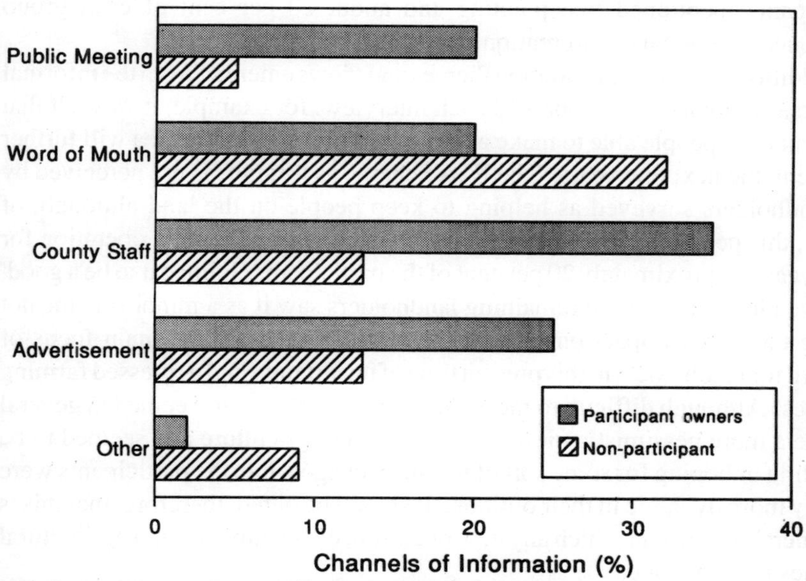


**Figure 5.8 Channels of information about the scheme**

as a method of channelling money to farmers.

In an attempt to gauge the level of awareness of the landholders about the influence of agriculture on the land in general, an open-ended question regarding this was asked. Forty per cent of the participants thought it had both an enhancing and a harmful effect as opposed to 26 per cent of the non-participants. Approximately 30 per cent of each sample thought that the only noticeable effects were harmful. It would be misleading, however, to consider these general comments as being indicative of a high level of awareness within the two sub-samples, since specific examples of either beneficial or harmful effects were mentioned by less than a fifth of the members in both groups. The most frequently cited major harmful effects were a reduction in wildlife, pollution, slurry, boundary removal and BSE disease, whilst the most frequently mentioned beneficial effect was improvement of land.

The general level of conservation awareness would appear, on first examination, to be relatively low in both groups (despite the conservation oriented work already undertaken by some of the participants) with conservation meaning "nothing" to 10 per cent of the participants and to almost 20 per cent of the non-participants. About 70 per cent of the participants and approximately 60 per cent of non-participants were able to offer only one or two suggestions of what is meant by conservation. The suggestions tended to be of a vague nature (e.g. tidy up the countryside, maintain the countryside as it is) with very few practical measures identified although 27 per cent of participants and 15 per cent of non-participants mentioned tree planting and about 20 per cent of each group mentioned maintenance or creation of wildlife habitats.

In addition, a number of common themes and views emerged from the informal conversations which accompanied each interview: for example, it was felt that the number of people able to make a living from farming in the area will further decline in the next few years. The ESA Scheme as it stands is not perceived by the landholders surveyed as helping to keep people on the land although, of course, this perception may change once the Scheme has been in operation for a few years; approximately 20 per cent of the participants claimed it to be a good, positive idea. Most of the remaining landholders saw it as a minor scheme not having too much impact on farms or incomes, which are the main focus of concern for landholders in this present time of uncertainty and depressed farming incomes. Although difficult to measure, the non-participants seemed in general to have a more pessimistic view of the future for agriculture and seemed to be expecting or hoping for some sort of rescue package while the participants were slightly more dynamic in their outlook. It should be noted, therefore, that this is the general scenario in which any new or current environmental and agricultural schemes must operate.

## Conclusions

The two sub-samples of landholders exhibited statistically significant differing characteristics. Participants are generally younger and more likely to be engaged in farming full-time, utilizing the more modern farming and land management techniques. They are also more likely to be known to official advisory staff and are generally more receptive to taking and acting upon their advice. Paradoxically more of them had also carried out conservation-type work on their farms prior to the Scheme, even if they were not fully aware of the environmental impact of the work.

It would appear, therefore, that the farmers or landholders most likely to take part in an environmentally orientated scheme such as the Mournes ESA are those that have been farming or managing their land in a less traditional manner in the immediate past. This would appear to be somewhat at variance with initial expectations - namely that such schemes (and the ESA Scheme in particular) would encourage retention of traditional farming practices. When one of the objectives of a scheme is to attract landholders farming in a traditional manner additional efforts may be necessary to recruit them, particularly those of an older average age. The presence or introduction of a stocking rate limitation could also have an effect on the type of landholder wishing to participate in the Scheme. The more intensive the farming system, then the greater the opportunity cost to the landholder of introducing stocking restrictions.

To return to the issue of environmental management on holdings, the survey identified a useful educational role for field staff when either extending an existing ESA or establishing a new one. This would include dissemination of information on the function or value of farm ponds, on the relevance of good wetland management to the encouragement of wildlife and on systematic heather regeneration techniques. There would also seem to be a need for more information on scrub/woodland management. The generally low level of positive activity or the tendency to consider these areas as waste ground is probably largely due to lack of knowledge on the landholders' part as to the intrinsic value of these habitats rather than to a wilful desire to destroy them whether through deliberate action or simple neglect. Thus, efforts must be made to heighten landholders' awareness of conservation matters to include more tasks (e.g. wetland management) and to make them more relevant to the landholder (e.g. recycling of resources, prudent use of artificial fertilizers and other inputs). The links between agriculture and conservation should then become more evident, so allowing conservation to play more than its current peripheral role in day-to-day land management. With environmental issues expected to take a higher priority in the formulation of new agricultural policies it is important that the ESA Schemes - which are the first serious attempt to integrate environmental management concepts with farm management practices - get off to a good start.

## Notes

1. As of November 1992 over 1000 farmers had signed management agreements covering some 19,000 hectares of land in Northern Ireland's two ESAs : Mourne Mountains and Slieve Croob, and the Glens of Antrim. It is proposed to extend the area of the existing Glens of Antrim ESA and to designate a new ESA in Co Fermanagh covering about 60,000 hectares. It is anticipated that this expansion will increase the area in Northern Ireland designated as environmentally sensitive to about 120,000 hectares or 11 per cent of the agricultural land area. (Department of Agriculture Press Release 291/92). In March 1993 the government announced proposals to designate a further 2 ESAs in the Sperrins and South Armagh as well as 3 new agri-environmental schemes: a moorland scheme; a habitat improvement scheme and an organic aid scheme (Department of Agriculture Press Release 68/93).
2. The first stage of the analysis led to determination of the sample parameters of discrete and continuous variables, while the second stage (chi-square test and t-tests) allowed comparisons between the two sub-samples to identify statistically significant differences. Following these tests, a Euclidean Dissimilarity Co-efficient matrix (measuring the level of similarity between different variables or cases: dissimilarity measures between entities decrease with greater similarity) was constructed to enable application of Hierarchical Cluster Analysis (using average linkage between groups) to a number of key variables in order to establish the existence, if any, of independent groups of linked variables to aid identification of participants or likely participants. The basic aim of cluster analysis is to find the natural groupings, if any, of a set of individuals. This set of individuals may form a complete population or be a sample from some larger population. More formally, cluster analysis aims to allocate a set of individuals to a set of mutually exclusive, exhaustive groups such that individuals within a group are similar to one another while individuals in different groups are dissimilar (Chatfield et al 1990). The process of hierarchical clustering (Gnanadesikan 1977) is one in which every cluster obtained at any stage is a merger of clusters at previous stages. Broadly speaking, a cluster analysis has been successful if it brings to light previously unnoticed groupings in a set of data or helps to formalize its hierarchical structure. Cluster analysis has been considered above in terms of the clustering of individuals rather than of variables. In view of the duality between measurements on variables and on

individuals (Chatfield et al, 1980), however, the techniques used to cluster individuals can also be applied to see if it is possible to discover subsets of variables which are so highly correlated amongst themselves that any one of them, or some average of them, can be used so as to represent the subset without serious loss of information. By using cluster analysis it was possible to take measurements on the variables (determined by the prior analysis as highly significant between participants and non-participants) important to the landholders to identify any relationships between those variables.

## References


Blunden, J. and Curry, N. (1988) *A future for our countryside*. Basil Blackwell, Oxford.

Chatfield, C. and Collins, A.J. (1980) Cluster analysis, in *Introduction to multivariate analysis*. pp. 212-215, Chapman and Hall Ltd, London.

Gnanadesikan, R. (1977) Multidimensional classification and clustering, in *Methods for statistical data analysis of multivariate observations*. John Wiley & Sons, Inc., Chichester.

Department of Agriculture for Northern Ireland (1987) *Mourne Mountains and Slieve Croob Environmentally Sensitive Area*. Belfast.

Department of Agriculture for Northern Ireland (1988) *Agricultural Census, Northern Ireland*. Belfast.

MAFF (1991) *Our farming future*. MAFF Publications, London.

# 6 Forestry and rural employment

*Áine Ní Dhubháin*

## Introduction

The Republic of Ireland has the smallest forested area of all EC countries, with only 7 per cent of its total land area under forest. In contrast, Greece has 44 per cent while the United Kingdom has almost 10 per cent. However, over the past decade the forestry sector has grown considerably in the Republic of Ireland. State planting rates have risen from 5,922 ha in 1980 to 7,855 ha in 1991. (These are afforestation rates only and do not include replanting.) The increase in private planting rates has been more spectacular rising from a mere 498 ha in 1982 to over 11,000 ha in 1991. As noted by Gillmor (1992) there is a distinct spatial pattern in the location and growth of private afforestation. It is concentrated on land which is marginal for agriculture in the west and south west. Up to 1981 it was usually the owners of large estates who planted trees on their land. In latter years financial institutions, particularly those specialising in pension funds, have invested in forestry, taking advantage of the new grants available for private planting. More recently farmers have accounted for a sizeable portion of the area being planted. In 1991, over 8,000 ha were planted by farmers. Further growth is predicted for the forestry sector and planting rates in 1993 are expected to be twice as high as they were in 1989 when the total area planted amounted to 15,000 ha. Since forestry is essentially a rural land-use enterprise, the increase in planting rates is having and will have various impacts on rural areas. These impacts must be identified and the expansion of the forestry sector planned in such a way as to minimise the negative impacts and maximise the positive impacts.

In various reports, it has been claimed that forestry has an important role to play in rural areas. In 1958 the report entitled *Economic development*, which formed the basis for Ireland's First Programme for Economic Expansion, stated that forestry provides "a substantial amount of employment in rural areas where there is little economic activity and considerable emigration" (Anon. 1958, p.144). Successive government White Papers on economic expansion have identified the importance of forestry in providing employment in rural areas. More recently in *The future of rural society*, published by the EC, forestry was described as an important component of any integrated rural development programme (Commission of the European Communities 1988). The development of woodlands and timber processing industries were deemed to represent a promising niche for rural development. On the other hand, forestry has been viewed by some as having a negative impact on rural areas. Gallagher (1991) reports that it has been perceived as contributing to rural depopulation. In New Zealand, where forestry has expanded at a rapid rate in a predominantly agricultural environment, it has been feared that forestry will depopulate the farming community with a resultant decline in rural services (Edmonds 1981). Furthermore, fears were expressed that workers employed by forest companies would not have a stake in the community and would replace the family owned and worked farm. Indeed forestry may be described as a two-edged sword. It offers the promise of employment and the prospect of repopulating rural areas, as well as acting as a resource with which to expand the regional economic base. On the other hand it may be seen to displace agriculture and disrupt farming communities (Fairgray, 1981).

## Forestry and employment in rural areas in the Republic of Ireland

### *Employment overview*

The most important impact that forestry has had on rural areas is employment generation. Forestry has been an important employer in rural areas and consequently has played an important role in maintaining the rural fabric (Gardiner 1991). At its peak in-forest employment in State forestry in the Republic of Ireland was some 5,000, all of which were rural jobs. With an increase in mechanisation, labour productivity and rationalisation and in the amount of work being done by contract, the number employed directly has decreased to a present low of 1,192 (see Table 6.1). Employment in the private sector has been more difficult to monitor as official statistics are not available. However, the increase in private planting coupled with an increase in the amount of work being carried out by contract in State forests suggests that private sector employment has increased considerably over the past ten years.

**Table 6.1**
**Area planted and numbers employed by State forestry in the Republic of Ireland**

| Planting Year | Area afforested (ha) | Number employed |
|---|---|---|
| 1930-31 | 1,442 | 462 |
| 1935-36 | 2,800 | 1,057 |
| 1940-41 | 2,412 | 1,340 |
| 1945-46 | 1,456 | 1,565 |
| 1950-51 | 3,792 | 2,734 |
| 1955-56 | 6,608 | 4,843 |
| 1956-57 | 7,044 | 5,048 |
| 1960-61 | 10,550 | 4,653 |
| 1965-66 | 9,004 | 4,668 |
| 1970-71 | 8,498 | 3,382 |
| 1975 | 8,961 | 2,659 |
| 1980 | 5,922 | 2,719 |
| 1985 | 4,625 | 2,400 |
| 1991 | 7,855 | 1,192 |

Source: Annual Reports, Forest Service and Coillte Teoranta

One of the significant aspects of employment in forestry is that direct employment accounts for only a small part of that generated from each hectare of forestry. Aldwell and Whyte (1984) indicate that downstream employment effects account for over 80 per cent of the total employment generated from domestic sawn timber. This would suggest that forestry may have a strong employment multiplier effect. Downstream jobs are generated primarily from the processing of materials and the transport to and from mills. In the Republic of Ireland the timber processing sector employs a considerable number of people in rural areas. At the present time there are two pulpwood processing facilities and approximately 100 sawmills in operation. The two pulpmills generate total employment, including transport and harvesting, for 800 people. It is estimated that the total employment in the private forestry and wood products sector (i.e. downstream industries) is about 10,500 people. From the above it is clear that there is quite a significant number of people employed in forest-related industries in Ireland and the majority of this employment is based in rural areas.

What effect will the expected two-fold increase in the planting rate, from 15,000 ha in 1989 (including both private and public planting) to 30,000 ha in

1993, have on rural areas? In the Forestry Operational Programme (FOP 1991), it is stated that every additional 1,000 hectares of planting generates 100 jobs, on average. Thus it is concluded that the doubling of the forestry planting programme will generate an additional 1,500 jobs in forest establishment work. An increase in the area of existing forest reaching clearfelling age will generate extra jobs in harvesting, bringing total job creation during the period 1989-1993 to 2,000. Many of these jobs will be in rural areas. In a more recent newspaper article however it was indicated that the doubling of planting and the increase in timber production would result in the generation of only 400 to 500 seasonal jobs. This suggests that initial FOP estimates may be much too optimistic.

Indications are that a new pulpwood mill, which would involve an investment of at least IR£150m, will be needed in the Republic of Ireland by 1995. This will be necessary to process the greater volume of thinnings becoming available and the residues from saw milling. At present a considerable volume of pulpwood is being exported and thus the added value which would be accrued from domestic processing of this material is being lost. Coillte Teoranta (the Irish Forestry Board) held negotiations with a Swedish industrial group regarding a joint venture to build a pulpmill and to plant trees for pulp production. While these plans with the Swedish group have been abandoned, Coillte Teoranta remains confident that a similar plant will come into operation but with a different partner. It was envisaged that the new pulpmill would create employment for up to 150 people with an additional 300 to 400 employed in establishment, harvesting and transport.

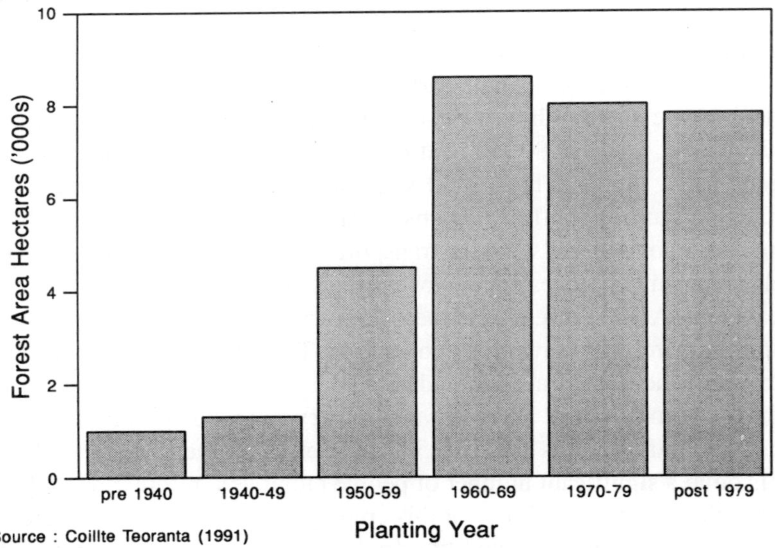


Source : Coillte Teoranta (1991)

**Figure 6.1 Forest area by age-class in the Republic of Ireland, 1990**

*Time-profile of forestry employment*

The distribution of jobs in forestry is affected by the age and maturity of the forests (Strak and Mackel 1991). Grundy et al. (1989) examined the pattern of employment over a typical 50-year+ rotation of a conifer forest. This report indicates that the establishment stages, i.e. the first 5 years of the rotation, have considerable employment potential. It is estimated that an average of 2 man weeks per hectare of forestry is required in the planting period. This falls to almost zero up until first thinning stage and rises to 3 man weeks per hectare in years 25-45, to 4 man weeks per hectare in years 45-55 and reaches 15 man weeks per hectare after 55 years, i.e. clearfell stage. Thus the bulk of employment is concentrated in the second half of the rotation and is associated with harvesting activity. Analysis of the age-class distribution of Irish forests (see Figure 6.1) demonstrates that over 52% of the forest area is under 20 years of age (1990 figures). Irish forestry is therefore at a juvenile stage of development. Figures for British forestry which is at a similar stage of development indicate that the present ratio of harvesting to other workers is 2:1. With a normal forest estate i.e. essentially one with an uniform age-class distribution, the ratio would be 5:1. Because of the age structure of Irish forests jobs in harvesting and processing have been relatively few to date. However, in the next 10 to 20 years many of the state forests in the Republic of Ireland will be reaching stages of development that require a high labour input. If the jobs that are created as a result of the doubling of the planting rate are to be maintained, it is essential that high planting rates continue for at least another 10 years. This should go some way to ensuring continuity of employment.

*Type of employment*

The skills required for employment in forestry tend to be basic, such as being able to use a selection of hand tools and possibly a selection of agricultural machinery and holding a driving licence. Thus employment in forestry is ideally suited to many who are used to working in rural areas, particularly in the agricultural sector. It is also attractive to those who are used to the open air and have a high level of self-motivation (Strak and Mackel 1991). On the other hand, because of the nature of forestry development, there is the difficulty of providing balanced employment to cater for the work needs of both women and men in various age-groups (Smith 1981).

The ability of farmers to manage and maintain forests on their land has been questioned. Many of the farmers who have established forests on their farms have been frequently criticised because of their poor management techniques. However, as there was no forestry extension programme available in the

Republic of Ireland, such criticism was unjustified. Under the recently announced forestry measures of the Operational Programme for Rural Development, courses are now available that provide for training in forest establishment, maintenance, harvesting and the marketing of forest products.

Of work that is presently part of forestry, chainsaw felling is the most physiologically demanding. However, the past five years have seen a considerable increase in the amount of harvesting being carried out mechanically. At present it is about 10-15 per cent, and this is expected to rise to a maximum of 25 per cent. This will reduce the demand for labour at the harvesting stage as one machine operator can now do the same amount of work as five men using chain-saws. However, the servicing and maintenance of the harvesting machines will require a larger indirect labour force than would be required for motor-manual felling. Increased mechanisation should also make harvesting work more accessible to women. The trend to mechanise forest operations will also increase the need for training. This training is likely to be provided in rural areas and should in itself generate demand for instructors.

*Assessing the employment impact*

In order to assess the impact of forestry on employment, it is necessary to recognise the distinction between unemployment and under- employment (Smith 1981). In rural areas there is considerable under-employment as well as unemployment. This is particularly true for the agricultural sector. Forestry can reduce both under-employment and unemployment in this sector. The extent to which it does so depends on how involved farmers and their families become in forestry. As indicated earlier many jobs in forestry are seasonal and could be fitted around work on the farm. Thus it would make sense for many farmers to plant some of their holdings with trees. In the case of farmers who become actively involved in the management of their woodland this would reduce their under-employment and might also generate additional employment for others. Many farmers who are already involved in forestry have not, however, become actively involved in the establishment and management of their woodlands. Instead they have employed forest management companies. As a result farmers have limited input to the management of the land under trees although employment for others is generated. Some farmers may sell their land for forestry development either to the State or to private individuals and gain income from the transaction but not gain any employment. However, other farmers and indeed non-farmers may gain work from the resulting forests. These would, in a statistical sense, add to the numbers at work.

Farming is not the only sector in rural areas to experience under-employment. In many parts of rural Ireland businesses find their turnover and workload falling as a result of the reduced spending power associated with the decline in the rural workforce and recently the decline in farm incomes. These local services face falling profitability and declining productivity which means that many of them are earning less than similar enterprises in urban areas. It has been suggested that where a development project such as forestry or forest processing occurs a considerable proportion of the employment impact can be expected to go towards increasing the productivity and earnings of people already in work outside the forest sector (Grant 1979). In other words there may be a strong income multiplier effect.

### Income and forestry

A development project can influence the incomes of people living in the development area in two ways - directly through salary and wage payments, and indirectly by purchasing materials and equipment in the region thereby creating new employment opportunities or higher wage payments in the local servicing and supplying industries (Grant, 1979). Those employed directly in forestry gain from an increase in income through salaries and wages. Farmers who plant their land with trees benefit financially from the premiums they receive. Furthermore as trees grow so too does their value and at the end of a forty year rotation the timber (at present prices) would be worth in the region of IR£25 per $m^3$ yielding approximately IR£10,000 per hectare. Thus with the present grant and premium scheme not only do farmers who afforest receive 85 per cent of the establishment costs (up to maximum of IR£2,000 per hectare for broadleaves and IR£1,100 per hectare for conifers) but they can also receive up to IR£116 per hectare for 15 years. At the end of the rotation the returns per hectare average at around IR£10,000 for conifer planting.

The indirect effect that forestry has on rural incomes depends on the type of inputs it requires and where these inputs are purchased. The establishment stage of the forest industry obtains most of its inputs from sectors supplying agriculture. For example both sectors have fertiliser requirements and transport requirements. The main difference would obviously be the growing stock requirements of the forest sector. The initial effect of increased afforestation would therefore be to strengthen the existing infrastructure rather than increase the diversification of the infrastructure (Aldwell and Whyte 1984). The extent to which existing infrastructure benefits from forestry will depend of course on the purchasing policy of the person or group afforesting. For example, State forestry has traditionally centralised purchasing. Thus many of the income benefits of forestry have been transferred outside of the area where development takes place. Private investors are less likely to have such a purchasing pattern and thus more of the benefits would stay in rural areas. As the forest estate develops diversification of the servicing infrastructure is more likely to occur with the increase in harvesting and processing (Aldwell and Whyte 1984).

## Other effects of forestry on rural areas

There are other, less tangible effects of forestry. For example, forestry may interfere with the decision-making process in rural areas. If State forestry or large scale private planting takes place in rural areas, decisions are made by individuals living outside these areas. Even when farmers themselves undertake the establishment and management of forest on their land, the conditions attached to planting grants are so rigid that farmers have little, if any, input into what type of forestry they want. Many would argue that similarly farmers have a minor decision-making role in relation to the agricultural systems that they employ, as subsidies obtained from the EC have conditions attached to them. The long time period associated with forestry further limits the range of decisions that can be made from year to year.

Other examples of potential effects of forestry include its impact on farmers' opportunities to interact with other farmers, as well as its impact on the social stratification. Firstly, many of the smaller, more isolated farmers depend considerably on their visits to co-operatives and marts for social contact. Such social contact is not associated with forestry. Secondly, State forestry and forest companies can increase the social stratification in rural areas because of the status differences that are found in their organisation at local level. For example, the local forester has a higher status than the assistant forester who in turn has a higher status than the forest labourer. This social stratification is not as marked in agriculture particularly where farmers and their families work the land and off-farm labour is not used. Any increase in social stratification can influence the way people interact with each other. If farmers gain employment in either State or forest companies such a move would take them from a high level in the stratification to a much lower one. These changes in status do not occur when farmers get involved in forestry on their own land. Farnsworth (1983) documented the social changes that accompanied the development of a forest company in an isolated rural farming community in New Zealand. He observed that a pecking order was produced amongst the resident families according to their relative position in the company hierarchy and that this flowed over into social events.

One of the main concerns of rural people is the sense of isolation that large-scale forests can create. In the more remote areas the planting of trees has meant that some rural residents can no longer see their neighbours, hence the resultant sense of isolation. Others, with houses formerly in view from a public road, have lost that benefit. No agricultural crop would have the same effect.

## Co-operative forestry

Co-operative forestry has developed considerably in Ireland in recent years. The co-operative forestry movement started in 1985 with the foundation of the Western Forestry Co-operative. Initially a group of 6 farmers planted 26 ha on a co-operative basis. By 1989 this figure had risen to 474 farmers planting over 2,000 ha. Gallagher (1991 p.75) states that the aim of the forestry co-operative movement is "to use forestry as the catalyst for self-help rural community enterprise, to exploit the possibilities of afforestation for the stabilisation of declining rural communities through the provision of jobs in remote rural areas and improve the viability of small farms, and to develop forestry in a way which would enhance the landscape and safeguard the natural environment". The orderly development of forestry is always stressed. Co-operative forestry offers many advantages to those farmers who have small areas of land that they wish to afforest as it allows them to do so and still retain ownership of their land. It groups the suitable forestry land available on adjacent farms into viable units and effects economies of scale in purchasing, fencing, and machine work.

Co-operative forestry has a particularly important role to play in rural development. It allows farmers to become actively involved in forestry and to have a greater input in the development of forestry in their area. Forestry can also form the focal point of a far wider community development programme. This aspect of forestry is being promoted by the co-operative movement and already some rural communities have included forestry in a development programme for their locality. For example, in Monasteraden in Co. Sligo a forestry/peat programme is being developed. Work in both aspects is seasonal so that during the summer workers prepare material for a small peat moss factory and in the winter they are deployed in forest work. The aim is to create 6 jobs. Another aspect of forestry that is being exploited in rural areas is its role in attracting tourists. In Killenkere in Co. Cavan, 80 farmers are afforesting 200 ha. of land as a community project. This project has now been expanded so as to exploit the tourist potential of the forests. Walks and picnic areas are being developed in the forests and a wildlife preserve is being created. In addition 4.5 miles of an adjacent river are being developed with riverside walks, broadleaf landscaping, fish pools and spawning beds.

## Conclusion

It is clear that there is a number of positive ways in which forestry can influence rural areas. It provides employment in areas where alternative employment opportunities are limited. It also generates income and in the long run creates a valuable asset. It can play an important role in an integrated rural development programme. If the maximum benefits are to be derived from forestry in rural areas local people must have a greater input into the development of forestry in their locality. It is also vital that the expansion of forestry be carried out in a planned way so as to maximise the benefits and minimise the negative impacts.

## Note

A joint research project between University College Dublin, The Queen's University of Belfast, and the University of Aberdeen commenced in 1991 on the socio-economic impacts of afforestation on rural development. It is proposed that the research will quantify some of the effects discussed in this chapter, in particular the contribution of afforestation to rural employment and income. It will also attempt to establish farmers' attitudes to forestry and to discover how forestry has affected those farmers who have already planted some of their land. In addition the contribution of the non-market benefits, i.e. the recreational benefits of forestry, to rural areas will be assessed. The work is being funded by the European Commission CAMAR Programme and should be concluded in 1994.

## References


Aldwell, P.H.B. and Whyte, J. (1984) Impacts of forest sector growth in Bruce County, Otago. A case study. *New Zealand Journal of Forestry*, Vol. 29. No. 2, pp. 269-295.

Anon. (1958) *Economic development*. Stationery Office, Dublin.

Commission of the European Communities (1988) *The Future of Rural Society*. Luxembourg.

Edmonds, K. (1981) The forestry debate. *People and Planning*, Vol.20, pp.7-8.

Fairgray, J.D.M. (1981) Regional afforestation issues. *People and Planning*, Vol. 20, pp. 17-19.

Farnsworth, M.C. (1983) The social impact of forest development in Northland. *New Zealand Journal of Forestry*, Vol. 28, No. 2, pp. 246-254.

FOP (1991) *Forestry operational programme 1989-1993*. Stationery Office, Dublin.

Gallagher, R. (1991) Co-operative farmer forestry and rural development, in *Post-Congress Proceedings IUFRO Division 3, XIX World Congress, Montreal, Canada, 1990*, pp. 74-79.

Gardiner, J.J. (1991) *The socio-economic impacts of forestry upon rural development.* Paper presented at EC workshop on Afforestation of Agricultural Land.

Gillmor, D. (1992) The upsurge in private afforestation in the Republic of Ireland. *Irish Geography*, Vol. 25, No. 1, pp. 89-97.

Grant, R.K. (1979) Managing the regional impact of forest development programmes. *New Zealand Journal of Forestry*, Vol. 24, No. 2, pp. 198-204.

Grundy, D.S., Hatfield, G.R. and Thompson, J. (1989) The contribution of forestry to rural employment. *NEDC Agriculture Ad Hoc Sector Group Report.*

Smith, B.N.P. (1981) Forestry and rural social change: a comment. *New Zealand Journal of Forestry*, Vol. 26, No. 1, pp. 103-107.

Strak, J. and Mackel, C. (1991) Forestry in the rural economy. Paper No. 12, in *Forestry expansion: a study of technical and ecological factors*. Forestry Commission.

# 7 Enterprise in rural areas

*Mark Hart*

## Introduction

Recent years have witnessed a major change in the manner in which many commentators analyse and discuss developments within the rural environment. Gone are the days when change in activities in rural areas was frequently interpreted as a reaction to changes elsewhere in the economic, social and political system (Bryant 1989). An excellent example of this exists within Northern Ireland where the physical planning strategy for the period 1975-1995 displayed little empathy with the concept of rurality in its pursuit of economic growth through urban-based policies. As Murray (1992) points out, "a misplaced paternalism that rural people can and want to avail of better social and economic opportunity in urban areas has held sway". However, this negative or passive view of the rural environment began to disintegrate in the face of a quite remarkable re-working of the urban and regional geography of all the developed economies. Of particular importance have been the changes that have occurred at the sub-regional level. The decline of the inner cities and the conurbations and the relative growth of outer metropolitan areas and smaller towns in rural areas represent the most significant shift in the geography of manufacturing since the mid-1960s (Fothergill and Gudgin 1982, Massey 1989). In essence, the nineteenth century impulse towards concentration of industry and population into cities has been reversed in the latter decades of the twentieth century.

With the persistence of spatial disparities in levels of socio-economic health throughout the 1970s and 1980s there has been an increased interest in locally-based economic development initiatives. As other contributions to this book illustrate, the status of rural areas within this overall policy approach has been growing throughout the 1980s and early 1990s. The benefits of local initiatives include the use of local knowledge and local resources in an effort to achieve community-determined goals and objectives. In the local economic development process (within or outside the urban arena), success must be measured in terms of the achievement of community goals. However, it should be stressed that these goals may include non-economic objectives and are, therefore, not necessarily synonymous with large factories and development projects.

The aim of this chapter is to concentrate upon one aspect of the rural economy, namely industrial development, in order to assess its potential contribution to economic growth in rural areas in the 1990s. The chapter is divided into 5 sections. The second section derived from Gudgin (1990), briefly outlines the nature of rural economies and reviews the major trends in sub-regional manufacturing employment change in the UK in the 1970s and 1980s. This is followed in the third section by a discussion of sub-regional employment trends in Northern Ireland for the period 1971-1990 with particular attention being given to the role of rural areas in the overall pattern of change. Turning to policy initiatives designed to promote industrial development in rural areas, the fourth section provides an assessment of the operation of the Local Enterprise Programme (LEP) in Northern Ireland with particular attention being focused on the activities of Local Enterprise Agencies (LEAs), the vast majority of which operate in rural areas. The fifth section continues this theme by concentrating upon the outcome of a 3 year pilot programme to stimulate Community Business in 5 localities in Northern Ireland (Mid-Ulster; Omagh; Newry and Mourne; Derry; and West Belfast). Of particular concern here will be an examination of the ability of rural areas within the overall programme to generate economically viable projects. The paper concludes with some policy recommendations for the process of rural enterprise development.

## Sub-regional employment trends in the United Kingdom, 1971-87

The difficulty of determining what constitutes urban and rural makes any analysis of the rural economy extremely problematic. In the following analysis, which is based on Gudgin (1990), rural areas have been arbitrarily defined as local authority districts in which all settlements had fewer than 35,000 people in 1971.[1] This definition results in a total of 175 rural areas out of a total of 484 local authority districts in Great Britain and Northern Ireland. They may be viewed as wholly rural in that they exclude local authority districts containing settlements of over 35,000, despite the fact that these contain large tracts of countryside. Wholly rural areas are characterised by small market towns as well as villages and isolated dwellings and range from those within commuting distance of large cities to remote uplands. Districts with towns of between 35,000 and 100,000 people are classified as "small towns". Some other urban categories are included in the analysis to illustrate the contrast between urban and rural areas in terms of employment change. The data source used in the analysis was the Census of Employment accessed through NOMIS.

A snapshot of the characteristics of the rural economy (defined as that of wholly rural areas) in 1987 reveals perhaps surprisingly that a minority of the workforce is directly employed in agriculture, forestry or fishing.[2] Out of a total employment base of 3.2m in 1987 only 189,000 (5.8 per cent) were employed in these sectors. These figures exclude the self-employed owing to data deficiencies. However, when adjusted for the self-employed, who form an important element in the farming and fishing sectors, this figure rises only to just under 10 per cent. The major sources of employment in rural areas are the same as those in urban areas with almost two-thirds of employees working in the service sectors. Of these most are in the private services which include retail and wholesale distribution, hotels and catering, finance, business and professional services and a range of entertainment, leisure and miscellaneous services. With one in five of all employees in government services, the rural areas have a similar proportion to that in the country as a whole. After private services the second most important sector in rural areas is manufacturing which has grown steadily in importance in rural areas. A quarter of all employment is now in manufacturing which is only slightly lower than the national average. As Gudgin (1990) asserts, "it is a little known fact that manufacturing is now as important a component of rural economies as it is of the economies of Britain's large cities".

Overall, therefore, the employment structure of rural areas is surprisingly similar to that of the UK as a whole. Rural areas have close to 14 per cent of national employment both in total and in most individual sectors. From the perspective of rural economic development the sectors of most importance are those capable of bringing income in from outside the individual rural area. These include agriculture, forestry, fishing, mining and quarrying and manufacturing. It is the contribution of the manufacturing sector which is the particular concern of this chapter and it is therefore pertinent to establish how this sector has been performing in recent years.

The UK economy has undergone profound changes since the early 1970s and has grown significantly less rapidly than in earlier decades. The urban-rural shift in employment is clearly evident in this period (Table 7.1). The less urban an area the more it has gained jobs. The general trend of falling employment over the period 1971-87 has been exacerbated in the cities by a shift of jobs to smaller towns and rural areas. Within the rural areas, however, the point to emerge is that the national decline in employment has been offset by an urban-rural redistribution to such a degree that these areas have gained substantial numbers of jobs. The statistics are most emphatic: over the period 1971-87 rural areas gained 496,000 jobs (19.2 per cent) while the national experience was a loss of 318,000 jobs (1.5 per cent). Furthermore, the rural areas were the only part of the UK to experience significant employment gains over this period of national employment decline.

**Table 7.1**
**Employment change in the UK by urban-rural category, 1971-87**

| | 1971-81 % | 1971-81 % | 1971-81 % |
|---|---|---|---|
| London | -10.5 | -0.2 | -10.6 |
| Conurbations | -12.2 | -4.8 | -16.4 |
| Free standing cities | -4.0 | -2.4 | -6.3 |
| Large towns | 3.1 | 3.1 | 6.3 |
| Small towns | 3.4 | 3.5 | 7.0 |
| Rural areas | 11.4 | 7.0 | 19.2 |
| United Kingdom | -2.1 | 1.0 | -1.5 |

Source: Department of Employment, NOMIS

The redistribution of economic activity out of the cities and into rural areas is immediately apparent when the growth in employment in each rural sector is compared with the national growth in that sector (Table 7.2). Rural areas have gained the greatest share of national activity in manufacturing: employment in this sector in rural areas grew 29 per cent faster than the national average. As a result by 1987 14.9 per cent of national manufacturing employment was in rural areas which contrasted with a figure of 9.5 per cent in 1971.

**Table 7.2**
**Employment change in rural areas relative to the UK (1971-87)**

| | % |
|---|---|
| Agriculture, forestry, fishing | -0.8 |
| Mining and quarrying | 3.4 |
| Manufacturing | 28.9 |
| Construction | 6.7 |
| Gas, electricity, water | 17.8 |
| Private services | 27.8 |
| Government services | 9.1 |
| Total | 17.8 |

Source: Department of Employment, NOMIS

One consequence of this redistribution of manufacturing activities into rural areas has been an increase in related activities most notably within non-tradeable private services. This movement of manufacturing jobs has caused population movement, and hence shifts in service sector jobs serving the rising rural population. Thus, an explanation of the overall urban-rural shift necessitates an understanding of the manufacturing shift. Table 7.3 presents data on the urban-rural differences in manufacturing employment change over the slightly longer time period 1960-87. The contrast is very clear with the general rule emerging that the larger the settlement the greater the rate of decline in manufacturing employment. It must be stressed at this stage that the shift of manufacturing to rural areas is not due solely to the relocation of companies. Far more important is the fact that existing rural factories grow faster than their urban counterparts and that new firm formation is higher in rural areas. Data on VAT registrations over the period 1980-90 for GB counties clearly indicates that the new firm formation rates are greater in rural localities (Keeble 1990, Hart et al 1993a).

**Table 7.3**
**The urban-rural contrast in manufacturing employment change in Great Britain, 1960-87**

| | Change in number of manufacturing jobs | as % 1960 |
|---|---|---|
| | (000s) | |
| Rural areas | 104.0 | 19.7 |
| Small towns | -136.0 | -8.3 |
| Large towns | -275.0 | -29.9 |
| Free standing cities | -551.0 | -41.4 |
| Conurbations | -1272.0 | -55.7 |
| London | -882.0 | -61.5 |
| Great Britain | -3012.0 | -37.5 |

Source: Department of Employment

How can these stark and consistent trends in sub-regional employment change be explained? The influence of industry mix can be dismissed immediately.[3] The most plausible explanation would seem to lie in the fact that rural areas receive a disproportionate share of new factory floorspace which is in abundant supply (planning legislation permitting) and this leads to an actual rise in manufacturing jobs (any expansion in industrial output requires an increase in the volume of factory floorspace). Such an explanation is consistent with the observation that the shift of jobs proceeds most rapidly in a period of economic boom (e.g. between 1983-89 London lost over one quarter of its entire manufacturing base). However, it must be acknowledged that this explanation is not without its problems, not least of which is that it concentrates on only one variable - land availability - and ignores cost factors such as land and labour. Although costs are important no strong pattern has yet emerged, and indeed some cities with very low land or labour costs still lose jobs to small towns and rural areas.

The conclusion to emerge from this analysis is clear. Rural industry has expanded and will continue to expand faster than the national average. The increase of industrial jobs attracts and retains population which brings with it incomes and purchasing power. This will in turn stimulate demand for private services. After some time the larger population will lead to an expansion in local public services. Through this mechanism rural economies are gradually becoming revitalised. These observations are given further weight by a recent study into the performance of rural enterprise in England (Keeble et al 1992). The aim of this large national-scale research project, which is based on interviews with over 1,100 enterprises, is to investigate the nature and possible causes of business creation, location and development in rural England. The main findings of the research which help explain the positive employment growth trends in rural areas are:

(1) most rural enterprises are relatively new reflecting the recent process of new firm formation in England's rural areas (see Hart et al 1993a);

(2) there was a clear connection between recent environmentally-influenced population migration to England's rural areas and high rates of new enterprise formation there - most rural entrepreneurs are in-migrants;

(3) company relocation from urban to rural areas is an important secondary influence on the growth of rural enterprise;

(4) employment has on average been growing faster in remote rural firms than in accessible rural businesses, while employment in urban firms has been declining;

(5) remote rural locations do provide important advantages for business development; for example, greater room for expansion, more modern, higher quality and cheaper freehold premises, and a more stable workforce.

However, the survey also acknowledges that rural enterprises, particularly those in more remote locations, do suffer some operating disadvantages which may prove detrimental to the performance of the rural economy in future years. For example, many firms have reported problems associated with shortages of skilled and technical workers, of management and professional staff, of larger local premises to facilitate expansion and, in a very small number of cases, with poorer telecommunications and transport infrastructure. The report concludes that a more pro-active response from government is necessary to overcome some of the constraints confronting rural enterprise.

## Sub-regional employment trends in Northern Ireland 1971-90

Although Northern Ireland was included within the analysis presented in the previous section it is desirable to explore in more detail the trends in sub-regional employment change within this region. Using data from the Northern Ireland Economic Research Centre (NIERC) databases for the period 1971-90 it is possible to examine employment trends within the rural areas of Northern Ireland.[4] As in the UK as a whole the nature of the rural economies in Northern Ireland is such that few people work directly in agriculture, forestry or fishing. Including the agricultural self-employed, out of a total of 226,000 employees in rural areas in 1987 only some 37,000 (16 per cent) were actually employed in the primary sectors. The employment structure of most rural areas is remarkably similar to that of their urban counterparts: 27 per cent of rural employment is in production industries compared to 25 per cent in urban areas; and 57 per cent of rural employment is in public and private services.

Before reviewing the temporal trends in sub-regional employment change it is appropriate to consider the nature and scale of the economic and social problems associated with rural economies in Northern Ireland. More important than the composition of employment in rural areas are the high and persistent levels of unemployment that prevail in these areas. For the past twenty years registered unemployment in rural Northern Ireland has outstripped urban unemployment by a constant margin of 4 per cent. Furthermore, unemployment is only part of the problem as it is coupled with a considerable margin of concealed unemployment in the form of on-farm under-employment. This bleak and depressing picture should be borne in mind as the comparative performance of urban and rural areas is examined.

Figures 7.1 to 7.4 provide an overview of the major trends in total employment and manufacturing employment over the period 1971-90. For the purposes of this analysis the 26 District Council Areas (DCAs) have been placed into 5 main groups (Fig. 7.1). A clear pattern emerges from an examination of total employment change in each of the DCA's (Fig. 7.3). Percentage decreases are recorded in the 4 Eastern DCAs of Belfast, Larne, Carrickfergus and Antrim,

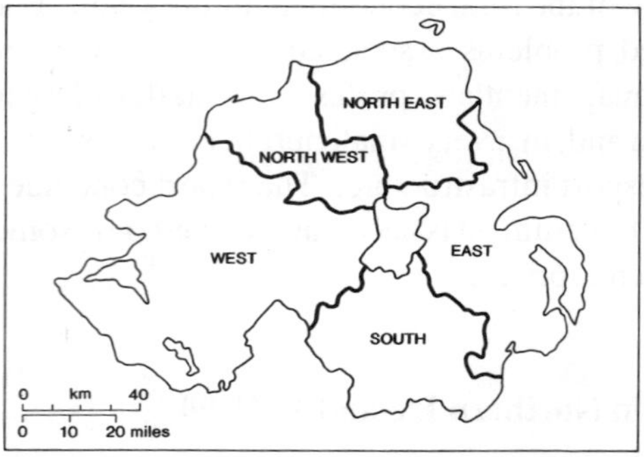


**Figure 7.1 The sub-regions of Northern Ireland**

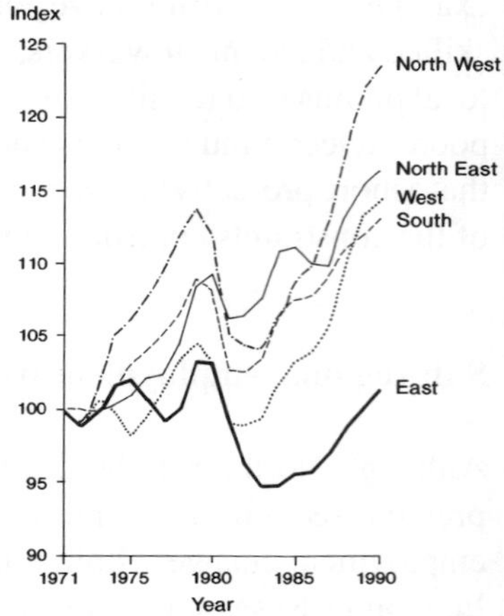


**Figure 7.2 Total employment change for sub-regions in Northern Ireland, 1971-1990**

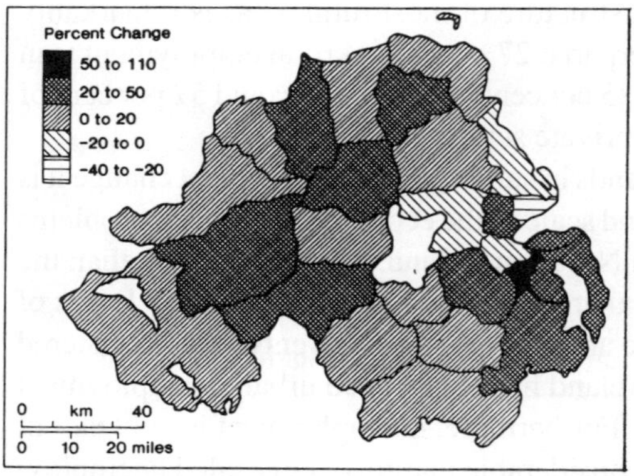


**Figure 7.3 Total employment change for district council areas in Northern Ireland, 1971-1990**

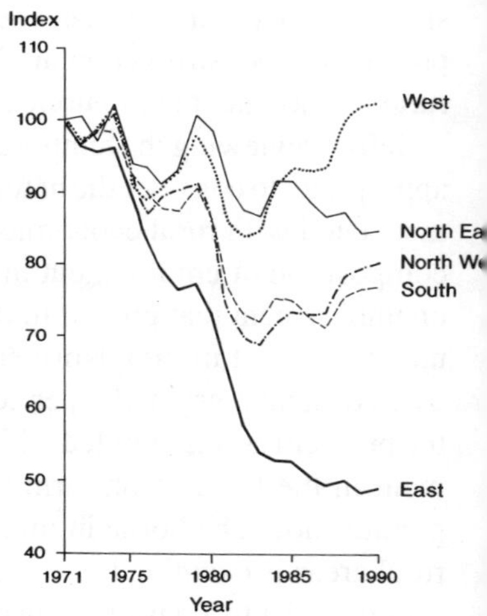


**Figure 7.4 Manufacturing employment change for sub-regions in Northern Ireland, 1971-1990**

while all other DCAs have experienced employment growth in the period. Of particular note is the performance of Omagh, Dungannon, Limavady and Magherafelt located outside the Eastern sub-region. Figures 7.2 and 7.4 provide a temporal analysis of the 5 sub-regions for total and manufacturing employment respectively. Since 1971 each of the 5 sub-regions has followed a broadly similar pattern in terms of total employment, although at differing scales (Fig. 7.2). The period 1971-79 is characterised by steady growth, although Belfast and the West were affected temporarily by the 1973/74 recession. In 1980-83 all sub-regions experienced a dramatic fall in total employment and this was followed by a period of recovery, albeit to greatly varying degrees. It is interesting to note that all sub-regions except the East increased their total employment levels in 1984-90 to above those in 1979. Although the East did grow in the 1984-90 period it was merely catching-up with its 1979 position. Throughout the study period the North West sub region has been one of the most impressive in terms of growth in total employment, apart from a short period in the mid-1980s when the North East outperformed it. Finally, since 1987 the West has dramatically improved its performance. From this analysis there is clear evidence that employment in rural areas has continued to grow in the 1970s and 1980s.

Has the manufacturing sector also displayed similar trends to those observed in the previous section for the UK as a whole? Against a background of manufacturing employment decline in the economy as a whole over the period 1971-90 the dramatic effects of the two major recessions of 1973-74 and 1980-81 can be clearly seen (Fig. 7.4). All sub-regions except the East displayed a recovery after the 1973-74 recession, and indeed the North East and West recovered to their pre-recession employment levels. The 1980-81 recession affected every part of Northern Ireland but with differing intensities - the East most dramatically. All sub-regions, except the East, underwent a slight recovery in the years 1983-84 which has been sustained through to 1990 with the exception of the North East. Indeed, since 1987 the performance of the Western, North-Eastern and Southern sub-regions has been very encouraging, with the Western sub-region now recovering to its 1971 position. A comparison of Figures 7.2 and 7.4 leads to the conclusion that a significant proportion of the growth in total employment observed in rural areas is the result of growth in service activities, both public and private. A more detailed appraisal of the types of service activity involved is necessary before any judgement can be made as to the long-term impact on economic development in these areas.

Clearly, the manufacturing sector in Northern Ireland's rural areas is not exhibiting as strong a growth profile as in rural areas in the rest of the UK, although the period between 1984 and 1990 showed encouraging growth. However, the onset of the recession in 1990 may well have reversed even that positive trend. Nevertheless, rural areas do portray a markedly different pattern of growth from urban areas and this would tend to confirm that some sort of urban-rural manufacturing shift is taking place. As discussed above manufacturing activity is seen as crucial to the revitalisation of rural economies. The evidence from Northern Ireland would suggest that from the mid-1980s some positive signs were emerging with respect to this sector. However, this needs to be placed in context. Unemployment in rural areas remains high and thus seems to be unaffected by increased levels of job creation. Indeed, it can be said that a positive relationship has emerged between areas which have experienced increased employment growth in recent years and areas with persistent high levels of unemployment. This is partly owing to the continuing high levels of population increase in these areas stemming from the maintenance of a high rate of natural increase and the decline in net out-migration (Shuttleworth 1992). Therefore, the scale of the problem in rural areas remains monumental and merits an active response by government. Accordingly, there follows a review of aspects of the policy framework designed to stimulate industrial development in rural areas.

## Local Enterprise Programme in Northern Ireland

Since the mid-1980s the promotion of enterprise in local areas has become an important aspect of industrial development policy in Northern Ireland. Under the auspices of the Local Enterprise Development Unit (LEDU) a number of Local Enterprise Agencies (LEAs) were established to assist the development of small firms and in particular new business start-ups. In the light of the previous section it might be tempting to draw some sort of correlation between the creation of a LEA network and the modest upswing in the fortunes of the rural economies in Northern Ireland. Such a conclusion needs to await a detailed consideration of the actual contribution the LEAs have made to local economic development.

The scale of job creation by government agencies in rural areas has been investigated by the Northern Ireland Economic Research Centre (NIERC). A recent report revealed that in the second half of the 1980s (1984/85 to 1988/89) LEDU managed to create just over 5,000 jobs in all locations beyond the responsibility of its Belfast Area Office as a result of job-related selective financial assistance schemes (Hart et al 1993b). With additionality estimated at around 50 per cent this means that approximately 500 additional jobs were created by LEDU on an annual basis. This is not a substantial contribution to the labour market deficiencies of rural areas. The remainder of this section will concentrate on the assessment of the economic impact of the LEAs. The commentary will draw upon a recently published report by the Northern Ireland

Economic Council (NIEC 1991) on the economic impact of the Local Enterprise Programme (LEP) of which the LEAs are an integral part.

In 1983 the Government sought to consolidate and add to the range of local initiatives that had already been in operation under a formal and co-ordinated network of agencies - the LEP. One objective of the LEP was to encourage the development of enterprise agencies across Northern Ireland to be administered by LEDU on behalf of the Department of Economic Development (DED). A further objective was to promote additional job opportunities through small business formation, survival and growth, and by integrating the skills, commitment and resources of local enterprise groups as a source of help and advice. The LEAs are financed almost entirely from public funds and in 1989-90 received £4.7m directly from LEDU. The International Fund for Ireland (IFI) is also actively involved and in the financial year 1989-90 committed £3.8m to LEP agencies. Although still in the early stages of development the LEP has become well established with a total of 32 LEAs operational at the end of June 1990. It should be stressed that other organisations exist outside the formal programme and make an active contribution to enterprise development in a range of localities. A final caveat is that not all these 32 LEAs are situated in rural areas, 7 being located in Belfast.

In the 20 LEAs surveyed in the NIEC report there were 408 firms or projects operating during the first half of 1990 generating a total employment of almost 3,000 with an additional 150 people directly employed by the agencies. However, as the NIEC report correctly points out, the vast majority of these firms serve the local market which suggests that the displacement effects on employment may be severe. In other words jobs created in firms assisted under this programme may be at the expense of jobs in other non-assisted firms which are competing against assisted projects for orders or resources. Just under half of the firms surveyed were in a manufacturing activity and they provided one-third of the total employment. A further 43 per cent of firms were in services (providing 23 per cent of total employment). The remaining 1,000 jobs were to be found in 25 community projects.

An important aspect of the performance of the LEAs is the turnover of tenant firms. Since the programme was initiated a total of 620 firms had at some time been operating from workspace provided by the agencies. Therefore, approximately one-third had moved out of the LEA. A level of turnover was meant to be a feature of the programme as companies became established and sought to expand outside the LEA. However, what is interesting is the follow-up on those firms that left. The NIEC survey managed to trace all these companies and revealed that 120 (58 per cent) did so because of closure while 90 (42 per cent) left in order to expand.

Measuring the effectiveness of the LEP is fraught with difficulties, not least because many of its activities are not of an economic nature. Nevertheless, on the basis of the headline statistics presented above it would be fair to conclude that despite the existence of a LEA infrastructure there has been very little impact upon the fundamental problem in these areas, namely high unemployment. Admittedly, the scale of the problem is immense and it would be rather optimistic to expect major changes in the short term. Evidence from the previous section indicated that the rural areas were showing signs of growth and this certainly needs to be exploited vigorously in the 1990s.

## Community Business Pilot Programme

To conclude this discussion of enterprise development in rural areas the experience of a 3 year pilot programme to stimulate community businesses in Northern Ireland will be examined. The importance of this initiative is that it does begin to address more forcefully the issue of the actual process of economic development from within local communities. This Community Business Pilot Programme funded by the IFI and LEDU and co-ordinated by Industrial Training Services Ltd as the Community Business Agency for Northern Ireland commenced in May 1989 and now encompasses the following areas: Mid-Ulster; Omagh; Newry and Mourne; Derry; and West Belfast. A LEA in each of these areas was chosen to host a full-time Community Business Development Worker. Community development initiatives are now being widely proposed as an appropriate means of stimulating economic development in economically depressed regions and localities. The community based approach recognises the need for more locally sensitive, accessible and targeted responses to employment change by providing funds to enable communities to analyse their local economy and develop a local economic strategy and by providing further finance to enable this strategy to be implemented.

The particular economic context within which a community business strategy has been proposed in Northern Ireland stems from the fact that conventional forms of local economic development have, for the most part, by-passed those most deprived in the labour market, that is those who lack skills, ideas, motivation, enthusiasm, self-confidence and self-esteem. As a potential third sector of the economy, set beside the private and public sectors, advocates of a community business strategy argue that community businesses give groups of people the capacity to engage in economic activity, to set up enterprises, to sponsor projects, to organise work, and to engage in negotiations with public and private organisations. In short, community business may permit such groups to exert some influence and control over the shape, structure and direction of their local economy (rural or otherwise) rather than depend solely on others to do something for it. In particular, the significance of community business as a local economic development strategy is threefold:

(1) it allows and encourages people to act in the economy by creating work, producing and recirculating wealth and providing services;

(2) it provides a mechanism for government (both central and local) and its agencies, and the private sector, to direct investment at poor communities with a greater assurance that the target population will benefit;

(3) it acknowledges that the majority of the unemployed do not want and do not have the capacity to become self-employed but prefer to work for someone else; the community business structure can serve this function.

One of the problems in developing community business strategies has been the lack of an agreed definition of the concept of community business itself. However, the following would seem to represent a suitable definition for most workers in the field of community business. A community business is a trading organisation which is set up, owned and controlled by the local community and which aims to create ultimately self-supporting jobs for local people, and to be a focus for local development. Any profits made from its business activities are used to create more employment, or to provide local services or to assist other schemes of community benefit. In summary, therefore, in a community business profit is a means of achieving goals, not the goal itself. The overriding objective is through sustainable trading businesses under the ownership and management of the community to support community development by:

(1) enhancing the quality of life of people in the community;

(2) making enhanced use of local human, cultural, institutional and physical resources;

(3) creating structures to enable communities to carry out economic functions;

(4) achieving greater community self-reliance and autonomy;

(5) developing the hidden potential and unrealised abilities of local residents;

(6) enabling community residents to participate directly in designing and implementing plans for development.

Between May 1989 and December 1991 a total of 71 groups had formally registered with the Community Business Pilot Programme across the 5 pilot areas. Out of that total 6 businesses were actively trading at the end of 1991. The main thrust of group activity has come from the rural areas within the pilot programme with Derry City forming an important urban dimension. The development of community businesses in West Belfast has been extremely difficult although one or two groups are moving towards the start line. Clearly, in economic terms the impact has been slight. However, a full evaluation of the Community Business Pilot Programme is to be published in 1993. The absence of such an analysis is not important for the purposes of this discussion because the example of the community business programme is meant to serve as an indication of the process whereby communities can initiate economic development.

One of the most important lessons to emerge from the Pilot Programme has been that simply to sit back and wait for groups of hitherto unorganised individuals to knock the door demanding the package on how to become a community business is unproductive. By their very nature marginalised local rural (or urban) communities have neither the experience nor the self-confidence to proceed down this route. The experience of the Community Business Development Programme has been that the dynamism comes from pre-existing groups formed as economic development organisations for their area. They usually comprise professional and business people whose prime motivation is to stimulate local/community based economic development. As Bryant (1989) argues,

> Development - however a community measures it - means change, and this means being ready to do things differently. Hence attitudes within the community are critical. It also means that there must be key individuals to assume leadership roles within the community. Without these people and a generally favourable attitude in the community to considering change, "entrepreneurial communities", cannot exist because communities are but the reflection of the individuals that comprise them.

## Conclusion

It has been argued in this chapter that industrial development in rural areas is important because it provides the base from which income can be earned within the local economy. Without income there can be no sustained economic growth over any time horizon. In Northern Ireland the current situation is one whereby many rural areas are experiencing severe economic difficulties. A basic absence of demand in the national, regional and local economies is obviously a major contributory factor to that situation. However, all is not doom and gloom on the horizon. Experience from Great Britain demonstrates that rural economies can create and sustain growth over a number of decades. Indeed, in Northern Ireland there are clear signs of the growth potential of rural areas, although any optimism must be tempered by the scale of the problem in the first instance and the very low employment base upon which some of that growth is taking place. Furthermore, population trends and structural rigidities in the labour market may tend to counteract any growth in employment that has taken place.

The problem is the design and implementation of an effective policy for the stimulation of rural enterprise in Northern Ireland. The framework of the LEP already exists but perhaps what is needed is more awareness of the process whereby economic growth can be achieved rather than the simple expedient of infrastructure construction in rural areas. Some of the results emerging from the experience of the Community Business Pilot Programme indicate one strand of a strategy which should be more firmly supported with the appropriate resources. Empowerment is an emotive word to use in any context but it is a vital and justifiable ingredient of any economic development strategy for rural areas. It should take the form of greater local decision-making, budgetary control and accountability. However, one of the major issues in this respect, which is perhaps currently operating as a major constraint on local economic initiative, would appear to be the apparent lack of trust that the existing statutory bodies and agencies have in the ability of rural communities to marshall their own resources effectively. Therefore, the challenge to those who seek to revitalise rural areas is as much a political one as it is an economic and social one.

## Notes

1. Coalfield areas, with an urban character but in scattered settlements, as well as surburban areas where several local authorities cover what is essentially a single urban agglomeration, have been excluded from this definition.
2. The focus in this discussion is on rural economies rather than rural dwellers. the location of employment is the workplace rarther than the residence.
3. Shift and Share analysis has revealed that industry mix explains only a small proportion of the difference.
4. Rural areas have been defined as any District Council Area (DCA) in which all settlements had fewer than 35,000 people; i.e. Belfast and Derry. In the case of Belfast all adjoining DCAs were also included in the urban category

as the suburban spread into these areas well exceeds the adopted dividing line. This definition is consistent with that used in the previous section.

## References

Bryant, C.R. (1989) Entrepreneurs in the rural environment. *Journal of Rural Studies*, Vol. 5, No. 4, pp. 337-348.

Fothergill, S. and Gudgin, G. (1982) *Unequal growth: urban and regional development change in the UK*. Heinemann, London.

Gudgin, G. (1990) Beyond farming: economic change in rural areas of the UK, in *Faith in the countryside*, Report of the Archbishops' Commission on Rural Areas, Churchman Publishing.

Hart, M., Harrison, R.T. and Gallagher, C. (1993) Enterprise creation, job generation and regional policy, in Harrison, R. and Hart, H. (eds) *Spatial policy in a divided nation*, Ch. 10, Jessica Kingsley, London.

Hart, M., Scott, R., Keegan, R. and Gudgin, G. (1993b) *Job creation in small firms: an economic valuation of job creation in small firms assisted by the Northern Ireland Local Enterprise Development Unit (LEDU)*. NIERC, Belfast.

Keeble, D. (1990) Small firms, new firms and uneven regional development in the UK. *Area*, Vol. 22, No. 3, pp. 234-245.

Keeble, D., Tyler, P., Broom, G. and Lewis, J. (1992) *Business success in the countryside: the performance of rural enterprise*. Department of the Environment, HMSO, London.

Massey, D. (1988) What's happening to UK manufacturing? in Allen,J. and Massey, D. (eds) *Restructuring Britain: the economy in question*, Sage, London.

Murray, M. (1992) *Paradigm redundancy and substitution: rural planning and development in Northern Ireland.* Dept of Applied Economics Seminar (mimeo), University of Ulster, Jordanstown.

NIEC (1991) *The Local Enterprise Programme in Northern Ireland.* Report 86, March, Belfast.

Shuttleworth, I. (1992) Population change in Northern Ireland, 1981-91: some preliminary results of the 1991 census of population. *Irish Geography*, Vol. 25, No. 1, pp. 83-88.

# 8 Rural tourism - The passport to development?

*Michael Keane*

## Introduction

There has been a dramatic increase in interest among rural communities in developing new tourism economies. One indication of this interest can be seen in the plans of local areas under the LEADER initiative. To date sixteen LEADER groups in the Republic of Ireland have been awarded IR£38m of public funding (IR£24m from the European Community and IR£14m from the Irish Government) to undertake rural development projects. Measures to promote tourism feature very prominently in the indicative funding plans of many areas. The indicative funding plans of five such LEADER groups are illustrated in Table 8.1. In all five cases tourism plans account for almost 50 per cent of the money available. Clearly the communities involved see tourism as a sector which can make a very positive contribution to local economic development. This chapter discusses the basis for this optimism. It suggests some a priori reasons why tourism, properly co-ordinated and managed, can be a potent vehicle for local regeneration. It then goes on to outline some of the key issues that must be addressed in local tourism development.

**Table 8.1**
**Indicative allocation of funds in five LEADER areas**

| Measure | Area 1 | Area 2 | Area 3 | Area 4 | Area 5 |
|---|---|---|---|---|---|
| Projects and Local Services | 21.2% | 15.0% | 10.2% | 12.6% | 17.3% |
| Farming/Forestry and Fishing | 14.1% | 17.4% | 16.3% | 5.1% | 8.0% |
| Tourism | 47.7% | 37.6% | 53.1% | 44.9% | 47.7% |
| Other | 17.0% | 30.0% | 20.4% | 37.4% | 27.0% |

## Tourism and rural economic diversification

Not everybody is convinced that rural areas have a bright economic future. Unless there is clarification of the nature of the economic potential of rural areas and of the manner in which this potential can be mobilised it will be difficult to identify the kind of policy measures that can be relevant and effective in meeting local aspirations. The correct test of rural policy should be how it fits with needs and solutions perceived at the local level. By concentrating on the local level it is possible to focus more clearly on ends and means and therefore fulfil what is a critical dimension of policy making, that of determining what institutions are best suited to make what decisions in a specific context.

Rural areas do not fit readily into neat and simple aggregates. The economic opportunity set for many of these areas is limited to, perhaps, three possibilities: (1) discovering and mobilising new resources; (2) creating new uses for existing resources; and (3) making better use of existing resources. In more differentiated areas, where the economic base is more assured and where economic activity is on a larger scale, the opportunity set may be more varied and the devising of development strategies less problematic. However, in the case of the more marginal areas, the problem is to find enough opportunities that can offer a sufficient rate of return to encourage new entrepreneurial activity. These areas are deeply vulnerable to economic conditions largely beyond their control. Indeed these economic difficulties are often beyond the capacity of regional or senior level agencies to resolve, at least with the traditional policy approaches and programmes. Some of these difficulties are due to location and size. Many rural areas, for example, have difficulties in capturing income and other economic benefits because of the dominance exerted by the larger urban and regional economy to which they belong. This puts a constraint on the scope for certain kinds of local economic diversification. It is, therefore, important that a realistic view is taken of the problems and possibilities in the rural economy.

While the challenge of rural development has a number of different dimensions it is fundamentally one of finding products and activities that will produce economic benefits at the local level. The increased disassociation of many rural communities from their traditional agricultural base has not been matched by sufficient growth in new manufacturing or locally created businesses. The out-migration, particularly of younger workers, has the effect of further weakening the local economic and social fabric, and the economies of many areas are in danger of becoming depleted. Strategies that can help stimulate entrepreneurship and generate opportunities for new work and income creation across a diversified set of sectors are needed if the continuity of many of these communities is to be secured.

The conceptual framework that is useful in formulating guidelines, and that is familiar to economists and planners, is one that looks for solutions to rural problems and opportunities in terms of correcting, or improving, market performance in rural areas. This framework does offer a number of worthwhile possibilities for guiding local economic development. Some of these possibilities are summarised in Fig. 8.1. The economic development problem is one of insufficient opportunities that can offer a sufficient rate of return (Michaelson 1979). It is possible to see this problem as lying with the quality and content of the market signals rather than with the lack of signals *per se*. It can be argued, for example, that the capital market is not quite perfect, that it operates through a number of layers, and that hidden opportunities may be present in a locality. It may be that because of unfamiliarity, or because of geographical distance, some potential entrepreneurs may feel that the expected rate of return in a local area is not sufficient, whereas the same opportunity, as seen from a local level, by a local person, may offer a quite acceptable rate of return. This is the principle that says that the only place where development opportunity can be seen is at the coalface. It points to the need for improvements in local capital markets and in entrepreneurial finance, and for better information, technical assistance and other non-pecuniary forms of assistance to potential entrepreneurs.

1. The key to development is capital placement. The question is how much capital to place where and in what form (factories or fish farms or interpretative centres or human capital etc).

2. Market signals about profitability and rates of return guide placement decisions.

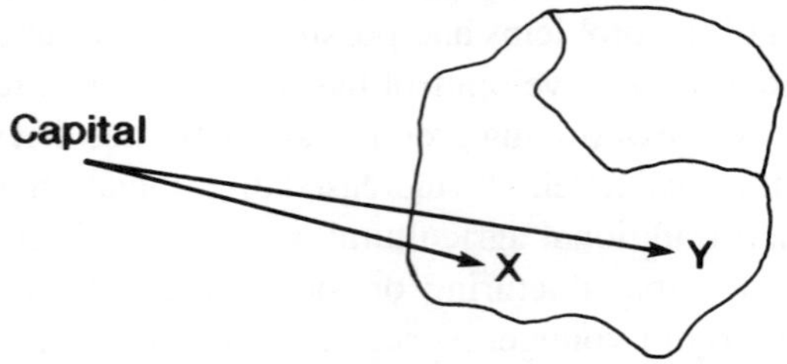


3. Development policy is a decision to interfere with this mechanism

To make different decisions? To make better decisions?

Policy rationale: only if current capital decisions are wrong or can be improved upon.

| Reason | Comment | Policy guideline |
|---|---|---|
| (1) Capital shuns opportunities in rural areas | Ignorance of opportunities, lack of information, lack of entrepreneurship | Find people who know about the opportunities; finance and assist them. Information, training and marketing |
| (2) The form capital takes affects the return | A potentially powerful argument | The particular development opportunity is such that the returns from it could be much greater, without increasing costs, if it were undertaken by a community or participative form of organisation than if it were left in private hands. |
| (3) Legal, institutional rigidities impede opportunities | Property rights, access issues at the local level | New institutions, co-ops, guilds, etc. to exploit natural resources. |
| (4) Market criteria and standard accounting frameworks are too narrow. | Social costs and benefits, a well known argument | Recognise external costs and benefits |

**Figure 8.1 Market-led responses to rural development**

Source: Michaelson 1979

Some of the market-failure arguments shown in Fig. 8.1 are well known. Perhaps the most powerful argument is that made under reason (2) in Fig. 8.1, which concerns a type of market-failure where the particular development opportunity is such that the returns from it could be much greater if, without incurring additional costs, it were undertaken by a community based and participative form of organisation than if it were left in private hands. For example, a collective approach may be able to call on resources that are unavailable to a private entrepreneur, or it may be able to achieve greater productivity from existing resources. This argument is particularly relevant to rural tourism development. Many local groups see opportunities in marketing their areas' uniqueness. This economic potential cannot be adequately exploited by an individual's initiative, but needs a broader-based approach. Rural tourism is a potent vehicle for local development, economic recovery, social progress and conservation of the rural heritage. Consequently it should be thought out, organised, marketed, and managed in accordance with the characteristics, needs, limitations, and potentials of the receiving area and its permanent residents (Thibal 1988). The effects of tourism development should be assessed primarily with reference to the rural receiving community, as it is the main potential beneficiary of any development. Similarly, many of the costs can be most efficiently met by the rural community, with assistance from the external agencies. The costs of marketing the product , for example, constitute a problem in that an individual operator, or a commercially oriented agency, cannot expect to recover benefits that will be in any way commensurate with these costs. But, unless these marketing development costs are incurred, there will be no significant market and the potential economic benefits from rural tourism to local communities will be minimal. A community based operation can internalise these costs, but to do so it will need suitable support from the government and its agencies. Local participation can be best encouraged through community co-ordinating structures. Such structures can mobilise resources which would not be available to the single individual. Furthermore, a community structure can internalise many of the risks and uncertainties which, the single individual would find it difficult to face. Community, or locally based, structures can best meet these various objectives and provide the kind of local focus and co-ordination that is required.

A community framework, where there is local co-ordination and community involvement, offers the best prospects for tourism development in rural areas (Keane and Quinn 1990). The development tasks involved in creating this framework are largely ones of managing human resources. These are infinitely more demanding than tasks that involve the management of grants or the management of physical capital. They pose a number of difficulties not the least of which is that of achieving some degree of balance at the local level between individual initiative and the local supports and institutions that are needed to promote local development.

## Developing the product

A detailed description of what might be called the rural tourism product is presented in Table 8.2. The product includes a range of activities, services and amenities promoted by farmers and rural people to attract tourists to their area in order to generate extra income and employment. The product emphasises the receiving area's natural,cultural and craft resources which offer water and land-based leisure activities, which provide opportunities for learning new skills and studying flora/fauna, heritage and archaeology and which encourage a holiday spirit through entertainment and other services. To a greater or lesser extent these have always been available in rural areas. Similarly there have previously been schemes to assist in the provision of accommodation and facilities and there have been some promotional activity and some marketing arrangements. However, few of these developments have taken place in an integrated and co-ordinated manner in any area. Gannon(1988) advances the particular term "community agri-tourism" to denote receiving areas where local people decide to co-operate to provide a range of activities, services and amenities, combine these elements in a package to attract visitors, and collectively market the agri-tourism package for their area. A hallmark of rural community tourism is that it is a community product and that it is developed from local structures. The model proposed by Gannon is a co-ordinated and community based initiative. It is a model that is closely tied to the concept of community development. It is also a model which has a good economic rationale. A community-based approach to rural tourism is specifically supported by Thibal (1988) who suggests that

> when a rural area chooses to bank on tourism as part of a local development programme, every inhabitant is potentially an interested party, not only because he may happen to have a project of his own, but above all as a member of the local community and potential beneficiary of the expected collective development.

Thibal goes on to argue that spontaneous initiatives are a thing of the past and that rural tourism must be everyone's business if it is to become, in small rural areas, simultaneously an incentive to the establishment of collective leisure facilities available to local people as well as to the tourists, a stimulus to local income and trade, an opportunity for job creation, a factor for the development of the area's economy and an instrument for re-awakening local culture and reviving the countryside.

**Table 8.2 The rural tourism product**

| | | |
|---|---|---|
| **Activities** | **Services** | **Amenities** |
| farm activities: | accommodation: | access |
| milking | farmhouse | signposts |
| turf cutting | self catering (gites) | viewing points |
| farm house cooking | camping | |
| | caravanning | **Visitor Farms** |
| **Rural Pursuits** | | cheese |
| fishing | **Food** | deer |
| rambling | restaurants | health farms |
| hill walking | coffee shops | open farms |
| bird watching | picnic areas | traditional farms |
| shooting | | |
| forest walks | **Activity** | **Activity Facility** |
| | bicycle hire | forests |
| **Outdoor Activities** | fishing rod hire | rivers |
| canoeing | boat hire | lakes |
| golf | golf clubs hire | walking trails |
| orienteering | | golf courses |
| cycling | **Domestic** | |
| rock climbing | babysitting | **Attractions** |
| | laundry services | abbeys |
| **Craft Studies** | | museums |
| lacemaking | **Entertainment** | caves |
| knitting | traditional pubs | churches |
| antique appreciation | barbecues | gardens |
| | dancing | castles |
| **Field Studies** | | |
| heritage trails | | **Language** |
| flora and fauna | | **Training** |
| rural studies | | |

Source: Gannon (1988)

The discussion so far has emphasised the importance of an integrated approach at the local level. This is a necessary condition but one that may be difficult to achieve, at least in the short run. It is difficult to see how any rural area can significantly impact on the highly competitive tourism sector without developing a local centralised system for co-ordinating the development of tourism products, information and other infrastructure and for marketing. Such a system also has the advantage of co-ordinating tourism planning so that the tourism which emerges has local community acceptance.The welcome of local people is a potentially massive competitive advantage in rural tourism (Quinn 1990). Competitiveness does not mean that rural tourism must seek to match the high-rise hotels of the cities or match what coastal resorts can offer. The strength of rural tourism lies in the special product that it has to offer - a product that is essentially the result of the spatial and human environment that can be found in the countryside.

## Community rural tourism

A considerable level of achievement in rural tourism development has been reached in the Ballyhoura area of Co. Limerick (Keane and Quinn 1990). Rural tourism development in Ballyhoura is part of an integrated programme which is well thought out and is co-ordinated at the local level. It has also been supported by the key state agencies. The level of involvement in rural tourism in the area, although small in absolute terms, has increased significantly since the initiative began in 1985. The community co-ordinating framework has facilitated and encouraged a wide degree of participation, a significant feature of which is the involvement of smaller farmers and their families and also of non-farming elements in the community. Economic results, by way of revenue, income and employment growth, have not been very significant. The reality is that tourism is not a panacea for the economic difficulties faced by rural areas.

Ballyhoura Failte was one of four communities who participated in a pilot rural tourism programme begun in 1989. The other communities involved were Corrib Country (Galway), Barrow/Nore (Kilkenny) and West Cork. Some details on how this programme evolved, and the key actors/agencies involved, are presented in Figure 8.2. This attempts to describe a complex and lengthy process that has managed to achieve results. The process shows that it is possible to derive public support measures that are compatible with one another and to achieve collaboration between agencies and local initiative provided that there is a common goal. The current position is that a National Rural Tourism Co-operative is in place. The Co-operative has a full-time co-ordinator and it has recently received funding for two years for a marketing executive from the Irish Tourist Board (Bord Failte). The Co-operative is currently working with 8 groups and aims to have 20 groups in place by 1994 with a revenue turnover of IR£6m.

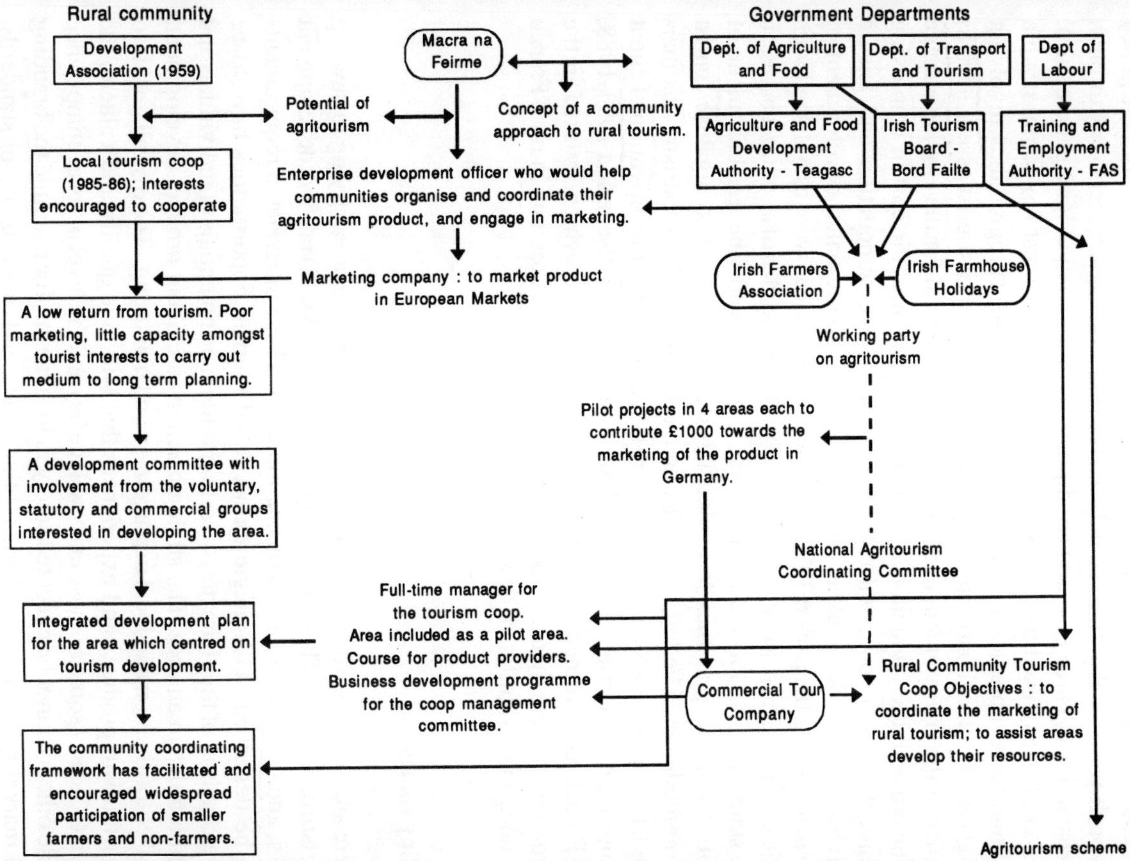


**Figure 8.2 Actors and actions in the development of rural tourism in Ireland**

Examples of collaborative arrangements exist in a number of other European countries. In relation to rural tourism France and Austria are perhaps the best known examples. In 1976 France introduced a new policy to exploit the tourism potential of rural areas, the Pays d'Accueil. Contiat (1988) describes the policy as a back-up to local initiatives and efforts to develop the local economy through tourist activity. Three essential conditions must be satisfied for a geographical area to be recognised as a Pays d'Accueil. The area must (1) demonstrate a willingness to implement concerted tourist development programmes, involving a high level of local participation; (2) enjoy a number of tourist assets, such as quality of the environment or natural habitats, potential for developing a range of leisure activities, and an active cultural life; (3) meet the cost of employing technical support to organise the provision of accommodation and leisure activities for holiday-makers and to ensure the co-ordinated development of tourism. During the period 1976-1980, ninety such areas were established with basic assistance from the state. From 1980 to 1983, the idea of a contract between the state and the Pays d'Accueil was explored with the establishment of multi-annual programmes to exploit leisure facilities and to organise tourist accommodation. The emphasis was on the terms on which tourism was marketed, the extent to which resources were taken up and the identification of client groups ( the need to tap all sectors of the community). In the period 1983-1988, the French Government established planning contracts which resulted in the formation of more than 200 extra Pays d' Accueil. Thus tourism in rural France has taken on a significant economic dimension.

**Policy issues**

There are many interdependent tasks that confront rural areas trying to develop tourism economies. These include: (1) marketing tasks, (2) product development tasks, and (3) control and co-ordination tasks. These interrelated requirements can be described in strategic terms. Rural tourism opportunities have to be developed out of the characteristics, limitations and potentials of individuals and communities in an area. The strategic actions are about product development, local co-ordination and local management and marketing. The overall goal is to offer tourism products and experiences that will give quality and value to the tourist. Clearly some of these tasks will be beyond the level of local competence while others cannot be executed solely in local terms, for example the branding and marketing of rural tourism and the setting and maintenance of standards. Local resources and constraints are such that external aid is indispensable for putting tourism plans, or indeed any rural programmes, into practice efficiently. The success of rural development depends on the way in which local initiatives and supra-local procedures and policies interlock.

There are no blueprints as to how these relationships might best work (Whitby 1986). The overall approach to rural policymaking, can be described as an effort to achieve an upward learning curve, with incremental improvements in the policy content and institutional arrangements taking place as more is learnt from specific situations and different policy experiments. The Irish agri-tourism grants scheme (Bord Failte 1989, 1990) is a good example of this. In 1989 the Irish Government, through the Department of Agriculture and Food, introduced an agri-tourism grants scheme. The objective of this scheme, when it appeared first, was to provide incentives to farmers by subsidising the cost of providing facilities. It applied only to farmers located within the areas designated as less-favoured within the meaning of Directive 85/350/EC. By the end of 1989, the total number of applications for support, if approved, would have taken up less than 2 per cent of the IR£3m. budget allocated to the scheme. A number of revisions were subsequently made to the initiative. All rural dwellers (albeit through partnerships with farmers) became eligible to participate in recognition of the principle that rural economic alternatives must go beyond agriculture. In the revised scheme there were significant increases made in the levels of investment deemed eligible for grant aid. New accommodation provision was also included. Some limited support was made available for marketing, and the geographical restrictions of the first scheme were also removed. The one major criticism of the revision is that it failed to recognise the need for local structures and to allow the supports that are necessary to help create such structures. Despite this shortcoming, the scheme has proved attractive and it has been fully taken up.

The various LEADER initiatives represent another important testing and learning ground. Having been successful in getting the long-sought-after global funding, the different groups are now addressing the formidable task of deploying this funding effectively in their respective areas. The conditions attached to this funding suggest that, in many cases, groups must still consult and negotiate with a very wide spectrum of agencies if they want to advance any development proposal. The way in which the wider policy community i.e. government departments, government agencies and local authorities, respond to the expectations and plans of the groups will be an important factor in determining the success or otherwise of the various initiatives that are planned. In relation to tourism development, groups will need help on issues like the provision of information, signposting, decisions about appropriate scale, on methods of converting and re-using derelict buildings as tourist facilities, on ways of improving the fabric of villages and small towns and on methods of managing recreational, habitat and scientific areas and the conservation of tourism assets in their areas. Local authorities are well placed to provide much of this expertise.

With sufficient resources they can play a very pro-active role, providing information and expertise to rural tourism initiatives, giving explicit recognition to area-based initiatives and incorporating local strategies in official development plans.

## Conclusion

The answer to the question posed in the title of this chapter is that tourism, while it may not be a complete solution, does have an important contribution to make to addressing the economic problems of rural areas. It is suggested that this potential is unlikely to be adequately realised if tourism is developed through a piecemeal and individual approach. The most effective structure is for tourism to be part of a community or area-wide integrated development plan. There are good *a priori* economic arguments, as well as positive pieces of empirical evidence, to support this view. However, the wider effect of rural tourism as a rural development strategy is ultimately dependent on a supportive policy environment.

## References


Bord Failte (1989) *Grant scheme for investment in agri-tourism under the revised Programme for Western Development.* Bord Failte, Dublin.

Bord Failte (1990) *Scheme of grant aid for investment in agri-tourism under the Operational Programme for Rural Development.* Bord Failte, Dublin.

Contiat, M. (1988) *The Pays d'Accueil in France.* Paper presented to a conference on Tourism and Leisure in Rural Areas, St. Peter Ording, Schleswig-Holstein.

Gannon, A. (1988) *A strategy for the development of agri-tourism.* Paper presented to the 4th Session of the Working Party on Women and the Agricultural Family in Rural Development, Rome.

Keane, M. J. and Quinn, J. (1990) *Rural development and rural tourism.* Research Report No.5, Social Sciences Research Centre, University College Galway.

Michaelson, S. (1979) Community-based economic development in urban areas, in B. Chinitz (ed) *Central city economic development.* Abt Books, New York.

Quinn, J. (1990) *Rural tourism and rural development.* Paper presented to Forschungspraktikum, Universitat Trier.

Thibal, S. (1988) *Rural tourism in Europe*. Paper presented to a meeting of the International Organising and Steering Committee of the European Campaign for the Countryside, Council of Europe, Strasbourg.

Whitby. M. (1986) An editorial postscript. *European Journal of Agricultural Economics*, Vol.13, pp.433-438.

# Section 3
# SOCIAL ISSUES

# 9 Land or landscape – Rural planning policy and the symbolic construction of the countryside

*Kay Milton*

## Introduction

Recent developments in political anthropology have been concerned with the use of language both as a resource and as an instrument of domination (see Grillo 1989, Fairclough 1989). Political discourse, it has been suggested, can usefully be seen as a "site of struggle in which social meanings are produced,...sustained and challenged" (Seidel 1985, 1989). This model of political discourse is used in this chapter to analyse the recurrent debate over rural planning policy in Northern Ireland, focusing specifically on the issue of new housing in the countryside.

The treatment of policy-making as a political discourse, in which meanings are negotiated and challenged, is founded on fundamental assumptions, once contentious but now generally accepted in social science, about the nature of social reality; namely that such reality is not given but constructed through social interaction, and that the extent to which it is shared is open to investigation. These assumptions are not only fundamental to the analytical approach of this chapter; they are also present, if not articulated, in the perceptions of those who engage in political discourse. While the individual participants in a debate necessarily conduct their lives on the basis of assumptions which they treat as axiomatic, they also recognise very well that others may hold quite contradictory assumptions, and that successful lobbying consists in persuading those in power that their view of reality should prevail. Of course, policy-making does not everywhere take a discursive form, much less one that is accessible to analysis. In a dictatorship policy-making can be expected to remain the preserve of an oligarchy and to be pursued behind closed doors. In a democracy it can be expected to pay some heed to the wishes of the majority, though the extent to which this is achieved through open debate will depend on a range of empirical factors. Northern Ireland is neither a dictatorship nor a democracy - it might best be described as a bureaucracy, with many of the important policy decisions being made by civil servants. Government ministers play their part, but they are appointed from Westminster and the people of Northern Ireland do not have the option of voting them out of office. In this, Northern Ireland is not dissimilar from Scotland, Wales or some regions of England.

Where the government of Northern Ireland does differ significantly from Great Britain, is in the power of local government, and this is particularly so in planning. Until 1972, responsibility for planning in Northern Ireland was divided, as it is in Great Britain, between local and central government. With the imposition of direct rule from Westminster, planning became solely a central government function. Since 1972, all planning decisions have been made by the Department of the Environment (NI) (or its predecessors);[1] district councils are consulted by the Department on planning proposals in their area, but they do not make the decisions. Besides being deprived of this and other responsibilities, Northern Ireland's local authorities also underwent a complete re-organisation in the early 1970s, with 26 new district councils being formed. Northern Ireland's political vacuum, as the effective absence of democratic processes is often called, has undoubtedly generated a feeling of powerlessness in the community in relation to policy-making in most fields, including planning. But it has also, arguably, had a significant effect on the way government planners operate.

## Rural planning policy 1972-90

The rationale for making planning a central government function in 1972 was to lessen the possibility of sectarian discrimination in planning decisions, a charge which had previously been levelled at local authorities. Against this historical background, planners have been sensitive both about their lack of accountability to public opinion, and about the possibility of being seen as unfair in their decisions. They have therefore been concerned to be seen to consult public opinion, and major changes in policy have usually been preceded by published discussion documents and requests for comment. Interested parties have thus been given repeated opportunities to make their views known to government, and have also submitted unsolicited views whenever they felt it appropriate. The pattern of rural housing policy over the past 20 years or so has been one in which first one lobby, then another, has tried to persuade the policy-makers in the Department that they have got it wrong.

*The pre-Cockcroft era*

Strategic planning policy for the whole of Northern Ireland was defined in the mid 1970s with the publication of the *Regional Physical Development Strategy* (RPDS) 1975-95 (HMSO 1977). Until then the policy had been one of encouraging development in designated growth towns around Belfast and key centres elsewhere in Northern Ireland. Following the administrative changes of the early 1970s, this policy was felt by the Department (of Housing, Local Government and Planning, as it then was) to be in need of revision. In 1975, the Department published a discussion paper (HMSO 1975) and invited the public to respond. This paper set out six options for the future of development in Northern Ireland. The Department's stated preferred option, and the one that was adopted in the RPDS, was the District Towns Strategy, in which one town in each of the new district council areas was selected as a centre for industry; some other towns were considered suitable for small-scale enterprises and some villages would be selected for residential development. Under the RPDS, residential development in the open countryside was to be discouraged for two reasons: to prevent the countryside being disfigured by unsympathetic development; and secondly to avoid the cost of providing services such as electricity, telephone and mains water to isolated houses (HMSO 1977). Planning permission for new houses in the countryside was to be granted only to those who demonstrated that they needed to live there, for employment, family or health reasons.[2]

The implementation of this policy provoked considerable opposition from district councillors, who were being lobbied by constituents whose planning applications had been refused. In some districts, councillors were said to have walked out in protest at the Department's decisions, and whole councils were said to be opposing every planning recommendation brought before them by the Department, in order to communicate their disapproval of what they perceived as an unnecessarily restrictive policy (Hansard 3.7.78: col 137). The opposition was such that in May 1977 the Government appointed a committee, under the chairmanship of Dr W H Cockcroft, to conduct a review of rural planning policy. The committee's report, the Cockcroft Report, was published in the spring of 1978. The committee's recommendation, with regard to rural housing, was that the restrictions on building in the countryside should be relaxed, both within and outside designated Areas of Outstanding Natural Beauty (AONBs)[3] (Cockcroft 1978). This recommendation was welcomed by the district councils and by Members of Parliament, but some conservation and amenity groups expressed concern at the possible consequences of a relaxed policy (see USPC 1978 and 1979). The Department's response to the Cockcroft Report was to make it no longer necessary, in most areas, to demonstrate a need to live in the countryside in order to obtain planning permission. The former restrictive policy was retained only in certain designated areas (Areas of Special Control) within AONBs and in the green belts around certain towns (Fig 9.1).

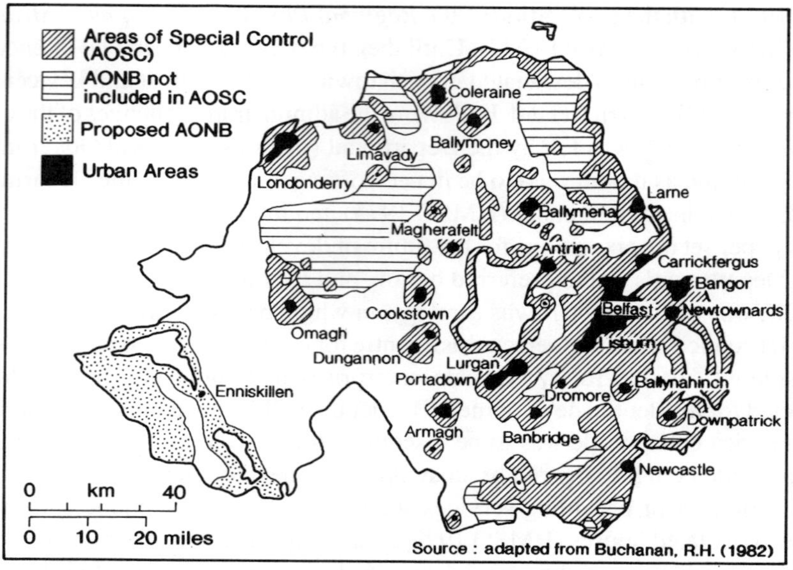


**Figure 9.1 Landscape policy in Northern Ireland, 1978**

*The post-Cockcroft era*

This change in policy is perceived by some participants in the rural planning debate as having opened the floodgates for speculative development. As long as an applicant had to demonstrate a need to live in the countryside before being allowed to build, any particular house was, in theory, tied to that applicant. An application was made, ostensibly, by the person who intended to live in the house, and the potential existed, whether or not it was used, for the Department to impose conditions on residence or sale. Opinions vary on the extent to which this system was abused and still is abused in the areas where the need criteria still apply, but the potential was there, at least, for the planning authority to exercise some control. Once the need restriction was removed, then new houses were no longer tied to the original applicants. A landowner could receive planning permission, and build a house for sale or sell the land for someone else to build on. Speculative development has become a valued source of income in some areas, particularly for farmers who feel that their economic stability is being threatened by changes in government agricultural policy. As the consequences of the more relaxed policy became evident, groups and individuals concerned about the appearance of the countryside increasingly voiced their concern. In particular, they criticised what they saw as an uncontrolled proliferation of houses inappropriate to the rural setting. These views appeared to be having some impact and in 1987 the Department tightened up its guidelines on the location (Fig 9.2), siting and design of rural houses, and ran a public awareness campaign, in an attempt to make development more sensitive to aesthetic concerns (DoE(NI) 1987, 1988). The opinion of amenity groups is that these measures have been ineffective (UAHS 1990).

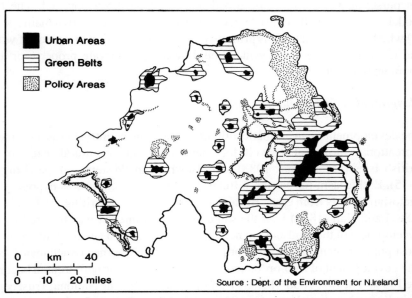


**Figure 9.2 Areas of strict rural planning control in Northern Ireland, 1991**

The pattern of rural planning policy in Northern Ireland since the early 1970s has thus been one of oscillation between extremes, with the Cockcroft Report as a watershed. During the pre-Cockcroft era a restrictive policy was in place and a broadly pro-development lobby was, so to speak, in opposition. In the post-Cockcroft era a relaxed policy has been implemented and the opposition has been represented by an amenity lobby.

## The symbolic construction of the countryside

In the rural planning debate the central concept, whose meaning has been contested with the policy-makers, is that of the countryside itself. Each lobby holds its own model which forms a basis for its views on how the countryside should be treated. In the course of the debate, each lobby has in turn attempted, with varying degrees of success, to persuade the Department that its model was the more valid one and should therefore form the basis of planning policy. The two opposing models, while undoubtedly consolidated and reinforced through the rural planning debate, were not generated in that context, but derive from the wider cultural context in which the debate has taken place. The models described have, therefore, drawn on this wider context, and in particular on other political discourses in which the same broad interests have been opposed. The two models, each internally consistent, conflict with each other on two main issues: (1) whether the countryside is primarily a place of recreation or a place of work, and (2) whether the countryside should be seen as private property or as a communal resource.

*Playground or factory floor*

The development of an aesthetic attitude towards the countryside as a source of recreational enjoyment is a well-documented trend in the cultural history of the British Isles (see Thomas 1983) and elsewhere in Western Europe (Lofgren 1985). Enthusiasm for Northern Ireland's scenic landscapes was expressed by Victorian tourists from Great Britain and enshrined in the writings of Thackeray (1887) and Hall (1843).[4] At the same time, local interest was fostered by the development of the road and rail networks linking Belfast and other towns to the most popular scenic areas, the north coast and the Mournes (Buchanan 1982). The development of a co-ordinated amenity lobby in Northern Ireland began in the 1930s. The first Youth Hostels were opened in 1931, the National Trust began operating in Northern Ireland in 1936 and the Ulster Society for the Preservation of the Countryside was founded in 1937 (Milton 1990). Pressure for legislation to protect scenic areas (see HMSO 1947) was resisted by government until the early 1960s, when Robert Matthew, in his planning recommendations for the Belfast area (Matthew 1963), persuaded the Government of Northern Ireland that landscape conservation was sound economic practice (see Buchanan 1982). The result was the Amenity Lands Act of 1965, which made provisions for the creation of National Parks and Areas of Outstanding Natural Beauty and set up the Ulster Countryside Committee to advise government on "questions affecting the natural beauty or amenity of any area or place in Northern Ireland".[5] By the time land-use planning became the full responsibility of central government in 1972, the protection of scenic beauty for recreation purposes was thus a statutory obligation.

Further provision for the recreational use of the countryside was made in the Access to the Countryside (NI) Order 1983, which obliged district councils protect public rights of way and enabled them "to create new public paths and long distance routes and to secure public access to areas of open country for recreational purposes."[6] This legislation was drafted during the existence of the Northern Ireland Assembly,[7] and the Assembly's papers and Official Reports provide a source of information on how the recreational use of the countryside was viewed by the different parties to the discussion. By government, and by recreation and amenity groups, the use of the countryside for recreation was treated as a public right, and the main issue in the debate was how an increasing demand for access should be regulated. The Ulster Countryside Committee, for instance, felt that "increasing interest in the countryside and the desire of a large number of people to use it regularly" was sufficient to justify the formalisation of rights of way (see NIA 40 1983: Appendix IX).

The debate concerning how recreational use of the countryside should be regulated dominated and effectively marginalised what was the main concern of farmers and their representatives, namely whether public access should be permitted at all in some areas. Farming interests, while prepared to concede that open, unenclosed country should be put to recreational use, tried to persuade government that enclosed fields should not be so used. In a written statement to the Assembly's Environment Committee, the Ulster Farmers Union (UFU) expressed the view that,

> . . . access to enclosed agricultural land should be visual access rather than physical access. Where footpaths are required across enclosed agricultural land, e.g. for access to open countryside, these should be fenced off from the land and well-marked. The proper use of minor country roads and lanes should mean that such paths would only rarely need to be created (NIA 40 1983: Appendix III).

The farmers' resistance to the model of the countryside as a place of leisure accords with their own perception of it as a place of work. The observation that those who make their living from the land tend to adopt a utilitarian view of their environment has been made in academic as well as public discourse (see Lofgren 1985). The emergence of an amenity lobby, the increasing public concern with the appearance of the countryside, and its increasing use as a place of recreation, have been perceived by farmers as a threat to their economic operations. In the face of this threat, farmers assert their own model of the countryside, as the place in which they, often with some difficulty, earn their livelihood:

> In the vast majority of the countryside, that is the ordinary enclosed green fields which we labour daily - and do not forget that grass is a...very expensive crop to grow... (NIA 40 1983 Appendix XII, p. 18)

> Farmers live and work in the countryside. The countryside is in effect the farmers' raw material...it is important that measures taken to open up the countryside recognise the very basic fact, that it is the same countryside from which the farmer obtains his livelihood (UFU 1990, p. 180).

The common perception of Northern Ireland as an economically depressed region gives economic arguments a strong appeal in any debate over the use of resources. In the Assembly discussions on public access to the countryside, the image of agriculture as Northern Ireland's most important industry, employing 13 per cent of the population, was used to counter the recreation threat. If agriculture is an industry, then the countryside becomes a factory floor, and what farmers do there is an important economic activity, in contrast to the idle pursuits promoted by the amenity lobby:

> . . . it needs to be recognised by the public that when they come onto this area for recreational activity...they are coming really onto the factory floor. Agriculture being the biggest industry in Northern Ireland, the land is the factory floor of that industry (NIA OR 15.2.83, p. 283; see also NIA 40 1983 Appendix XII, p. 18).

In the context of the rural planning debate, the issue of whether the countryside should be seen as playground or as factory floor is essentially a question of which takes priority, aesthetics or functionality.

If the countryside is primarily a place of recreation, then its appearance matters because aesthetic appreciation is part of the recreational enjoyment of the countryside. An attempt to have it perceived by policy-makers as a place of recreation is a bid to put aesthetic considerations high on the planners' list of priorities, to have planning decisions made on aesthetic grounds. Not surprisingly, the Department was perceived by some members of the amenity lobby to be acting inconsistently, by supporting the recreational use of the countryside through the Access Order, while at the same time pursuing a planning policy which appeared, to them, to be destroying its aesthetic quality. If, on the other hand, the countryside is primarily a place of work, then it can reasonably be argued that functionality should take precedence over aesthetic considerations. An attempt to have the countryside perceived by policy-makers as a place of work is an attempt to give aesthetic considerations a low priority in planning decisions. In terms of this model, what matters about a building is not its visual impact, but whether it is of the right kind, and in the right place, to serve the economic interests of those who intend to use it.

*Communal resource or private property*

Underlying many of the arguments over the use of resources is the common understanding that rights derive from ownership. The rights in question are not only rights of access and use, but also rights to influence, rights to have a say in how a resource should be managed.[8] In the rural planning debate, the interest group that can most convincingly argue that the countryside is "theirs" may have the best chance of persuading the policy-makers that their views on its management are valid.

The amenity lobby presents the countryside as a communal resource in which everyone has rights: "Fine landscapes are a priceless part of our national heritage" (Voluntary Amenity Group 1983).[9] Amenity groups aim to conserve the countryside, not only for those who live there or use it for recreational purposes, but also, most importantly, for future generations (ibid and USPC, no date). Since those as yet unborn cannot speak for themselves, they need someone to defend their rights, to protect their communal heritage. For farmers, the right to decide how the countryside should be managed derives from its status as the private property of individual landowners. As one farmer expressed it in the debate over the Access Order:

> . . . it must be said that this Order is really an infringement on us, the owners of the land. We are actually the owners and therefore it is a very great infringement (NIA 40 Appendix XII, p. 30)

The contrast between these two images could not be greater: on the one hand the individual property owner whose personal rights are threatened by public interference; on the other the entire population, present and future, whose rights may be infringed by the actions of that individual. This contrast may be appropriately illustrated by the material used by the opposing lobbies to support their views.

The following anecdote, quoted from the Assembly discussion on the Access Order, was told several times, during research interviews, by farmers and their representatives:

> I heard a story about a farmer who found a group of people picnicking in a meadow near his farm where there were a lot of cattle. They had not asked his permission, and when he went down to chide them gently he got into quite a big argument about it. He took the number of their car, found out where they lived, and on the next Sunday afternoon he and his family picnicked in their front garden (NIA OR 15.2.83, p. 284).

Another version continued with the suburban householder calling the police to have the farmer removed from his garden. The tale contains several facets of the farmers' image of their own self worth *vis-a-vis* those by whom they feel their rights are being threatened. The hardworking, religious (only on a Sunday did he and his family relax) and reasonable farmer, who intended, not to expel the picnickers from his land but merely to chide them gently for not asking permission, is contrasted with the argumentative and unreasonable householder. In this image the virtues of the rural dweller and the evils of the urban dweller are encapsulated. In the context of the present argument, the importance of the story lies in what it says about ownership. The householder regards his front garden as his personal property, and is affronted when others treat it as their own. And yet this householder not only treats the farmer's fields as his own, but protests when his right to do so is questioned. The farmer's claim to ownership rights is legitimised through comparison with the householder's claim; if a garden is private property, then why not a meadow?

The state of Northern Ireland's countryside is occasionally given critical attention in the national press. In 1988 Marion Shoard, in an article entitled *Ulster, the need for control*, attacked the relaxed, post-Cockcroft approach to rural planning (Shoard 1988).[10] In 1990 Simon Courtauld expressed similar views in an article entitled *The plain face of Ulster*. He began by extolling the beauty of both the natural and the man-made landscape:

> Just south of Newcastle in County Down, the Mountains of Mourne really do sweep down to the sea...Only the name (sic) of the nearby border towns of Newry and Warrenpoint remind you that this is a land of trouble, for the beauty and peace of the countryside make it hard to believe...the hedgerows here still look as Rupert Brooke described them, "little lines of sportive wood run wild" (Courtauld 1990).

Then comes a change of tone:

> But then you look - you cannot avoid looking - at the houses. It is said that the Ulster landscape gives the impression that a giant, having filled a pepperpot with bungalows, has scattered the contents...What Northern Ireland needs and deserves, in addition to a better "image", is a more sympathetic attitude to its housing and environment (ibid).

Within Northern Ireland these observations were quoted and cited by members of the amenity groups in representations to government (see USPC 1990 and CNCC 1990b), and generally discussed as legitimate vindications of their own views. The fact that the criticisms came from outside observers made them more rather than less acceptable. Undoubtedly this acceptability derives partly from the knowledge that government is concerned to promote a positive image for Northern Ireland, and is therefore likely to be influenced by external criticism. But it also demonstrates how the right to have a say in the future of Northern Ireland's countryside is conferred by the amenity lobby on those living elsewhere. The community to which "Ulster's heritage of natural beauty" (USPC, no date) belongs extends beyond its borders. The presentation of the countryside as a communal resource is a necessary part of the amenity lobby's strategy. The strength of their argument rests on their claim to be speaking on behalf of the community, present and future, as a whole; if the countryside were not public property, their claimed right to have a say in its future would have no foundation.

**Land, landscape and rural housing**

The two opposing models of the countryside are encapsulated in the concepts of land and landscape. Land is a physical, tangible resource which can be ploughed, sown, grazed, built on. It is therefore a place of work; it is more important for it to be functional than beautiful. As a tangible resource it can be bought and sold, inherited and left to children; it is personal wealth which can be used to generate more personal wealth. Landscape is an intangible resource, whose definitive characteristic is its appearance; landscape is viewed, not worked. It is equally accessible to all who can see it and is therefore owned communally by them.

| LAND | LANDSCAPE |
|---|---|
| Place of work | Place of recreation |
| Functionality | Appearance |
| Private property | Communal resource |
| Personal heritage | Communal heritage |
| (farmer's children) | (future generations) |

In the debate on rural housing, those who argued, in the pre-Cockcroft era, for a relaxation of controls on rural development, constituted a land lobby. The restrictions were seen as an infringement of landowners' rights to make the best use of their property. Much of the evidence used to support the opposition to the pre-Cockcroft restrictions consisted of reports of farmers' sons who had been denied the right to build where they wished to on their fathers' land (see Hansard 3.7.78: col 115, 139-40). Those who have argued, in the post-Cockcroft era, for a tightening of controls, constitute a landscape lobby. Post-Cockcroft planning policy has, they argue, allowed landowners and developers to destroy the appearance of the countryside, a communal resource.

## Shifting the ground, winning the arguments

Describing the conceptual models that underlie the arguments presented in debate can throw considerable light on those arguments and help to explain the stances and strategies of the participants. But it does not go very far in elucidating the course of the debate; it does not show how arguments are won and lost. To do this attention must be paid not only to the meanings that are contested in discourse, but also to the process whereby they are negotiated and established. The most significant shift in the Department's rural housing policy occurred following the Cockcroft Report, when restrictions on building in the open countryside were relaxed in most areas. Not surprisingly, this is perceived, on both sides of the debate, as a victory for the land lobby. Before the Cockcroft Report, the discourse was effectively a head-on collision between the two opposing models. The Department's policy had been defined, at least partly, on the basis of a landscape model, in which the protection of amenity took precedence over individual property rights. Representatives of the land lobby could only protest, through their district councillors, that their rights were being infringed. Their views, founded on a land model of the countryside, were incompatible with those of the Department. The result was a breakdown in communication, with councillors walking out in protest or opposing the Department's recommendations on principle.

The Cockcroft Report provided the mechanism whereby this deadlock could be broken, by introducing into the debate the possibility that the two models might, after all, be reconciled. Cockcroft questioned the Department's assumption that buildings were detrimental to the quality of the landscape, and suggested that, in certain circumstances, they might improve its appearance:

> ...we would suggest that planning permission could be given for the building of well-sited houses of good design in some of the more sparsely populated areas, thus enhancing the natural beauty of the landscape (Cockcroft 1978, p. 14).

This sentiment was embraced with unrestrained enthusiasm by Northern Ireland's MPs, for whom the Cockcroft Report was "a breath of fresh air blowing through 'the planning offices":[11]

> Many old and new buildings enhance the countryside...They belong to it, are part of it and give it its character.[12]
>
> All of us from Northern Ireland are very much aware of the scenic beauty in the place, and we want to preserve it...But the countryside consists of people and houses. If there are not people and houses what is there to

> look at? Where is the beauty? Where is the life?...I do not think that I have ever seen a photograph or a landscape of Northern Ireland without a pretty bungalow or a pretty cottage in it...I can safely say that we want to see a nice countryside, with the beauty preserved, and with quite a lot of houses and people living there to ensure that it stays beautiful.

Thus the central focus of the debate was shifted away from the irreconcilable issues of what the countryside is for and who has rights in its management, towards the question of what makes the landscape beautiful. Scenic beauty became the newly contested concept. Those in favour of increased development openly conceded the landscape lobby's view that the beauty of the countryside is important, but then defined that beauty in terms that suited their purpose, in terms of the presence, rather than the absence, of houses. This move effectively swept the ground from under the feet of the landscape lobby, most of whom would probably not agree that buildings are a necessary component of scenic beauty, but who certainly would have to concede that some buildings enhance some landscapes. To deny this would make nonsense of the efforts of organisations such as the National Trust, the Ulster Architectural Heritage Society and the Ulster Society for the Preservation of the Countryside, some of whose activities are directed at conserving the built environment. Robbed of an effective counter-argument, the landscape lobby could only express concern at the possible consequences of a change in policy (USPC 1978, 1979).

The understanding that the conservation of landscape did not require a total absence of new buildings provided the Department with a basis for changing its policy without needing to choose between the opposing models of the countryside as land and landscape. The deadlock of disagreement with the district councils could now be broken without the Department having to abandon its stance as a protector of scenic beauty. This is what has made post-Cockcroft planning policy so difficult to challenge. In practice it may appear, to the landscape lobby, to favour private interests at the expense of a communal resource, but the Department can argue, given the nature of the Cockcroft proposals, that communal interests still form a basis for their decisions.

**Re-opening the debate**

During the post-Cockcroft era, the landscape lobby has made repeated attempts to re-open the rural planning debate and instigate further changes in policy. Little progress was made, however, until March 1990, when the House of Commons Select Committee on the Environment announced its intention to review environmental issues in Northern Ireland, and invited views from interested parties.

Virtually all the amenity bodies responding to the invitation expressed concern about the effects of rural housing on the landscape. The Historic Buildings Council (HBC) for Northern Ireland[14] referred to,

> . . . the peppering of "Spanish style" and other inappropriate new buildings throughout the countryside, and a disastrous "ribbon" type development pattern along roadways (HBC 1990, p. 157).

The Council for Nature Conservation and the Countryside (CNCC),[15] in its evidence to the Select Committee, stated,

> Northern Ireland is cited by Planning Departments in Scotland and Wales as the worst-case example, on no account to be followed (CNCC 1990, p. 16).

These and other similar views (HMSO 1990) clearly impressed the Select Committee who, in their report, recommended,

> . . . that the DoE(NI) carry out a review of the effects of current policies on residential development in the countryside and reconsider the changes introduced following the Cockcroft Report (ibid, p. xxix).

In August 1991, in response to this recommendation, the DoE(NI) published a consultation leaflet entitled, *What kind of countryside do we want?* (DoE(NI) 1991), and invited responses from interested parties. The results of this exercise, in the form of further consultation documents or new policy statements, are expected to be published during 1993.

## Models of change, changing models

The debate which preceded and surrounded the Cockcroft proposals was relatively narrow in focus, arose out of conditions peculiar to Northern Ireland, and employed clearly distinguishable models of what the countryside is for and whom it belongs to. The re-opened debate is more broadly based and is part of a wider discourse about the future of rural society, not only in Northern Ireland, but in the rest of the UK and beyond. Although the main concerns of the current debate are still being negotiated, it is already clear that they cannot be reduced to oppositions between aesthetics and functionality, and between private and communal ownership. A new model, of "a changing countryside", has emerged at the centre of the discourse. An examination of the relationship between this model and the more established perceptions of the countryside as land and landscape may give some indication of the directions the debate is now taking.

The image of a changing countryside has arisen primarily out of the Europe-wide reform of the Common Agricultural Policy (CAP) which, since the mid-1980s, has introduced a series of measures aimed at decreasing agricultural production and diversifying land use. Post-Cockcroft planning policy has also played its part, in changing the structure of the rural population. Between 1979 and 1988, about 31,000 applications were granted for new rural houses (CNCC 1990b), and building has continued at the rate of 2,500-3,000 new houses per year (HMSO 1990). While some of these houses are certainly for the use of farming families, many are bought by professional people who work in the towns. A significant proportion of the rural population now has little direct contact with farming and treats the countryside as somewhere to live and spend leisure time.

The observation that changes have taken place is not a sufficient basis on which to argue that a model of a changing countryside is now central to the debate. It needs to be shown that change is perceived by the participants as an important factor. Several recent documents on planning policy present images of transition and uncertainty. The CNCC, introducing its proposals for a reform of rural planning policy, comments, "We are certainly living in a time of rapid and not always predictable change" (CNCC 1990b). The DoE(NI)'s consultation leaflet on rural planning begins, "Considerable changes are taking place today in Northern Ireland's rural areas. The people who live there are faced with many new 'challenges" (DoE(NI) 1991). The question posed by this leaflet, *What kind of countryside do we want?*, implies that the options are open, that there are a number of routes which could be chosen. The House of Commons Environment Committee conveys a similar impression: "As far as the environment is concerned, Northern Ireland is now at a crossroads" (HMSO 1990). Interestingly, the model of a changing countryside is also being reinforced through academic research (see Dawson 1992). The model of change, and the perceived nature of the changes taking place, throw into question two aspects of the more established models: the notion of the countryside as private property and the opposition between work and recreation.

*From ownership to stewardship*

The understanding that farmers not only work the countryside but also care for it has an established place in debates on land use. In Northern Ireland it is often pointed out that the attractive landscape of small fields bounded by hedgerows is a result of many generations of farming. This view is not only asserted by agricultural interests,[16] but is also acknowledged by conservation bodies. Further recognition of the farmers' role as carers of the rural environment is expressed in government publications offering advice on conservation,[17] and through the DANI's advisory service; advice on environmental matters is one of the few services still given free of charge (Milton 1990). Nevertheless, conservation of the countryside has been seen, until recently, as little more than a by-product of agricultural activities, whose main purpose has been food production. This view is changing under the reform of the CAP. Conservation bodies lobbying for change have suggested that the goals of farming be redefined to include environmental and cultural benefits:

> As well as food and a basic need for safety and security, Europe's public also want a rural environment that provides for wider cultural and personal needs. The public want a countryside rich in wildlife; one that is unpolluted and attractive; recreational opportunities to satisfy populations with increased leisure time. To be successful and sustainable a future policy must satisfy these other goals (Taylor and Dixon 1990).

Although government's response has been slower than many of the conservation bodies would have wished, a steady stream of new grant schemes and initiatives, many of which support conservation measures, has communicated the clear message that the role of farming is being changed through government policy. The values of high productivity and intensification, which guided agriculture through the past fifty years, are being replaced by a new regime in which stewardship of the rural environment is a central concept. There are also indications that many of Northern Ireland's farmers would be willing to adopt this new role, provided adequate financial support is available. A survey conducted in 1988 indicated that 90 per cent of farmers felt they should be paid to preserve the rural environment (NIAPA 1989).

This redefinition of the farmers' role is having a subtle effect on the model of the countryside as privately owned land. This model was based on the perception of land as a raw material in a manufacturing process. Farmers used land to produce a commodity, food, for which the community was willing to pay. Their income depended on their ownership of the means of production. In their new role as stewards, farmers are still producing a commodity, but that commodity, a diverse and attractive rural environment, is inseparable from the land itself. The land, refashioned as landscape, is the new product, for which the community pays through government grants. Furthermore, the concept of stewardship is incompatible with that of private ownership, since it implies that the resource is being cared for on behalf of someone other than the carer. When owners become stewards, what could once be presented as private property is redefined as a communal resource.

*A place of work and recreation*

Changes in government policy have also engendered a shift in the relationship between work and recreation in the countryside. While the economic activities of farmers were directed almost entirely towards food production, recreation could be presented as a conflicting interest. Farmers are now being encouraged to diversify out of food production into other enterprises, some of which - guest houses, golf courses, craft workshops, riding and shooting facilities - cater for the recreation market. Rural tourism is being actively promoted by the Northern Ireland Tourist Board, and is seen by the DoE(NI) as having particular potential in the future of the rural economy (DoE(NI) 1991). The significance of these developments is that they help to integrate the interests of work and recreation in the countryside. If, as the DoE(NI) suggests, the outlook for the growth of conventional farming is limited, the provision of recreation facilities may become an important alternative source of rural employment. The continued status of the countryside as a place of work, far from conflicting with its status as a place of recreation, will depend on its use as a leisure resource.

## Looking back, looking forward

It remains to be seen whether the House of Commons Environment Committee Report will become a second watershed, and usher in a new era of rural planning policy. What is certain is that the issues involved in the current debate are different and more complex than those that were negotiated in the late 1970s. Some of the current shifts in the way the countryside is perceived appear, on the face of it, to favour the interests of the landscape lobby. Through the redefinition of farmers as stewards, the status of the countryside as a communal resource appears to be taking precedence over its status as private property; while recognition of the countryside as a place of recreation, as well as a place of work, is being promoted through pressures to sustain rural employment in the face of a declining agriculture industry. However, in assessing the possible consequences of these shifts for future planning policy, it needs to be understood that the policy-makers have always treated the countryside as both land and landscape, as both private and communal property, as both a place of work and a place of recreation. If the interests of the landscape lobby have suffered as a result of post-Cockcroft planning policy, this is not because they lost the battle to have the countryside defined as landscape; in fact, the land lobby effectively conceded victory in this particular struggle. The success of the land lobby rested on the way in which scenic beauty was defined in line with private ownership interests. Given that the perception of the countryside as a communal resource and a place of recreation has always been present as a basis for planning policy, it may be unrealistic to expect major policy changes simply because these ideas are now more prominent in the debate than they were.

On the other hand, new conflicts can be envisaged arising out of the changing nature of rural recreation. When, in the late 1970s and early 1980s, the landscape lobby argued for the public right to experience and enjoy the countryside, rural recreation was envisaged as an escape from pressures of modern life, achieved through activities which brought people into close contact with nature e.g. walking, climbing and angling. None of these activities requires the sort of facilities likely to sustain rural employment. Rural recreation is now being defined increasingly in terms of economic development. The creation of a mass market in rural recreation, whether it means the commercialisation of conventional rural pursuits, the expansion of urban and suburban facilities into rural areas, or the generation of new rural activities, is unlikely to satisfy a lobby concerned with the preservation of scenic beauty. The landscape lobby may find itself increasingly having to oppose the recreational use of the countryside in order to protect its interests.

The once clear boundaries between the land and landscape models of the countryside are breaking down as a result of current shifts in the perception and use of resources. It is impossible to predict whether new models, with similarly clear boundaries, will emerge. Nevertheless, given the nature of administrative processes in Northern Ireland, the struggle for symbolic ownership of the countryside will almost certainly continue to play a major part in the determination of planning policy.

## Acknowledgement

This paper was originally prepared for the Workshop on Social Anthropology and Public Policy, held in the Department of Social Anthropology at the Queen's University of Belfast in December 1991. I am grateful to the convenors of the Workshop for allowing it to be included in this volume.

## Notes

1. Unless otherwise stated, references to "the Department" are references to the Department of the Environment (NI).

2. The Department's Practice Notes of November 1976 list categories of people whose applications would be treated with sympathy: full- and part-time farmers, farm workers, retired farmers, members of farmers' families, managers of rural businesses, and so on (DoE(NI) 1976).
3. Area of Outstanding Natural Beauty (AONB) is a statutory designation used for landscape conservation purposes, implemented initially under the Amenity Lands Act 1965, and later under the Nature Conservation and Amenity Lands (NI) Order 1985.
4. Cited in Buchanan 1982: 269.
5. Amenity Lands Act 1965, Article 4(1)(b).
6. The Access to the Countryside (Northern Ireland) Order 1983: Explanatory Note.
7. The Assembly was a non-legislative elected body set up in an attempt to encourage power-sharing between Northern Ireland's Loyalist and Nationalist communities
8. I am grateful to Hilary Tovey for help in developing this idea.
9. The Voluntary Amenity Group, formed in 1980, was an informal association of voluntary amenity and conservation groups in Northern Ireland. In 1983 it changed its name to the Northern Ireland Environment Group and, in 1990, was formally constituted as the Northern Ireland Environment Link.
10. Marion Shoard is widely respected in conservation and amenity circles as an outspoken defender of the public right to use the countryside (see Shoard 1980, 1987).
11. From a speech by Ian Paisley MP during the Parliamentary debate on the Cockcroft Report (Hansard 3.7.78: col ).
12. From a speech by Enoch Powell MP during the same debate (Hansard 3.7.78: col 118).
13. From a speech by William Ross MP during the same debate (Hansard 3.7.78: col 154).
14. The Historic Buildings Council is a committee appointed by government to advise the DoE(NI) on the conservation of the built environment.
15. The Council for Nature Conservation and the Countryside (CNCC) is a committee appointed by government to advise the DoE(NI) on the conservation of landscape and nature.
16. "For centuries, farming has been the dominant land use in the Ulster countryside and through time has produced an attractive rural landscape" (from a booklet on Trees on the Farm, produced by the Ulster Tree Committee, the DoE(NI) and the DANI, see also DANI 1990).
17. See, for instance, DoE(NI) and DANI (nd) and booklets produced by the two government departments on hedges, ponds and trees on the farm.

## References


Buchanan, R.H. (1982) Landscape: the recreational use of the countryside, in J.G. Cruickshank and D.N. Wilcock (ed), *Northern Ireland: environment and natural resources.* The Queen's University of Belfast and the New University of Ulster.

CNCC (1990a) *Memorandum by the Council for Nature Conservation and the Countryside to the House of Commons Environment Committee,* in HMSO (1990) pp.15-18, Belfast.

CNCC (1990b) *Rural planning policy in Northern Ireland: time for change.* CNCC Belfast.

Cockcroft, W.H. (1978) *Review of rural planning policy: report of the committee under the chairmanship of Dr. W.H. Cockcroft.* HMSO, Belfast.

Courtauld, S. (1990) The plain face of Ulster. *Weekend Telegraph*, 10th February 1990.

DANI (1988) *At your service 1988-89: an outline of advisory and other services, grants and subsidies available to farmers and horticulturalists.* Department of Agriculture (NI), Belfast.

DANI (1990) *Countryside management: the DANI Strategy.* Department of Agriculture (NI), Belfast.

Dawson, A. (1992) Changing farm economies in Northern Ireland: research report. *Anthropology Ireland*, Vol.2, No. 1, Anthropological Association of Ireland

DoE(NI) (1976) *Residential development in rural areas: development control policy note.* Department of the Environment, Belfast.

DoE(NI) (1987) *Location, siting and design in rural areas.* Department of the Environment, Belfast.

DoE(NI) (1988) *Houses in harmony with the countryside.* Department of the Environment, Belfast.

DoE(NI) (1991) *What kind of countryside do we want? Options for a new planning strategy for rural Northern Ireland.* Department of the Environment, Belfast.

DoE(NI) and DANI (nd) *Farming and the countryside.* HMSO, Belfast.

Fairclough, N. (1989) *Language and power.* Longman, London.

Grillo, R. (1989) Anthropology, languaage, politics, in R. Grillo (ed), *Social anthropology and the politics of language.* Sociological Review Monograph 36, Routledge, London and New York.

Hall, S.C. (1843) *Ireland, its scenery and character*, etc. London.

Hansard (1977-78) *House of Commons official report*, Fifth Series, Vol 953.

HBC (1990) *Memoranda by the Historic Buildings Council for Northern Ireland to the House of Commons Environment Committee*, published as Appendix 22 in HMSO 1990.

HMSO (1947) *The Ulster countryside.* Report by the Planning Advisory Board on Amenities in Northern Ireland. HMSO, Belfast.

HMSO (1975) *Northern Ireland discussion paper: Regional Physical Development Strategy 1975-95.* Department of Housing, Local Government and Planning, Belfast.

HMSO (1977) *Regional Physical Development Strategy 1975-95.* HMSO, Belfast.

HMSO (1990) *House of Commons Environment Committee first report: environmental issues in Northern Ireland.* HC Paper 39.

Lofgren, O. (1985) *Wish you were here! Holiday images and picture postcards Ethnologia Scandinavia,* pp. 90-107.

Milton, K. (1990) *Our countryside our concern.* Northern Ireland Environment Link, Belfast.

NIA OR (1984) *Northern Ireland Assembly official report,* 1983-1984. HMSO, Belfast

NIA 40 (1983) *Northern Ireland Assembly report on the proposal for a draft Access to the Countryside (Northern Ireland) Order.* HMSO, Belfast.

NIAPA (1989) *Newsletter.* Northern Ireland Agricultural Producers' Association, Draperstown.

Seidel, G. (1985) Political discourse analysis, in T.A. van Dijk (ed) *Handbook of discourse analysis, Volume 4: discourse analysis in society.* Academic Press.

Seidel, G. (1989) We condemn apartheid, BUT . . . a discursive analysis of the European Parliamentary debate on sanctions, in R. Grillo (ed), *Social anthropology and the politics of language.* Sociological Review Monograph 36, Routledge, London and New York.

Shoard, M. (1980) *The theft of the countryside.* Temple Smith, London.

Shoard, M. (1987) *This land is our land: the struggle for Britain's countryside.* Paladin, London.

Shoard, M. (1988) Ulster, the need for control. *Landscape,* February 1988.

Taylor, J.P. and Dixon, J.B. (1990) *Agriculture and the environment: towards integration.* RSPB, Sandy.

Thackeray, W.M. (1887) *The Irish Sketch Book.* London.

Thomas, K. (1983) *Man and the natural world: changing attitudes in England 1500-1800.* Allen Lane.

UAHS (1990) *Memorandum by the Ulster Architectural Heritage Society to the House of Commons Environment Committee,* published as Apendidix 29 in HMSO 1990.

UFU (1990) *Memorandum by the Ulster Farmers' Union to the House of Commons Environment Committee,* published as Appendix 30 in HMSO 1990.
USPC (no date) *Ulster needs you.* Campaign leaflet and membership application form.
UPSC (1990) *Letter to the Clerk of the House of Commons Environment Committee,* published as Appendix 32 in HMSO 1990.
Voluntary Amenity Group (1983) *A policy for landscape conservation.* Paper presented by the Northern Ireland Environment Group to the Northern Ireland Assembly Environment Committee, in response to the proposal for a draft Nature Conservation and Amenity Lands (NI) Order 1983.

# 10 The rural housing problem in Northern Ireland*

*John McPeake and Brendan Murtagh*

## Introduction

There is a long-established tradition of research into rural issues in Britain, Ireland and further afield with the result that the literature is voluminous. In terms of housing in rural areas, researchers have been interested in a wide diversity of matters including planning and development, demography, supply issues, rural services, poverty, self-help, conservation and housing conditions (Birrell et al 1991). In recent years, the focus, particularly in England, has been on the problems generated by the desirability of rural living and the effect that more affluent former city-dwellers are having on existing rural communities (Best, 1990). Issues such as affordability (ACRE 1988), second homes and development pressures, particularly from commuters (Blunden and Curry 1988, Clark 1989, Shucksmith 1981) have been emphasized. Referring to Great Britain, Rogers notes that "rural housing conditions now generate relatively little concern" (Rogers 1976, p.85). However, some recent initiatives suggest that rural housing conditions are beginning to receive more serious attention once again, and this is particularly the case in the "Celtic fringe" of Scotland (Scottish Homes 1990), Wales (Tai Cymru 1991) and Northern Ireland.

In 1974, the first comprehensive house condition survey in Northern Ireland showed that 1 dwelling in 5 was unfit for human habitation, 1 in 4 lacked basic amenities and 1 in 3 was in need of major repairs (NIHE 1974). Overall, 38 per cent of the stock required some form of remedial action. Conditions in Belfast were particularly poor: the city accounted for one third of all unfit dwellings and almost 40 per cent of dwellings in need of remedial action. These results

* *The views expressed in this paper are those of the author and are not necessarily those of his employer, the Northern Ireland Housing Executive.*

heralded a major programme of urban redevelopment and rehabilitation, a programme that resulted in a 73 per cent reduction in the number of unfit dwellings in Belfast by 1987 (NIHE 1988). However, the 1974 survey also showed that poor conditions were not confined to the urban areas of Northern Ireland. Indeed, more than half (54 per cent) of all unfit dwellings were in rural locations. Moreover, while the 1987 survey showed that unfitness levels in rural areas had been reduced, at 42 per cent the improvement rate was substantially below that achieved in urban areas. As a result, by 1987 more than two-thirds of all unfits were in rural areas and the great majority of these (81 per cent) were individual dwellings outside the existing village and hamlet network. This increasing concentration of unfitness in more isolated locations lies at the core of the rural housing problem in the region. Concern over rural dwelling conditions represents an interesting departure from the traditional focus.

It is suggested that the contemporary rural housing problems of the province have to be viewed in their historical context. Thus, the chapter opens with a brief examination of the origins and development of rural housing problems up to 1971. Attention then shifts to consider the contribution of the Northern Ireland Housing Executive over the past two decades. Comparative information on the nature of the rural and urban stock is presented, together with a review of the major trends in housing conditions over the 1970s and 1980s. In recognition of the differential progress made in tackling rural housing problems the Housing Executive has recently completed a comprehensive review of its rural housing policy. This initiative is considered in some detail and the chapter concludes by drawing out important implications for policy planning in rural areas in Northern Ireland.

## The historical background

### *1883-1939*

The housing condition problems of Northern Ireland almost certainly represent an inherited situation. Although very little objective data exist on the nature of housing conditions in the years before the twentieth century, some indication of the situation can be gauged from the report of the 1885 Royal Commission on the Housing of the Working Classes. The Commission reported that conditions in Londonderry and Belfast were very favourable in contrast to conditions in other urban centres in Ireland. Brett (1986), however, sounds a warning note:

> Of course, it would be wrong to paint too rosy a picture: there were certainly appalling slums, over-crowded and insanitary alleyways, rack-

> rented mill-workers' hovels, byres and stables used for human habitation. But, by the standards of the day, Belfast was an uncommonly well-housed city. (Brett 1986, p.16)

The Commission did not, however, consider conditions in rural areas. Brett (1986) goes on to note that rural conditions were little better but, if anything, conditions were worse in the small towns and villages than in the countryside in general. It is reported that in 1861, there were some 600,000 occupied mud cabins in Ireland. Increasingly landlords were called upon to provide better accommodation for their tenants and this pressure culminated in a series of Labourers (Ireland) Acts, the first of which was in 1883. The 1883 Act established the principle that public authorities had a role to play in the area of rural housing provision and the dwellings constructed under the Act and its revisions may be regarded as the forerunners of general council housing (Haddon and Trimble 1986). The Acts provided powers for the raising of loans to finance local authority building and introduced Government subsidies on loan charges. Although some 21,000 rural cottages were built between 1883 and 1906, very few were in present-day Northern Ireland. Rural living conditions remained poor well into the twentieth century.

In 1919, two years before the partitioning of Ireland, a new Ministry of Health was established at Westminster and the scene was set for a more direct role for local authorities in housing provision. The more enlightened approach to housing provision in Britain was not embraced in the province. Indeed, following partition, subsidies for new house construction failed to keep pace with those in Britain and little was done to encourage local authority building (Murie 1992). As a result, house-building activity in the inter-war years remained relatively low-key. Singleton (1989) reports that 51,000 houses were built between 1919 and 1939, only 7,500 of which were by local authorities. Furthermore, the peak of this activity was not reached until 1931. The house-building record of some rural local authorities was particularly disappointing with, for example, no rural cottages built in rural Fermanagh up to 1933 leading Bardon (1992) to comment that this "is merely the worst example of Northern Ireland's dismal housing record in this period" (p.532). Nevertheless, between 1919 and 1939, some 4,300 rural cottages were built in Northern Ireland, a meagre but important contribution. In addition to the relatively small numbers of properties built in the period, concern has also been expressed that the standards of construction were much lower in rural areas than in urban areas (Birrell et al 1971). In summary, the inter-war period was characterised by a strong reliance on the private sector, with a minimum of subsidy and a general dislike of direct provision on the part of local authorities -a situation strangely familiar to students of contemporary British housing policy.

## Table 10.1
## Rural and urban housing conditions, 1943

| Characteristic | Belfast County Borough | | Other Urban Areas | | Isolated Rural Areas | | Total | |
|---|---|---|---|---|---|---|---|---|
| **Structural Condition** | No. | % | No. | % | No. | % | No. | % |
| No repairs required | 13040 | 12.5 | 13590 | 23.3 | 24500 | 15.2 | 51130 | 15.8 |
| Minor repairs (up to £20) | 40750 | 39.0 | 21010 | 36.1 | 38730 | 24.1 | 100490 | 31.1 |
| Extensive repairs (£20-£100) | 38800 | 37.1 | 15830 | 27.2 | 51240 | 32.0 | 105880 | 32.8 |
| Major repairs (£100-£200) | 7040 | 6.7 | 3000 | 5.2 | 13510 | 8.4 | 23550 | 7.3 |
| Totally unfit (repairs >£200) | 4840 | 4.7 | 4780 | 8.2 | 32390 | 20.2 | 42010 | 13.0 |
| All dwellings | 104470 | 100.0 | 58210 | 100.0 | 160370 | 100.0 | 323050 | 100.0 |
| **Overcrowding** | No. | % | No. | % | No. | % | No. | % |
| Not overcrowded | 74590 | 76.1 | 40490 | 77.3 | 85380 | 68.9 | 200460 | 73.1 |
| Overcrowded | 23480 | 23.9 | 11900 | 22.7 | 38530 | 31.1 | 73910 | 26.9 |
| All inhabited fit or repairable dwellings | 98070 | 100 | 52390 | 100.0 | 123910 | 100.0 | 274370 | 100 |
| **Lighting & Ventilation** | No. | % | No. | % | No. | % | No. | % |
| Satisfactory | 91090 | 91.4 | 44470 | 83.2 | 88590 | 69.2 | 224150 | 79.8 |
| Not Satisfactory | 8540 | 8.6 | 8960 | 16.8 | 39390 | 30.8 | 56900 | 20.2 |
| All fit or repairable dwellings | 99630 | 100.0 | 53430 | 100.0 | 127980 | 100.0 | 281040 | 100.0 |

Source: PAB (1944). Figures rounded to nearest 10 dwellings.

Less than 1,000 dwellings were constructed in Northern Ireland during the second world war, further exacerbating the neglect of the inter-war years. This lack of activity led to the appointment of a Planning Advisory Board with a brief to "consider and report on the general housing problem in Northern Ireland with particular reference to the clearance of slums and the provision of housing in the post-war period" (PAB 1944, p.6). The Interim Report of the Board constitutes a damning indictment of the years of neglect in the pre-war period. The report, which was based on a survey of housing conditions across Northern Ireland, represents an important landmark in housing information. Although simplistic by to-day's standards, the report provides the first detailed comparative analysis of urban and rural housing conditions in Northern Ireland. Table 10.1, which has been compiled from information contained in the Planning Advisory Board report, clearly shows that rural conditions were worse than those in urban areas. On all three measures employed in the survey, the rural stock fared worse than its urban counterpart. For example, 20 per cent of rural dwellings were described as totally unfit compared to less than 5 per cent of the Belfast stock; 31 per cent were overcrowded compared to 24 per cent in Belfast; and, 31 per cent had unsatisfactory lighting and ventilation compared to just 9 per cent in Belfast. Indeed, the report comments that

> In the rural areas the survey has shown that the number of houses regarded as unfit by modern standards is extraordinarily high. (PAB 1944, p.15)

Furthermore, in the rural areas of Fermanagh and Tyrone more than 95 per cent of dwellings had no piped water supply, no gas or no electricity. The report called for a comprehensive programme of new construction which should aim to provide 100,000 new homes to meet immediate needs, 60 per cent of which were to be targeted at rural areas. Information is not available that would permit an assessment of the degree to which this rural target was met, but official figures show that the global target was not reached until the early 1960s (HMSO 1979).

One of the most important events that followed the publication of the Planning Advisory Board report was the establishment of the Northern Ireland Housing Trust (NIHT) in 1945. The NIHT, which was modelled on the Scottish Special Housing Association, had a remit to complement local authority new building activity. Initially, the Trust was to provide 25,000 of the needed 100,000 dwellings, with the remainder to come from the local authorities and private enterprise. Unfortunately, the standards of new construction, whilst far superior to the standards of the dwellings that they replaced, fell short of that being provided in England (O'Brien 1951). One of the early initiatives of the Trust was the introduction of non-traditional forms of construction into Northern Ireland, partly in response to a shortage of traditional building materials and partly because of a lack of skilled labour. This decision was to have unforseen ramifications: many of these industrialized building forms proved to have basic design defects that required dwelling replacement well inside the planned life span. O'Brien (1951) argued that such methods were essential in order to meet the Trust's new-build targets. In the event, as the 18th Annual Report of the Trust shows, the target of 25,000 new homes by 1955 was not reached until 1963 (NIHT 1963). Nevertheless, almost from its inception the Trust acknowledged the importance of tackling rural housing problems, perhaps reflecting the fact that its general manager had been secretary to the influential Planning Advisory Board. In its 2nd Annual Report, the details of the first rural schemes in Fermanagh are outlined (NIHT 1947) and of the 48,532 dwellings built by the Trust over its life, some 21,000 were built on lands acquired from the rural district councils. However, only about 2,200 of these were completed in locations that accord with contemporary definitions of rural areas (Conway 1991a).

In the period 1944-1972, approximately 75,000 dwellings were completed by local authorities, but some were of an appallingly low standard. Brett (1986) reports that even in the late 1950s, many of the smaller councils, hampered by the antiquated legislative framework and a lack of rate income, continued to build new houses — the so-called "Ulster Cottages" — without running water, sewerage systems or electricity. Although detailed information is not readily available, it seems likely that most of these inadequate dwellings were built in the rural districts. In addition to building sub-standard dwellings, local authorities had limited powers to deal with unfit housing conditions. Such powers were not introduced until 1956 at which time tackling unfitness became a statutory duty and improvement grant procedures were brought into line with those in Great Britain (Murie 1992). Unfortunately, as far as local authorities were concerned it was a case of too little, too late.

Brett (1986) is also dismissive of the private sector contribution in the post-war period describing it as "uninspired and uninspiring" (p. 36). Nevertheless, some 76,000 dwellings were built, the great majority with government subsidies. In addition, some 9,500 farmhouses were modernized or replaced through Department of Agriculture grants between 1944 and 1972, going some way towards addressing Mogey's (1947) finding that buildings designed for animals were often in better condition than those occupied by the farmers themselves. Taken together, the three main housing suppliers provided something in the order of 213,000 houses between 1944 and 1972 (HMSO 1979), a programme of building on a scale comparable with that in Britain (Singleton 1989).

As the 1960s came to a close, there was growing community disaffection with the administration of public housing in Northern Ireland. In particular, there was concern that some local authorities were using their housing powers to gain political and electoral advantage (Murie 1992) and, although there was no evidence of systematic discrimination in the location and allocation of new housing, there was sufficient evidence of malpractice in specific local areas (Rose 1971). Singleton (1989) notes that concern over malpractice in the housing field "led to the first civil rights marches and the outbreak of violence in 1968-1969 which followed them" (p.631). The Cameron Commission was set up to investigate the disturbances in 1969 and it placed considerable emphasis on complaints about public housing, pointing particularly to housing shortages in Roman Catholic areas and unfair allocation procedures (HMSO 1970). Following the publication of the Cameron Report, the Government decided that all public housing should be removed from political control and all housing powers were to be centralized with a single housing authority. Thus, the Housing Executive was formed by the Housing Executive (NI) Act 1971. Between 1971 and 1973 the Executive inherited a stock of some 150,000 dwellings, about 42,000 of which were in rural locations, and it assumed the housing functions of 65 separate housing authorities.

## The Housing Executive and rural housing

### *The first decade - an urban focus?*

The planning guidelines for the early years of the Executive's operations were set out in the Northern Ireland Development Programme 1970-1975. This established a target of 73,500 dwellings over the five year period, 49,000 to be publicly provided (HMSO 1970). However, at the same time as suggesting an ambitious house-building programme, the 1970-1975 Development Programme highlighted the benefits of strict control over countryside development and urged a concentration of new housing in key settlements. This policy is likely to have hampered the ability of the Executive to tackle housing conditions in rural communities. In his first Annual Report, the Chairman of the Executive noted:

> A tentative assessment of housing need shows that 50 per cent of replacement dwellings should be built in areas which the 1970-1975 Development Programme does not designate as Growth or Key Centres. As with redevelopment the speed of operation for this type of replacement is necessarily slow. (NIHE 1972, p.14)

The Executive did not begin its operations with a clean slate: rather, it inherited a substantial programme of new-building and slum-clearance from its predecessors and these programmes formed the backbone of its building activities in the early years of the 1970s (NIHE 1991a). In any case, the 1970-1975 Development Programme targets proved somewhat optimistic with some 67,000 dwellings completed, including 41,300 provided by various public agencies. It is difficult to estimate how this was distributed across urban and rural areas. An analysis of the first four Annual Reports of the Housing Executive suggests that somewhere between 15 per cent and 20 per cent of new-build was in rural locations, but reliable information is not available on the location of private new-build.

The 1974 House Condition Survey (NIHE 1974) revealed the enormity of the task facing the newly-formed organization: 20 per cent of the stock was unfit for human habitation; 26 per cent lacked at least one basic amenity; and, 38 per cent was in need of urgent repair. Bardon (1992) reports that "The Labour government, shocked by the evidence of the 1974 House Condition Survey, more than doubled the resources available to the Housing Executive in real terms between 1974 and 1977". The situation in Belfast was of major concern because of the intense concentration of the problems and the sheer numbers involved. The publication of the Regional Physical Development Strategy 1975-1995 (HMSO 1975), with its forecast of a reduction in household growth rates, "enabled a shift in resources to be made to concentrate upon the needs of Belfast." (NIHE 1977, p.8). In other words, the reduced requirement for new dwellings to cater for newly forming households allowed an increased emphasis on meeting replacement needs,and the bulk of these needs were seen to be in Belfast. This renewed emphasis on Belfast occurred in spite of the mounting evidence of a major concentration of deprivation and poor dwelling conditions in the predominately rural west of the region (NIHE and UU 1976).

The redevelopment programmes of the former Belfast County Borough Council formed the basis for the replacement building throughout the 1970s and into the early 1980s (NIHE 1982). At the same time, more than 45 Housing Action Areas (HAAs) were identified in the city following the 1976 Housing (Northern Ireland) Order. Overall, between 1972 and 1982, more than 6,000 new houses were provided in Redevelopment Areas (RDAs)and some 3,500 dwellings in HAAs were rehabilitated. Area-based schemes such as Enveloping, together with individual renovation grants, also made a significant contribution to the improvement of the Belfast stock.

Similar, although less pronounced, progress was made in tackling unfitness in urban areas in general. Thus, by 1979, the number of unfit houses in urban areas had been reduced by one third and by more than 40 per cent in Belfast (NIHE 1980). In contrast, the reduction in rural areas was less than 20 per cent. As a result, the unfitness rate in rural areas, at 25 per cent, was almost three times that in the urban areas of Northern Ireland (Tables 10.2 and 10.3). It is interesting to

**Table 10.2**

**Urban and rural unfitness, 1974 - 1987**

| | Urban | | | Rural | | | Total | | |
|---|---|---|---|---|---|---|---|---|---|
| 1974: | No. | Col % | Row % | No. | Col % | Row % | No. | Col % | Row % |
| Fit Dwellings | 228100 | 84.7 | 62.3 | 138040 | 74.2 | 37.7 | 366470 | 80.4 | 100.0 |
| Unfit Dwellings | 41330 | 15.3 | 46.0 | 47710 | 25.8 | 54.0 | 89040 | 19.6 | 100.0 |
| All Dwellings | 269430 | 100.0 | 59.1 | 186080 | 100.0 | 40.9 | 455510 | 100.0 | 100.0 |
| 1979: | No. | Col % | Row % | No. | Col % | Row % | No. | Col % | Row % |
| Fit Dwellings | 292350 | 91.3 | 72.2 | 112830 | 74.6 | 27.8 | 405180 | 85.9 | 100.0 |
| Unfit Dwellings | 27770 | 8.7 | 41.9 | 38440 | 25.4 | 58.1 | 66210 | 14.1 | 100.0 |
| All Dwellings | 320120 | 100.0 | 67.9 | 151270 | 100.0 | 32.1 | 471390 | 100.0 | 100.0 |
| 1984: | No. | Col % | Row % | No. | Col % | Row % | No. | Col % | Row % |
| Fit Dwellings | 314020 | 93.9 | 71.3 | 126200 | 80.3 | 28.7 | 440220 | 89.6 | 100.0 |
| Unfit Dwellings | 20420 | 6.1 | 39.8 | 30910 | 19.7 | 60.2 | 51330 | 10.4 | 100.0 |
| All Dwellings | 334440 | 100.0 | 68.0 | 157110 | 100.0 | 32.0 | 491550 | 100.0 | 100.0 |
| 1987: | No. | Col % | Row % | No. | Col % | Row % | No. | Col % | Row % |
| Fit Dwellings | 326130 | 95.6 | 69.6 | 142190 | 83.5 | 30.4 | 468320 | 91.6 | 100.0 |
| Unfit Dwellings | 14900 | 4.4 | 34.7 | 28000 | 16.5 | 65.3 | 42900 | 8.4 | 100.0 |
| All Dwellings | 341030 | 100.0 | 66.7 | 170190 | 100.0 | 33.3 | 511220 | 100.0 | 100.0 |

Sources - House Condition Surveys for 1974, 1979, 1984 and 1987 (NIHE 1974; 1982; 1985; 1988). Figures rounded to nearest 10 dwellings.

**Table 10.3**
**Inter-survey changes in unfitness by location, 1974 - 1987**

| Period | Urban | | | Rural | | | Total | | |
|---|---|---|---|---|---|---|---|---|---|
| | No. | % Change | Annual rate | No. | % Change | Annual rate | No. | % Change | Annual rate |
| 1974 - 1979 | -13530 | -33.7 | - 6.5 | -9600 | -33.7 | - 6.5 | -22830 | -25.6 | - 5.1 |
| 1979 - 1984 | - 7350 | - 26.5 | - 5.3 | - 7530 | - 26.5 | - 5.3 | - 14880 | - 22.5 | - 4.5 |
| 1984 - 1987 | - 5520 | - 27.0 | - 9.0 | - 2900 | - 27.0 | - 9.0 | - 8430 | - 16.4 | - 5.5 |
| 1974 - 1987 | - 26430 | - 63.9 | - 4.9 | - 26430 | - 63.9 | - 4.9 | - 46140 | - 51.8 | - 4.0 |

set the differential progress in rural areas against the, somewhat premature, claim that "the housing problem outside Belfast . . . has largely been resolved". (NIHE 1978, p. 8).

*The second decade - the emergence of the rural problem*

The 1980s saw a continued concern with conditions in the urban areas of Northern Ireland in general, and Belfast in particular. The Belfast Housing Renewal Strategy presented a comprehensive plan aimed at tackling the continuation of poor housing conditions in the city (NIHE 1982). The area based programmes of the 1970s were extended with the identification of a further 42 Redevelopment Areas and 15 Housing Action Areas. The new Private Investment Priority Area (PIPA) concept further bolstered the Executive's efforts at tackling housing condition problems in Belfast. Some of the fruits of this activity were apparent in the results of the 1984 House Condition Survey (NIHE 1985). Between 1979 and 1984, unfitness in Belfast was reduced by a further 25 per cent. Interestingly, the difference between progress in urban and rural areas had narrowed: over the same period rural unfitness declined by 20 per cent. Nevertheless, a very substantial investment continued to be made in Belfast and between 1983 and 1986 the Housing Executive spending in the city averaged almost £100m per year (NIHE 1991a). Unfortunately, comparable figures are not available for rural areas but the spending levels are likely to be considerably smaller. Some commentators went so far as to suggest that in funding terms rural issues were not on the agenda (Conway 1990). This is not wholly accurate because throughout the 1970s and 1980s the Executive continued to build new houses in rural areas, almost exclusively in villages and hamlets; it maintained and improved its existing rural stock; and it funded a high volume of renovation grant activity. In addition, a number of important rural initiatives were introduced following the results of the 1984 House Condition Survey which confirmed the now well-established trend of increasing concentration of unfit dwellings in the rural stock (NIHE 1985).

*Rural initiatives*

The profile of rural housing was raised with the launch of the Roslea Study by the Executive's west region and the subsequent publication of its findings (NIHE 1987). The study notes:

> Since the publication of the 1984 House Condition Survey the Executive has been pursuing with renewed vigour the quest for more meaningful housing solutions and opportunities within rural areas. It is not that rural

> areas have been ignored but in the past the scale of urban decay has overshadowed all other areas. . . The case for rural housing initiatives is borne out from the realisation that although the problems experienced by individual urban and rural dwellers are in many ways similar, the solutions open to them are not. (NIHE 1987, p. 4)

In essence, in urban areas the range of policy instruments available are many but in rural areas they are limited to renovation grants or re-housing in a nearby village. Both rural options are highly problematic. The Roslea Study showed a very marked reluctance among rural dwellers to leave their homes and move to nucleated settlements. It also confirmed the difficulties of effectively targeting grant aid to the worst of the stock, and suggested that a major reason for the limited success of the grants scheme in rural areas was household fear of bureaucracy and/or an inability to cope with the administrative requirements of a grants application. This led to the formation of the Rural Action Team (RAT) specifically charged with assisting potential applicants through the grants process.

The idea of on-the-ground help, advice and assistance underpins the success of the HAA and PIPA concepts in Belfast. The RAT concept is simply an extension of this idea to the rural areas of Northern Ireland. In reviewing the effectiveness of the initiative, Conway (1991b) pointed out that the success of the scheme was hampered by a number of significant stumbling blocks. These included the inability of many rural dwellers to afford home improvements, their inability to raise additional finance (i.e. above and beyond any grant amount) from the major lending institutions, and the "persistent reality that the existing grants regime was simply not sufficiently tailored to rural requirements" (Conway 1991b, p. 9).

*Contemporary rural housing*

The publication of the 1987 House Condition Survey completes the time series of unfitness information. As far as rural housing is concerned, the 1987 survey shows that the gap in urban and rural improvement rates widened significantly between 1984 and 1987 primarily reflecting the impact of the Belfast Renewal Strategy. As Table 10.3 shows, the annual rural improvement rate (3.1 per cent) as only one third of that achieved in urban areas (9 per cent) thus leading to an intensification of the rural unfitness problem. Tables 10.4 and 10.5 present a more detailed comparison of the characteristics and condition of the urban and rural stock. These tables do not require detailed comment but, in short, show that the nature of the rural stock is significantly different from that in urban areas. The main points of difference are the high levels of owner-occupation in rural areas,

## Table 10.4
## Characteristics of the rural and urban stock, 1987

| Characteristic | Belfast Urban Area | | Other Urban | | Small Rural Settlements | | Isolated Rural Dwellings | | Total | |
|---|---|---|---|---|---|---|---|---|---|---|
| **Tenure** | No. | % | No. | % | No. | % | No. | % | No. | % |
| Owner occupied | 97760 | 57 | 83200 | 49 | 40090 | 50 | 72210 | 81 | 293260 | 57 |
| Private rented & other | 12620 | 7 | 5750 | 3 | 2770 | 3 | 4960 | 6 | 26100 | 5 |
| NIHE | 52270 | 30 | 72430 | 43 | 32450 | 40 | 4090 | 5 | 161240 | 32 |
| Housing Association | 2960 | 2 | 1560 | 1 | 1270 | 2 | 350 | * | 6140 | 1 |
| Vacant | 6290 | 4 | 6920 | 4 | 3950 | 5 | 7320 | 8 | 24470 | 5 |
| Total | 171900 | 100 | 169860 | 100 | 80530 | 100 | 88930 | 100 | 511220 | 100 |
| **Dwelling Age** | No. | % | No. | % | No. | % | No. | % | No. | % |
| Pre 1919 | 32120 | 19 | 17800 | 10 | 13050 | 16 | 48030 | 54 | 111000 | 22 |
| 1919 - 1944 | 28150 | 16 | 14660 | 9 | 6400 | 8 | 9360 | 11 | 58580 | 11 |
| 1945 - 1964 | 41680 | 24 | 28470 | 17 | 14850 | 18 | 8170 | 9 | 93170 | 18 |
| 1965 - 1980 | 38340 | 22 | 44960 | 26 | 20970 | 26 | 5560 | 6 | 109840 | 21 |
| Post 1980 | 31610 | 18 | 63970 | 38 | 19980 | 25 | 17800 | 20 | 138630 | 27 |
| Total | 171900 | 100 | 169860 | 100 | 80530 | 100 | 88930 | 100 | 511220 | 100 |
| **Net Annual Valuation** | No. | % | No. | % | No. | % | No. | % | No. | % |
| Under 61 | 17370 | 10 | 5150 | 3 | 7060 | 9 | 24850 | 18 | 54420 | 11 |
| 61 - 130 | 79700 | 46 | 68440 | 40 | 42580 | 53 | 31770 | 31 | 222490 | 44 |
| 131 - 225 | 56810 | 33 | 72330 | 43 | 19700 | 25 | 21520 | 31 | 170360 | 33 |
| Over 225 | 18020 | 11 | 23900 | 14 | 11190 | 14 | 10750 | 19 | 63850 | 13 |
| Total | 171900 | 100 | 169860 | 100 | 80530 | 100 | 88930 | 100 | 511220 | 100 |

Sources - 1987 House Condition Survey, NIHE (1988). Figures rounded to nearest 10 dwellings. Percentages may not add to 100 due to rounding errors. *indicates < 0.5%

**Table 10.5**
**Condition of the rural and urban stock, 1987**

| Characteristic | Belfast Urban Area | | Other Urban | | Small Rural Settlements | | Isolated Rural Dwellings | | Total | |
|---|---|---|---|---|---|---|---|---|---|---|
| **Unfitness** | No. | % | No. | % | No. | % | No. | % | No. | % |
| Fit | 162310 | 94.4 | 164550 | 96.9 | 75170 | 93.3 | 66290 | 74.5 | 468320 | 91.6 |
| Unfit | 9590 | 5.6 | 5310 | 3.1 | 5360 | 6.7 | 22640 | 25.5 | 42900 | 8.4 |
| Total | 171900 | 100.0 | 169860 | 100.0 | 80530 | 100.0 | 88930 | 100.0 | 511220 | 100.0 |
| **Amenity Provision** | No. | % | No. | % | No. | % | No. | % | No. | % |
| Lacks 1 - 4 amenities | 7350 | 4.3 | 3180 | 1.9 | 2930 | 3.6 | 7590 | 8.5 | 21040 | 4.1 |
| Lacks all 5 amenities | 310 | * | 580 | * | 540 | 0.7 | 5860 | 6.6 | 7290 | 1.4 |
| Has all 5 amenities | 164240 | 95.6 | 166100 | 97.8 | 77060 | 95,7 | 75480 | 84.9 | 482890 | 94.5 |
| Total | 171900 | 100.0 | 169860 | 100.0 | 80530 | 100.0 | 88930 | 100.0 | 511220 | 100.0 |
| **Disrepair (£)** | No. | % | No. | % | No. | % | No. | % | No. | % |
| Nil | 49550 | 28.8 | 74960 | 44.1 | 28520 | 35.4 | 27190 | 30.6 | 180190 | 35.2 |
| 1 - 3000 | 83760 | 48.7 | 69890 | 41.1 | 38730 | 48.1 | 23720 | 26.7 | 216100 | 42.3 |
| 3001 - 8000 | 25740 | 15.0 | 17520 | 10.3 | 7100 | 8.8 | 12040 | 13.5 | 62400 | 12.2 |
| 8001 - 15000 | 9810 | 5.7 | 4890 | 2.9 | 3580 | 4.4 | 12420 | 14.0 | 30700 | 6.0 |
| 15001 - 20000 | 1630 | 0.9 | 1420 | 0.8 | 1220 | 1.5 | 6460 | 7.3 | 10730 | 2.1 |
| Over 20000 | 1400 | 0.8 | 1180 | 0.7 | 1380 | 1.7 | 7130 | 8.0 | 11090 | 2.2 |
| Total | 171900 | 100 | 169860 | 100.0 | 80530 | 100.0 | 88930 | 100.0 | 511220 | 100.0 |

Sources - 1987 House Condition Survey, NIHE (1988). Figures rounded to nearest 10 dwellings. Percentages may not add to 100 due to rounding errors. *indicates < 0.5%

reaching 81 per cent in isolated rural locations; the more aged stock profile which is particularly pronounced in isolated areas where 54 per cent of the stock was built before 1919; and the over-representation of dwellings with low rateable valuations in rural areas. The planning policies of the 1970s which targeted development to Growth and Key Centres and District Towns can be seen to have strongly influenced the profile of these areas. Two thirds of these dwellings were built after 1960 and 43 per cent are Housing Executive dwellings (Table 10.4). Rural dwellings are in much worse condition than their urban counterparts. In terms of unfitness, relatively uniform rates are recorded in all forms of nucleated settlements, including small rural settlements (6.7 per cent). In contrast, however, more than 25 per cent of isolated rural dwellings, representing some 22,500 dwellings, were recorded as unfit for human habitation in 1987. A similar profile emerges in respect of dwelling amenities and disrepair (Table 10.5).

Throughout this section comparisons between the urban and rural stock have been presented on a range of dwelling indicators. In addition, a comparison of changes in unfitness over time has illustrated that improvements in rural areas have not kept pace with those in the towns and cities of Northern Ireland. However, this time series analysis suffers from an important weakness: it relies on a comparison of several snap-shot surveys at different points in time. Although the methodologies of the various surveys, and their standards, are compatible, such an analysis reveals very little about the individual components of change.

As all of the properties included in the 1987 survey had previously been inspected in 1984, it is possible to examine the dynamics of change within a fixed pool of dwellings. This longitudinal analysis provides much greater depth of understanding than can be achieved from a simple comparison of two cross-sectional surveys. For example, it was noted above that between 1984 and 1987 the number of rural unfits was reduced by 9 per cent, in contrast to 27 per cent in urban areas. These figures might suggest a low level of activity in the rural areas. In fact, as Table 10.6 demonstrates, a considerable amount of change occurred over the three years. Of the original 30,960 rural unfits in 1984, 24 per cent were improved into fitness, 12 per cent were closed or demolished under the 1981 Housing (Northern Ireland) Order, and 64 per cent remained unfit. In addition, a further 8,220 dwellings became unfit over the period, representing 27 per cent of the opening balance. If demolition and closure are set aside, the rural stock is deteriorating more quickly (marginally) than it is being improved. The dynamics in urban areas are very different. Here, of the original 20,370 unfits in 1984, 32 per cent were improved, 24 per cent were closed or demolished, and just 44 per cent remained unfit. Although in relative terms proportionately more urban dwellings deteriorated into unfitness (29 per cent) the net effect of the components of change clearly favours a reduction in unfitness. The importance

## Table 10.6
## Dynamics of urban and rural unfitness, 1984 - 1987

| Change Category 1984 - 1987 | Urban | | Rural | | Total | |
|---|---|---|---|---|---|---|
| **OPENING UNFITNESS BALANCE 1984** | 20370 | | 30960 | | 51330 | |
| **"Losses" to the unfit stock 1984 - 1987** | No. | % | No. | % | No. | % |
| Single unfit - sound | 1470 | | 4850 | 16 | 6320 | 12 |
| Single unfit - repair | 260 | 1 | 1660 | 5 | 1920 | 4 |
| Single unfit - improvement | 240 | 1 | 370 | 1 | 610 | 1 |
| Area unfit - sound | 2740 | 13 | 670 | 2 | 3410 | 7 |
| Area unfit - repair | 970 | 5 | 40 | * | 1010 | 2 |
| Area unfit - improvement | 860 | 4 | 0 | 0 | 860 | 2 |
| Single unfit - void | 1006 | 5 | 3130 | 10 | 4140 | 8 |
| Area unfit - void | 3830 | 19 | 440 | 1 | 4260 | 8 |
| **Dwellings remaining unfit 1984 - 1987** | No. | % | No. | % | No. | % |
| Single unfit - single unfit | 1380 | 7 | 17450 | 56 | 18830 | 37 |
| Single unfit - area unfit | 540 | 3 | 1030 | 3 | 1580 | 3 |
| Area unfit - area unfit | 6210 | 30 | 470 | 2 | 6680 | 13 |
| Area unfit - single unfit | 870 | 4 | 830 | 3 | 1700 | 3 |
| **Additions to the unfit stock 1984 - 1987** | No. | % | No. | % | No. | % |
| Sound - single unfit | 700 | 3 | 2720 | 9 | 3410 | 7 |
| Repair - single unfit | 2070 | 10 | 4480 | 14 | 6550 | 13 |
| Improvement - single unfit | 600 | 3 | 720 | 2 | 1320 | 3 |
| Sound - area unfit | 1450 | 7 | 0 | 0 | 1450 | 3 |
| Repair - area unfit | 860 | 4 | 150 | * | 1010 | 2 |
| Improvement - area unfit | 210 | 1 | 150 | * | 360 | 1 |
| **CLOSING UNFITNESS BALANCE 1987** | 14900 | | 28000 | | 42900 | |

Sources - 1987 House Condition Survey, NIHE (1988). Figures rounded to nearest 10 dwellings. Percentages may not add up to 100 due to rounding errors. *indicates < 0.5%

of area based action is underlined in the high level of demolition and closure activity in urban areas over the period.

*The need for a review*

Although the Executive billed its exercise as a review of rural housing policy, in reality there was no rural housing policy as such. Rather, there was a broad set of housing policies, the objectives of which were set out each year in the government's expenditure plans. These objectives have remained fairly stable over the years emphasizing a desire to promote owner occupation, to reduce the number of households in "urgent housing need" and to reduce dwelling unfitness. As has been shown, there are high levels of owner occupation in rural areas, and so a desire to extend home ownership further is of limited relevance. Similarly, there is a question about the extent to which need expressed in terms of waiting lists is of value in a rural context. The basic argument that has been advanced is that as dwellings are not available in the preferred rural locations, households in need simply do not register. This has been referred to as latent demand and was one of the features of presumed importance in the Executive's rural policy review outlined below.

Although it is suggested that there was no such thing as a rural policy to review, following the Roslea Study (NIHE 1987) there was a genuine concern that the range of general policy instruments available were inappropriate in the rural environment. These instruments have primarily been area based and statutory in nature and often backed by compulsory purchase powers. They have been particularly effective, especially in Belfast. In rural areas the primary policy instrument has been the renovation grant scheme, with particular emphasis on the improvement grant as a means of reducing unfitness. For some time, however, it had been realized that the improvement grant was not particularly well-focused on unfit houses. An analysis of renovation grants completed between 1979 and 1984 revealed that less than 40 per cent of improvement grants, and just 16 per cent of repair grants, went to unfit houses (NIHE 1983). The Northern Ireland Economic Development Office commented that

> the grants system is not closely targeted on the Housing Executive's objective of reducing the level of housing unfitness. (NIEDO 1985, p. 23)

Similar results are reported in the 1987 House Condition Survey (NIHE 1988). Over the period 1984 to 1987, just 42 per cent of properties improved out of unfitness had received improvement grant aid, although grant penetration was actually slightly higher in rural areas (44 per cent). A further problem with the grants scheme, aside from poor targeting, was the high incidence of drop-out, hence the Executive's earlier RAT initiative.

In order to stimulate grant activity in rural areas, the Executive launched a further initiative in September 1989 in which it identified 67 Rural Priority Areas (RPAs). Arising from the results of the 1987 House Condition Survey (NIHE 1988) this was an attempt to bring an area based approach to rural locations. By March 1992, £7.3m in renovation grants had been approved in these areas. However, monitoring information on RPA dwellings shows a very high level of dwelling obsolescence with, for example, 47 per cent without an internal WC and 48 per cent without a wash hand basin. In addition, 27 per cent had no piped water supply, 30 per cent had no electricity and 46 per cent had no sewerage system (NIHE 1992). The high incidence of service deficiency led the Executive to boost grant levels to allow for first-time service provision in rural dwellings. Under the Higher Eligible Expense Limits, some 200 grants were approved up to March 1992. However, under the revised renovation grants scheme introduced in the Housing (Northern Ireland) Order 1992, grant-aid is confined to the curtilage of the dwelling, although the Executive is currently discussing options to allow aid up to an additional £7,000 for such works subject to value-for-money criteria.

In summary, the evidence suggests that the main tools of housing policy have been most effective when applied to urban concentrations of problems. Given the scale, complexity and longevity of the rural housing problem, the Housing Executive embarked on a major review of its policy in respect of rural housing. The purpose of the review was to formulate a revised approach to rural housing problems through which progress could be made in meeting housing need throughout rural areas. The next section considers the structure and method of that policy review and details the programme of consultation and research on which it was based.

## The rural housing policy review

### *The structure of the review process*

It is often reported that large, centralized bureaucracies tend to be remote from their clients and run the risk of developing policies, procedures and services that are not wholly appropriate to those who receive and depend upon them (Singleton 1989). Conscious of this criticism, in conducting its review of rural housing policy in Northern Ireland, the Housing Executive strove to tailor the review process specifically to the needs of those people who live and work in the countryside. In particular, the review was based on the principles of consultation and research (Fig. 10.1). The main events in the review process are outlined in Table 10.7.

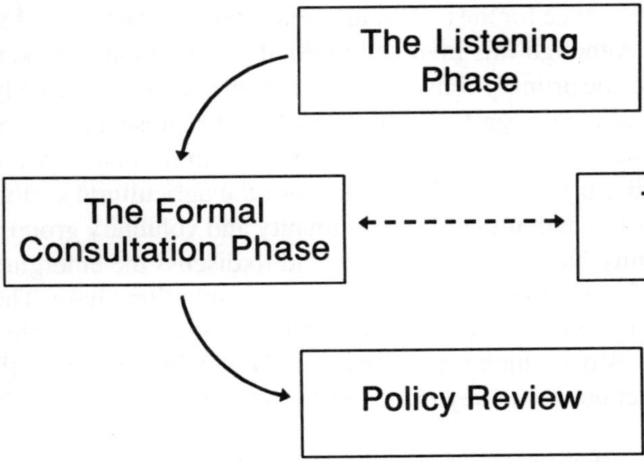

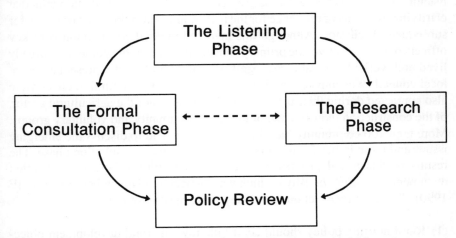


**Figure 10.1 The Northern Ireland Housing Executive rural housing policy review process**

**Table 10.7**
**Rural policy review - timetable of main events**

| Date | Event |
|---|---|
| May 1990 | Launch of review process. Secondment of senior manager to lead the review. |
| July 1990 | Structure of research programme agreed. Research commisioned. |
| October 1990 | Presentation and discussion of issues emerging from the listening phase together with preliminary research results at Rural Housing Policy Symposium. |
| November 1990 | Publication of consultation document *Leading the way.* |
| June 1991 | Publication of proposals document *The Way Ahead.* |

*Consultation*

The Executive launched its review in May 1990 with what it referred to as the listening stage. This was essentially a period of informal consultation aimed at clarifying the terms of reference for the review and compiling a list of issues for subsequent discussion. Although this involved internal consultation with key officers of the Executive, the primary consultation was with people who already lived and worked in rural areas together with their elected representatives, at local council, Westminster and European levels. Specific rural interests were also contacted during this stage, e.g. representatives of the agricultural sector, of the construction industry, and of the local community and voluntary groups. More than 100 community-based meetings were held to discuss the emerging issues and these issues formed the basis of the formal consultation phase. The results of this initial process were consolidated into a formal consultation document - *Leading the Way* - which was launched in November 1990 (NIHE 1990). The document set out seven key principles as follows:

(1) Rural housing policy should contribute towards rural development objectives;

(2) Partnership with others in developing and implementing a rural housing policy is critical for success;

(3) A new rural approach is necessary, not a revised urban approach;

(4) Tailoring to local circumstances is a critical success factor;

(5) Working with rural communities is essential for effective rural development;

(6) Affordability lies at the core of potential housing solutions;

(7) Investment and resources should be directed to where they are needed and to those who need them most.

The consultative document presented a range of issues and proposals for consideration under the following headings:

(1) Improving housing conditions;

(2) Assessing housing need;

(3) The sources of supply - increasing housing choice;

(4) The affordability dimension;

(5) Care in the community;

(6) Community participation.

Over 2,000 copies of the document were distributed and a three month period was set aside for the consultation process. The Executive was particularly keen to obtain the opinions of rural community groups. To facilitate this, the Rural Action Project and Community Technical Aid were asked to help by organizing a series of housing clinics. In total, Housing Executive representatives were invited to 112 meetings in order to discuss the proposals included in the consultation document and more than 10,000 people attended these various meetings. In addition, 65 written submissions were received, the sources of which are summarised in Table 10.8. Most written submissions were supportive of the Executive's efforts and the guiding principles outlined in the consultation document.

**Table 10.8**
**Written submissions following formal consultation**

| Source of Written Submission | Number |
|---|---|
| District councils | 18 |
| Statutory bodies | 12 |
| Trade bodies/associations | 11 |
| Housing associations | 8 |
| MPs/MEPs | 6 |
| Community/pressure groups | 4 |
| Private individuals | 3 |
| Other | 2 |
| Total | 65 |

*Issues emerging from the consultation*

*1. Should housing play the lead role?* This is an important issue. The Executive acknowledges that housing is but one component of rural development, but it sees itself as having a leading role. A number of responses questioned the validity of this assumption, stressing the importance of jobs and employment issues. Nevertheless, housing was seen as a key factor in stemming further rural depopulation as well as improving the conditions of those already living and working in rural areas. The ability of the Executive to facilitate greater co-operation between the various agencies, both public and private, with a contribution to make would seem to be important.

*2. Grants.* The Executive's grant policy was widely regarded as having a crucial role to play in rural housing improvement but it was criticised on a number of grounds: the inability of rural dwellers to raise the necessary top-up funds in order to be able to complete grant-aided work diminished the usefulness of the scheme; the two year occupancy rule before repair grant applications can be made reduced opportunities for re-use of vacant stock; and, the excessive demolition rule that can make certain properties ineligible for grant-aid. In addition, the Executive was criticised for being too slow in paying out grants. The consultation also raised the important issue of self-help, particularly in respect of grant-aided improvement work and self-build. The general view was that the Executive's requirement that a warranted builder be used on grant schemes was a reflection of an urban approach that was not merited in rural communities. In addition, such builders added an unnecessary additional cost that could not be afforded by the majority of rural households living in poor housing conditions.

*3. Planning.* This emerged as the most common cause of complaint. Responses from district councils, voluntary bodies, elected representatives and private individuals all criticised the Department of Environment's rural planning policy. Many voiced concern that it was very difficult to obtain planning permissions for new construction in the countryside and that the Department's Location, Siting and Design policy criteria (DOE 1987) were particularly restrictive. Recent figures, showing that during 1992 some 70 per cent of the 3,400 planning applications in rural areas received approval, challenges the validity of this view (Belfast Telegraph 1993). Almost without exception, district council responses were highly critical of the Planning Service and its perceived lack of sympathy for the needs of rural communities. This is particularly interesting in light of recently published research on local government in Northern Ireland which indicates that it is the planning function that local councillors most want to see returned to local government control (Johns 1993). It seems, therefore, that the planning issue is a significant area of conflict between the rural community, its elected representatives, and the government, in the form of the Planning Service. The Planning Service is caught "between a rock and a hard place": on the one hand, there is strong and mounting community-based criticism that planning is highly restrictive; on the other, peer review suggests that, in the context of the United Kingdom, rural planning in Northern Ireland is a worst case example (see Milton in this volume). The Rural Planning Policy has been under review since 1989 and publication of the review findings is overdue. Whatever the outcome, it seems likely that there is scope for conflict between the Planning Service and the Housing Executive, most notably in respect of the "crossroads" initiative discussed below.

*Assessing the results of the consultation exercise*

It is clear from a detailed analysis of the responses that, in spite of the extremely detailed nature of the consultative process, very few new ideas or perspectives were generated. Although this is somewhat disappointing, it could be argued that the lack of new ideas suggests that the listening phase had been particularly successful in identifying the relevant issues. Furthermore, there is more to consultation than generating new ideas: consultation is important in developing a sense of involvement and ownership; a wide consensus may be expected to smooth the path of new policy implementation; and consultation helps to develop a wider understanding of what is and is not possible in policy terms. For example, one of the proposals concerns the siting of possible future new dwellings at "crossroads" locations. From the consultation responses it is apparent that many rural communities do not wholly support this idea: they would prefer dispersed new-build. The Planning Service, on the other hand, is strongly opposed to dispersed new-build and local communities are aware of this position. Thus, the consultation process enabled the Executive to present the "crossroads" idea as a compromise which local communities could accept as a second choice option. There is little doubt that awareness of rural housing issues has been raised amongst the general public over the period of the review. A simple comparison of the 1990 Public Attitudes Survey (McPeake 1990a) with the 1992 survey (Montieth forthcoming) shows a significant reduction in popularity of the view that the Housing Executive is dominated by urban housing problems and a corresponding increase in the opinion that the organization has a well-balanced approach. It is, of course, not possible to prove a causal link between the conduct of the review and this change in public opinions, but it does seem possible that the two are related.

*Research*

As indicated above, the initial impetus for the review came from the recognition that progress in improving rural housing conditions had not kept pace with achievements in the urban areas of Northern Ireland. However, whilst extensive information was available on the nature of rural housing conditions, the information on wider social and economic issues in rural communities was less well developed. Virtually nothing was known about the attitudes and preferences of rural dwellers. Furthermore, no information was available on the links between housing and other services such as health, education, leisure and transport. Consequently, the Executive developed and funded an intensive programme of research aimed at clarifying what was already known or suspected, and extending the knowledge base to cover those areas where identifiable gaps existed. The research programme involved both the secondary analysis of existing datasets and published materials, together with new empirical research.

*Issues emerging from the research*

*1. Poor housing conditions and the inadequacy of the renovation grants scheme.* The correlation between poor housing conditions and owner occupation had already been established. In addition, in these cases, it had been demonstrated that the main instrument of housing improvement was the Renovation Grants system. Indeed, about half of existing households had applied for grant aid (49 per cent) and of these applications, two thirds (67 per cent) were granted and the improvement work carried out. However, applicants complained that the grant aid did not cover all the problems that required attention (33 per cent) and 16 per cent felt that they should have been able to replace the dwelling because of the complex condition deficiencies associated with non-traditional rural dwelling designs. A further 16 per cent found the grant process bureaucratic and difficult to understand.

The rural household survey focused on the particular problems of occupants of dwellings with a low rateable value (under £60 per annum), which was used as a proxy indicator for dwellings in poor condition. When this analysis considered the profile of non-grant aided households, inherent weaknesses in the grant system as a method of improving rural conditions were revealed. Nearly two thirds (63 per cent) of non-grant aided households living in poor conditions were classified as elderly. In addition, only 45 per cent of the economically active population were in full time work compared to 63 per cent of all households and 64 per cent of grant aided households. Finally, nearly half of these households received an annual income of less than £5,000 compared to 31 per cent for all rural dwellers. Therefore, even with generous grant assistance many households living in the poorest conditions could not even afford the portion to be financed by applicants. Thus, the analysis revealed three basic problems in the grant system. First, the economic and demographic circumstances of those living in the poorest conditions inhibited effective use of a grant based renovation policy. Second, there were administrative problems that made it difficult for applicants, particularly the elderly to work their way through the grant process. Finally, many of the dwellings have severe problems, leaving them beyond the scope of the current grants system.

2. *Rural housing supply.* When the problems of rural housing conditions are considered along with difficulties in supply, the serious structural weaknesses in the rural housing market are revealed. The dominance of owner occupation is at the root of these weaknesses. Only one quarter (25 per cent) of owners purchased their dwelling from a previous owner. A further 29 per cent had inherited their dwelling and a large portion (20 per cent) had built their own dwelling, most since the relaxation of planning policy following the Cockcroft Report (1978). Housing Executive house sales (12 per cent) and purchase from speculative developers (10 per cent) were the other main routes to home ownership. Significantly, sites were more likely to have been a parental gift (27 per cent) or to have always been in the family (24 per cent) rather than to have been purchased through the open land and property market. A major untapped supply source is the vacant stock in rural areas, estimated at around 11,000 dwellings (McPeake 1990b). For the first time information became available on the intentions of the owners of dwellings: about half of owners intended no action, one third would consider letting unimproved dwellings and 1 in 8 would consider improvement for letting if grant-aid was available. Much more needs to be done to encourage the re-use of these properties. Clearly the private sector housing market in rural areas is restricted. Relatively few dwellings were exchanged on the open market. A large volume of the current stock had exchanged hands through inheritance and sites for new development were traditionally donated or sold by relatives. Problems with the restricted supply should also be seen in the context of rural housing need.

3. *Housing need and attachment to rural living*. The rural household survey emphasised a strong attachment to place. Three quarters of rural households had connections with their locality spanning one generation and more than one-third had links beyond three generations. Most people would not consider moving away (84 per cent) and the overriding choice was more housing opportunities in the area. The research showed that 40 per cent of respondents felt that there was a need for specialist housing provision for the elderly and 48 per cent felt that more family housing was needed. This was also felt by the 40 per cent who

thought that the Housing Executive should intervene directly to resolve housing shortages in their areas. Low cost dwellings were another option favoured to provide low income groups access to the housing market (46 per cent). These attitudes led the Housing Executive to rethink the relationship between housing need and latent demand. In recognising that rural dwellers have a strong attachment to place and want to stay in their locality, the policy review agreed that the traditional method of assessing urgent housing need failed to reflect the reality of housing preference in rural areas.

> There is evidence that the need is not necessarily registered for those requiring accommodation beyond the larger settlements due mainly to a judgement that additional public sector accommodation will not be provided there. This is the basis for latent housing demand (Conway 1991c, p. 33).

In short, the research revealed a distorted rural housing market with restricted and often poor quality supply coupled with local housing demand. In response, the Housing Executive's strategy attempted to address the structural weaknesses in a way that responded to local housing concerns. The key elements of that policy are set out in the next section.

## The policy response : *Rural Housing Policy - The Way Ahead*

The policy proposals are contained in *The Way Ahead*, published by the Executive in June 1991. Proposals and recommendations are made under 4 main headings: improving housing conditions, assessing housing need, improving housing supply and care in the community (Table 10.9). These broad categories fall within the main thrust of the Executive's Annual Housing Strategy Review process and reflect the traditional issues of housing need on the one hand and supply on the other. They are overlain by a concern for providing housing options that are both attractive and affordable. In addition, there is a general desire to develop proposals in a bottom-up rather than a top-down fashion. Part of this desire finds expression in a willingness to work with other agencies on an integrated approach to rural problem solving.

The key proposal in improving housing conditions is the introduction of a new Replacement Grant which is to be made available when, on technical and cost grounds, replacement of the dwelling is a more effective solution than improvement. An extra-statutory scheme was introduced just as the review process was drawing to a close, but this has been replaced by a new scheme following the introduction of the revised Renovation Grants Scheme under the 1992 Housing

## Table 10.9
## Summary of main proposals

| Proposal category | Proposals |
|---|---|
| IMPROVING HOUSING CONDITIONS | 1. Introduction of a Replacement Grant for properties where, on technical and cost grounds, replacement is more effective than improvement.<br>2. Removal of 2 year rule that had access to Higher Eligible Expense Limits for service provision.<br>3. Relaxation of requirement to use warranted builders in case of self-improvers.<br>4. Introduction of Staying Put initiative in association with Fold Housing Trust.<br>5. Application of Group Repair approach in villages and small settlements.<br>6. Greater priority within the IPBS programme to poor condition, isolated properties already in the ownership of the Executive.<br>7. Review of the boundaries of the current (67) Rural Priority Areas. |
| ASSESSING HOUSING NEED | 1. Latent demand will, as far as possible, be quantified and pilot schemes will be identified to test its importance.<br>2. Include the need for low-cost private accommodation in the Annual Strategy Review.<br>3. Introduce an urban/rural segregation in housing programmes beginning in the programme year 1992/1993.<br>4. Introduce integrated waiting lists for Housing Executive and Housing Association properties.<br>5. Investigate the feasibility of small-scale sheltered housing provision suited to village and hamlet settings.<br>6. Seek to retain a balanced rural public sector stock.<br>7. Revision of Housing Application Form to allow identification of areas that applicants would like to live (irrespective of whether housing available at that location or not) and to record interest in low-cost private schemes. |
| SOURCES OF SUPPLY | 1. Introduction of a "Crossroads Initiative" where the Executive will primarily act in a facilitating and enabling capacity.<br>2. Attempt to make better use of existing vacant dwellings, with an emphasis on Housing Association activity.<br>3. The possible use of comprehensive development powers in particularly poor areas.<br>4. Review the potential for better use of land in the Executive's ownership.<br>5. There is no proven case for limiting future house sales to sitting tenants but there is a need to monitor sales activity carefully in certain localities to ensure that a public rented option remains available. |
| AFFORDABILITY | No specific proposals were made. However, a number of the earlier proposals (e.g. 2-year rule and replacement grant) should help to reduce the costs of access to good quality housing in rural areas. |
| CARE IN THE COMMUNITY | Here the proposals are essentially a re-statement of current practice, namely:<br>1. Joint-planning between the Executive and the Area Health Boards.<br>2. Continued Housing Executive provision of wheel-chair and mobility dwellings in new-build schemes on a needs basis. The role of the Executive is seen as important in rural locations because of low Housing Association presence.<br>3. Sensitive application of the Housing Selection Scheme rules.<br>4. Adaption of existing stock to meet special need criteria. Consideration of measures to improve transfer scheme in respect of special need tenants.<br>5. Continued provision of grants for adaption work in the private sector stock. |
| COMMUNITY PARTICIPATION | 1. A general statement of intent to work with others to encourage a more integrated approach to rural problems.<br>2. In conjunction with the Northern Ireland federation of Housing Associations, produce an advisory pack on housing co-operatives. |

(Northern Ireland) Order. The new grant is subject to means testing but in some circumstances could cover 100 per cent of the cost of the required work. The two year occupation requirement that was previously conditional on grant awards has been removed as it is acknowledged that it was a disincentive to bringing vacant rural stock into the housing market. Self build is also encouraged by the relaxation of the need for an approved builder to carry out the work. The review has also proposed the use of forthcoming Group Repairs Scheme powers to improve blocks or terraces of substandard dwellings in hamlets or small villages. At the same time, the Executive has also introduced proposals to improve its dispersed stock in rural areas (some 4,000 dwellings) using planned maintenance and improvement programmes. As noted above, in 1990 the Executive had designated 67 Rural Priority Areas comprising some 6,500 dwellings. The purpose of the designation is to increase the level of awareness by occupiers of grant availability through visits by Executive staff. The policy statement proposes to extend these boundaries based on more up to date and detailed data from the 1991 House Condition Survey (NIHE forthcoming).

A key priority in the policy statement is the effective analysis and assessment of rural housing need. In particular, the Executive proposes to assess latent demand with small scale locally based market research. This will include liaison with existing community groups and the local public and will be complemented by advertisements in the local press that aim to elicit interest in proposed developments. However, in order to place this initiative within an effective analysis of need, the Executive proposes to formally include these assessments in both the housing strategy review and the annual District Housing Plans. In addition, the housing application form is to be altered to include a question on where applicants would like to live together with first and second preferences. Finally, small scale sheltered schemes are proposed initially on a pilot basis to accommodate the specific needs of the elderly population in rural areas.

In terms of actually increasing housing supply and choice, the Executive has introduced a range of specific development proposals. The "crossroads" initiative aims to develop small scale housing schemes in "small settlements beyond existing villages which have, over time, evolved around a church, hall, school or shop or some combination of these facilities and which are considered by residents to be a primary focal point for their communities" (NIHE 1991b, p.36). In these schemes, the Housing Executive will act as land assembler, with acquisition taking into account the need for mainstream renting, Housing Association special needs accommodation and shared ownership through the Northern Ireland Co-ownership housing scheme. Typically, the Housing Executive envisages about six dwellings in any one proposal comprising two built by the Executive, two by a Housing Association and two by a self builder or developer. In addition, the Executive proposes to make more effective use of the vacant housing resource in rural areas. It may develop a programme of acquisition for sale or lease and possibly use selected Housing Associations to undertake such initiatives on a limited scale. A further source of supply is the sale or development of Housing Executive land banks in rural areas. This will help ease the problem of site acquisition for development although the Executive's preference for these sites is for low cost or shared ownership schemes.

All these development concepts seek to ensure that housing opportunities are affordable by local people. Specifically, the Executive has suggested that the means-tested replacement grant option, the "crossroads" initiative, the encouragement of low cost shared ownership in development schemes and the Rural Priority Areas programme should ensure that housing resources are targeted at the most vulnerable groups in the rural housing market. The Executive has also specifically recognised the role of rural housing policy within the Care in the Community initiative of the Department of Health and Social Services. In encouraging care in the home or in a homely setting, the Executive recognises that the main client groups in rural areas are elderly persons, the disabled, people suffering from mental illness and those with severe learning difficulties. Joint planning agreements exist with each of the four Health and Social Services Boards in regard to special housing needs including those in rural areas. Within this context Housing Associations complement the Executive's role in the provision of special needs housing, warden support and specially adapted dwellings for those with a specific illness or disability.

The final theme of the policy statement is community participation. The policy commits the Housing Executive to structured and regular consultations with tenant and community groups in the identification of local housing needs and in the development of specific housing proposals to meet those needs. The proposals also recognise the role of the Housing Executive within the broader framework of rural regeneration strategies, developed at both government and European Community levels.

In order to resource the strategy the Executive has initially devoted £50m per annum to rural housing. The main elements of this expenditure are the construction of 200 new dwellings per annum, repair and improvement of 34,000 public sector dwellings and 1,750 renovation grants per annum. During the three years following the launch of the programme the level of expenditure may rise incrementally to £65m per annum.

## Conclusion

This chapter has provided an insight into rural housing policy and practice in Northern Ireland. A number of matters need to be raised by way of conclusion.

The first relates to the style of the policy making process which, it is argued, provided an effective mechanism for public participation in rural areas. In his analysis of planning and power, Forester (1989) draws a distinction between hearing and listening in approaches to public consultation:

> When planners face heated arguments, for example, but hear only words, they may easily dismiss the ambiguities of interests as expressions of anger, muddle-headedness or inner confusion. The impulse to avoid ambiguity can have substantial psychological costs. Yet when planners listen in such situations, they will be more likely to expect and respect ambiguities of meaning, probe and explore them and actually build on them to reach practical agreements. Hearing passively records, listening helps us to learn (Forester 1989, p. 110).

The basis for rural housing policy formulation was a twofold research and consultation strategy. The involvement of community groups, locally elected representatives and statutory bodies was important and helped to shape final policy outcomes. Nevertheless, there are limits on the extent to which organisations such as the Housing Executive can implement policy objectives. Overall responsibility for devising housing policy is located within the housing and planning divisions of the Department of the Environment (NI). Thus, while the Housing Executive has "considerable autonomy" (Connolly 1990, p.120) in the development and delivery of housing policy, it must work within the framework of a central government department which has its own policy and programme priorities. The Housing Executive can formulate policies based on an analysis of rural needs but its ability to deliver on these policies is circumscribed by this wider administrative structure. It remains to be seen, for example, whether the Executive can successfully pursue a significant programme of dispersed housing schemes at "crossroads" sites given the traditional thrust of rural settlement policy. Progress on the implementation of the rural housing initiative as a whole will need to be closely monitored and evaluated.

A related issue is that of resource allocation. The Housing Executive's research paper on rural deprivation (NIHE 1991b) highlighted the severity of rural conditions relative to socio-economic problems in urban areas. The analysis of selected indicators from the House Condition Survey further emphasised this disparity. In the Health Service, much of the debate regarding regional health needs is based on the conclusions of various methodologies, such as the Jarman index (Jarman 1983) and the Townsend index (Townsend et al 1988) that map a range of indicators of social deprivation. In response to the policy review, the Housing Executive has addressed rural priorities within the strategic framework of the three year rolling Housing Strategy and at an operational level, through the annual District Housing Plans. However, given the increasing restrictions on housing expenditure in Northern Ireland, the utility of more rigorous methodologies for targeting scarce resources should be investigated. For the first time the Northern Ireland House Condition Survey (NIHE 1993) and the Northern Ireland Census of Population (HMSO 1992) were carried out in the same year (i.e. 1991). This affords a unique opportunity to use comprehensive and detailed area-based data to devise new deprivation-based methodologies for targeting expenditure. In this way the housing problems of rural Northern Ireland would receive in-depth scrutiny thus providing for a more equitable response over future years.

## Notes

1. Throughout this chapter, the term "rural" generally adheres to the Housing Executive definition as outlined in Conway (1991a). In essence, this involves the division of Northern Ireland into 5 zones, the first 3 of which (BUA, District Towns, other Towns) are referred to as urban, while the remainder (small settlements and isolated dwellings) are referred to as rural. In the historical sections of the chapter, however, it has not always been possible to remain consistent to this definition - mainly because the historical uses of the term "rural" are mostly undefined.
2. The term "unfit" in the context of the Planning Advisory Board Report should not be confused with the statutory concept of unfit dwellings. This latter category is defined in legislation and forms the basis of the Housing Executive's house condition survey programme. The Planning Advisory Board's application of the term is less clearly defined and is related to properties which are so defective as to require replacement.
3. All four House Conditions Surveys between 1974 and 1987 are compatible in terms of the Fitness Standard. The 1991 Survey breaks this trend because it presents information on the revised Fitness Standard introduced in the Housing (Northern Ireland) Order 1992. Although still called the Fitness Standard, the revised standard is fundamentally different from the standard that it replaces. Published results from the 1991 survey will not be directly comparable with previous surveys.

## References

Action with Communities in Rural England (1988) *Who can Afford to live in the Countryside?* ACRE, Cirencester.

Bardon, J. (1992) *A History of Ulster.* The Blackstaff Press, Belfast.
*Belfast Telegraph* (1993) Planners come under spotlight. January 29th, 1993, p. 15.
Best, R. (1990) Idyll or exile. *Search*, August 1990, pp. 7-13
Birrell, D., Gray, P. and Mackay, C. (1991) *Rural housing literature review: II summary of key literature.* NIHE, Belfast.
Birrell, D. and Murie, A. (1980) *Policy and government in Northern Ireland: lessons of devolution.* Gill and Macmillan, Dublin.
Birrell, D., Murie, A. and Roche, J. (1971) *Housing in Northern Ireland.* Centre for Environmental Studies, Working Paper No. 12, London.
Blunden, J. and Curry, N. (eds) (1988) *A future for our countryside.* Basil Blackwell, Oxford.
Brett, C. E. B. (1986) *Housing a divided community.* Institute of Public Administration, Dublin and The Institute of Irish Studies, The Queen's University of Belfast.
Clark, M. (1989) A countryside for all. *Town and Country Planning*, Vol.58, pp. 241-243.
Cockcroft Report (1978) *Review of rural planning policy.* HMSO, Belfast.
Community Technical Aid (NI) (1991) *Rural housing policy review - leading the way: a community response.* Report prepared for Rural Action Project, February 1991, Belfast.
Connolly, M. (1990) *Politics and policy making in Northern Ireland.* Philip Allen, London.
Conway, M. (1990) *Rural communities do not have a voice.* Theme Group discussion, International Symposium on Rural Policy, October 1990, Enniskillen.
Conway, M. (1991a) *Definitions of rurality.* Rural Housing Policy Review Research Paper No. 1, NIHE, Belfast.
Conway, M. (1991b) *An evaluation of rural action to date.* Rural Housing Policy Review Research Paper No. 3, NIHE, Belfast.
Conway, M. (1991c) *Rural housing demand.* Rural Housing Policy Review Research Paper No. 4, NIHE, Belfast.
Department of the Environment (Northern Ireland) (1975) *Regional physical development strategy 1975-1995.* HMSO, Belfast.
Department of Environment (Northern Ireland) (1987) *Location, siting and design in rural areas: statement on the standards to be applied to new development in the countryside.* Town and Country Planning Service, Belfast.
Forester, J. (1980) *Planning in the face of power.* University of California Press, Berkeley.
Hadden, T. and Trimble, D. (1986) *Northern Ireland housing law.* SLC Legal Publications, Belfast.

HMSO (1969) *Disturbances in Northern Ireland.* Report of the Commission appointed by the Governor of Northern Ireland. Cmnd 532, HMSO, Belfast.

HMSO (1970) *Northern Ireland development programme 1970-1975*, HMSO, Belfast.

HMSO (1971) *Housing Executive Act (Northern Ireland) 1971.* HMSO, Belfast.

HMSO (1976) *Housing (Northern Ireland) Order 1976.* HMSO, Belfast.

HMSO (1979) *Digest of housing statistics for Northern Ireland: 1st June 1944 - 31st December 1978.* HMSO, Belfast.

HMSO (1992a) *Housing (Northern Ireland) Order 1992.* HMSO, Belfast.

HMSO (1992b) *Northern Ireland census of population: summary report.* HMSO, Belfast.

Jarman (1983) Identification of underprivileged areas. *British Medical Journal.* Joseph Rowntree Foundation, York.

McPeake, J. (1990a) *1990 public attitudes survey.* Occasional Papers in Housing Research, No. 1, NIHE, Belfast.

McPeake, J. (1990b) *The Northern Ireland dwelling stock: a case study in occupancy dynamics.* Paper presented at International Symposium on Rural Housing, 25th October, 1990, Enniskillen.

McPeake, J. and Murtagh, B. (1991) *Rural household survey 1991.* NIHE, Belfast.

Montieth, M. (forthcoming) *1992 public attitudes survey.* NIHE, Belfast.

Mogey, J. (1947) *Rural life in Northern Ireland.* Oxford University Press, Oxford.

Murie, A. (1992) *Housing policy in Northern Ireland: a review.* Research Paper No. 3, Centre for Policy Research, University of Ulster.

Northern Ireland Economic Development Office (1985) *Review of recent developments in housing policy.* NIEDO, Belfast.

Northern Ireland Housing Executive (1974) *The Northern Ireland house condition survey 1974: principal characteristics of the Northern Ireland dwelling stock by district.* NIHE, Belfast.

Northern Ireland Housing Executive (1977) *Housing Executive 6th annual report.* NIHE, Belfast.

Northern Ireland Housing Executive (1978) *Housing Executive 7th annual report.* NIHE, Belfast.

Northern Ireland Housing Executive (1980) *The Northern Ireland house condition survey 1979: main report.* NIHE, Belfast.

Northern Ireland Housing Executive (1982) *The Northern Ireland house condition survey 1979: final report.* NIHE, Belfast.

Northern Ireland Housing Executive (1982) *Belfast housing renewal strategy.* NIHE, Belfast.

Northern Ireland Housing Executive (1983) *House renovation grants in Northern Ireland: an appraisal of improvement, intermediate and repair grants completions April 1979 - March 1982*. NIHE, Belfast.

Northern Ireland Housing Executive (1985) *The Northern Ireland house condition survey 1984*. NIHE, Belfast.

Northern Ireland Housing Executive (1987) *The Roslea study: an investigation into rural housing in West Region*. NIHE, Belfast.

Northern Ireland Housing Executive (1988) *The Northern Ireland house condition survey 1987*. NIHE, Belfast.

Northern Ireland Housing Executive (1990) *Rural housing policy review: leading the way - a consultative paper*. NIHE, Belfast.

Northern Ireland Housing Executive (1991a) *Brick by brick: a short history of the Northern Ireland Housing Executive*. NIHE, Belfast.

Northern Ireland Housing Executive (1991b) *Rural housing policy, the way ahead: a policy statement*. NIHE, Belfast.

Northern Ireland Housing Executive (1993) *Rural priority areas survey*. NIHE, Belfast.

Northern Ireland Housing Executive (forthcoming) *1991 Northern Ireland house condition survey: the physical survey report*. NIHE, Belfast.

Northern Ireland Housing Executive and the Department of Environment (NI) (1987) *The search for rural policy*. Joint Working Group Report, Internal Document, Belfast.

Northern Ireland Housing Executive and the University of Ulster (1976) *Northern Ireland regional household survey 1975*. NIHE, Belfast.

Northern Ireland Housing Trust (1947) *Northern Ireland Housing Trust: annual report 1946-1947*. NIHT, Belfast.

Northern Ireland Housing Trust (1963) *Northern Ireland Housing Trust: 18th annual report*. NIHT, Belfast.

O'Brien, L. (1951) *The Northern Ireland Housing Trust*. Paper presented at the Housing Centre, 27th February 1951, London.

Planning Advisory Board (1944) *Housing in Northern Ireland, Interim Report*. HMSO, Belfast.

Rogers, A. W. (1976) Rural housing, in Cherry, G. E. (ed) *Rural planning problems*. Leonard Hill, London.

Rose, R. (1971) *Governing without consensus*. Faber, London.

Scottish Homes (1990) *The role of Scottish Homes in rural Scotland*. Edinburgh, Scottish Homes.

Shucksmith, M. (1981) *No homes for locals?* Gower, Aldershot.

Singleton, D. (1989) Housing in Northern Ireland: the problems of a divided community, in Smith, M. E. H. (ed) *Guide to housing*. 3rd Edition, Housing Centre Trust, London.

# 11 Rural primary schools - Policy, planning and curriculum

*Leslie Caul*

## Introduction

Northern Ireland has an education system which is both similar to and different from that evident in other parts of the United Kingdom. It is not typical nor indeed is it atypical of British education but reflects a culture and society that are particular to the region. (see for example, McKeown and Connolly 1992, Strain 1992). The large proportion of schools in relatively isolated areas and school management divided on religious grounds are inescapable elements of the education system[1]. Problems as to the financial viability of the small rural school and the curriculum it provides have been addressed over many years without resolution. Quite simply, the answers change with the criteria being used to define the problem. A key issue is the definition of a rural school. In 1965 Pahl identified the differences between rural and urban life as those related to low population densities and small settlements that give rise to problems in the provision of services such as education. There often exists in such circumstances a conflict between national and local needs which when resolved in favour of apparent wider interests can lead to the decline of remote communities. School closure is evidence of that decline. Yet rural schools contribute not only to the educational welfare of their locality but also to cultural, religious and community vitality. Public policy relating to resource allocation must have regard to these many dimensions. This chapter provides an analysis of the current provision of rural schools in Northern Ireland and considers their future as education reform and the application of market principles redefine educational and social provision.

## Education in the small primary school

If all the criticisms levelled at small rural schools were true of each of those schools they would represent a substantial defective and disadvantaged element in the regional system of education. However, such schools are subject to the same swings in strengths and weaknesses as all others. Various waves of closures have thrown up new explanations of the weaknesses of the rural school. Yet much has been made of innovative educators such as L.R. Russell who in *The child and his pencil* (1935) provided inspiration to a generation of teachers who worked in less disadvantaged circumstances. The rural school has a history extending beyond its urban equivalent. In *Schools under scrutiny* (Caul 1990) the manoeuvring of the churches in Ireland in the nineteenth century to maintain parish and denominational schools, often in rural areas, was identified. Boyd (1972) records how in the 1890s the government in Dublin Castle was preoccupied by an over provision of schools in Ireland. Accordingly, it would seem that the position of the rural school at the centre of a crisis about over-provision and rationalisation of places is not a new phenomenon.

In 1926 the Consultative Committee led by Sir Henry Hadow recommended in *The education of the adolescent* that all-age elementary schools should become distinctive primary and secondary schools. Although this change did not come about until the 1950s it was as a result of this recommendation that the small rural primary school came into existence. In a second report Hadow (1931) exemplified good primary practice using evidence gleaned from rural schools:

> We have received a large number of interesting memoranda from headteachers of rural schools describing the internal organisation and methods of instruction adopted. The impression gained from these memoranda and from our oral evidence is that the teachers in schools which have converted into primary schools for pupils between the ages of 5-11 are developing a technique and a type of organisation which are yielding good results ... In a small country school in the north with an average attendance of twelve children under one teacher, the pupils are grouped for different branches of the curriculum. The teacher makes full use of individual effort on the part of children by training them to work at their own pace... In another primary school which is staffed with two teachers it has been found possible to make the work as individual and progressive as it has in small rural schools ... (pp. 81-2).

The small rural school emerged with much credit from the second Hadow Report as an institution with much to teach larger urban schools. It was recommended that teaching practice for young teachers should be in rural and small schools so that the student teacher could gain valuable knowledge of the methodologies used and benefit from the wider classroom experience available in such schools. Yet using the best psychological evidence available at the time Hadow did criticise the smaller school's ability to maintain a progressive course of instruction. This view was in obvious contradiction to the committee's insistence upon pupil progress as continuous rather than subject to administrative age-graded class based arrangements. It would appear that Hadow's view had become tainted by an urban view of progress of age-grade inevitably related to school form. Similarly the committee's view of the rural schools' organisation was coloured by an urban perspective:

> We think however that ... even in small rural schools there should be a well defined line of demarcation between the younger and older children (p. 68).

The committee's perception of the value of the small rural school had become clouded in an attempt to reconcile educational theory with practice in and organisation of the school. Thus the small rural school while a model of good practice became an anomaly in a system of schools based on age-grading and streaming.

In 1959 the Ministry of Education published *Primary education* to replace its *Handbook of suggestions* (1937) and thereby reflect a wider professional perspective which had developed in the immediate post war years. In Northern Ireland the 1947 Education Act had established primary schools as a distinct element of the region's education system. Both primary education and the teacher training colleges were heavily influenced by Piagetian theories of child development and attempted to link them with educational practices. This was evident in *Primary education* which renamed arithmetic mathematics, encouraged free writing and proposed discovery learning. However, little was said about rural schools except to remove from them the stigma of being unable to stream - this had been seen as one of their disadvantages:

> In the small school, to the range of ability is added the wide age range within one class, though this is not necessarily a disadvantage if the numbers are small. Many devices are used in schools to give each child work which is suitable for him and to ensure progress in accordance with his rate of learning (p. 68).

This freedom did little to change either practice or attitudes. The use of group work which was central to the ideas contained in *Primary education* did not become universally accepted in Northern Ireland. While accounts of rural education, such as that of Russell (1935) and Claypole's *James Boyce is late* (1990), suggest progressive ideas the main body of rural education remained conservative and tied to the 11+ examination. The ideology of relating academic development to streaming and setting became cemented as a corner-stone of education in Northern Ireland. The implementation of these organising principles was dependent upon school size and consequently the small rural schools continued to be seen as deficient because they were not large enough to conform to this prescription.

The Gittins Report (1963) in Wales and the Plowden Committee (1967) devoted particular attention to rural schools and were influential in determining their ethos at the time. The reports emphatically rejected streaming:

> We welcome streaming in the infant school and hope that it will continue to spread through the age range of the junior and middle schools (Plowden, para. 819).

Both committees commented unfavourably on the generally poor condition of village schools and especially their physical facilities. The reports also drew attention to the higher costs, measured in terms of unit costs per pupil, of providing a network of small schools across an area of low population density. Gittins argued:

> Where there is a number of small schools needing very generous staffing, education is likely to be more expensive than in a compact area within a small number of larger schools (para. 7.5.8).

The Gittins Report revealed clearly the relationship between density of population, teacher-pupil ratio, size of school and unit costs. It suggested that there was nothing to indicate that the greater expenditure by most rural authorities resulted in the provision of better education. There was no evidence that the measured attainment of rural children differed from that of their urban peers. The only point was that rural schools were simply more expensive to run than urban schools.

In the area of the curriculum offered by the primary school both Plowden and Gittins challenged the rural school. Up to this point in the development of the national system of schooling the curriculum was not seen as a problem. Neither Hadow (1931) nor the subsequent *Handbook of suggestions* had expressed any reservations about what constituted the curriculum. By the 1960s, however, the definition of an appropriate curriculum had altered and so that which was formerly considered to be suitable was now seen to be deficient:

> The curriculum of the primary school is now much wider and richer than when many primary schools were first built. The goals proposed by modern education challenge the limited space and resources of the small school. Teachers must between them cover a wide range of activities and attempt to be equally effective in all fields. Some aspects of the curriculum such as drama, physical education, and expressive movement and science tend to be weak ... In larger primary schools ... teachers with a particular qualification can help to draw up schemes of work ... The opportunity for this kind of cooperation is limited in the small school (para. 7.5.6).

Both committees regarded the small primary school as inevitably under-resourced and reflected Hadow's view of the importance of pupil interaction with peer age groups. This led to the view that the size of a small school was in itself a limiting factor in its potential to provide a modern education. But above all it was the small number of teachers and the assumption that this inferred a narrow curriculum that led Plowden to recommend that schools with an age range of 5-11 years should have at least three classes each covering two age ranges. Gittins more emphatically recommended the minimum size of schools is fifty to sixty pupils with three teachers. In addition Gittins suggested that the optimum solution for the rural school was to be found in the centrally located area school of six teachers. Gittins more than Plowden rejected the local rural school for the urban model.

This debate did not go unnoticed in Northern Ireland. In 1983 The Northern Ireland Council for Educational Development, in its primary guidelines programme, published a paper on the small school. The Council recognised the sheer number and importance of small primary schools in the more isolated parts of the region. But in the same year the Department of Education for Northern Ireland issued *Demographic trends* which for the first time directly addressed the question of the minimum size of school. The prescription was arrived at in the face of falling rolls and empty school places which had ultimately to be managed by the local Education and Library Boards. It had little to do with educational viability. The document simply set out standards on minimum school size as summarized in Table 11.1 below. Policy formulation in Northern Ireland had belatedly adopted the resources led rationale of Gittins and Plowden.

**Table 11.1**
**Recommended school size in Northern Ireland**

| | | |
|---|---|---|
| **Secondary Schools:** | **Urban** | Minimum Size - 600 pupils |
| | **Rural** | Minimum Size - 300 pupils |
| **Primary Schools:** | **Urban** | Minimum Size - 300 pupils |
| | **Rural** | Minimum Size - 100 pupils |

Source: DENI (1983)

## Rural primary schools in Northern Ireland

From the discussion above it is clear that value for money and quality of education are key policy issues. Accordingly, there appear to be four significant questions in addressing the management of primary education delivery to rural populations in Northern Ireland:

(1) how many schools exist in rural areas?

(2) where are they located?

(3) do rural schools cost more to manage than their urban counterparts?

(4) do rural schools have educational deficiencies?

The rest of this chapter seeks to provide answers to these questions.

In 1992 there were 905 primary schools in Northern Ireland. Of these some 436 (48.2 per cent) were controlled schools under the auspices of the 5 Education and Library Boards (Fig. 11.1). The Catholic maintained school sector numbered 461 (50.8 per cent) while the remaining 8 schools were Church of Ireland maintained, integrated and Irish speaking schools.

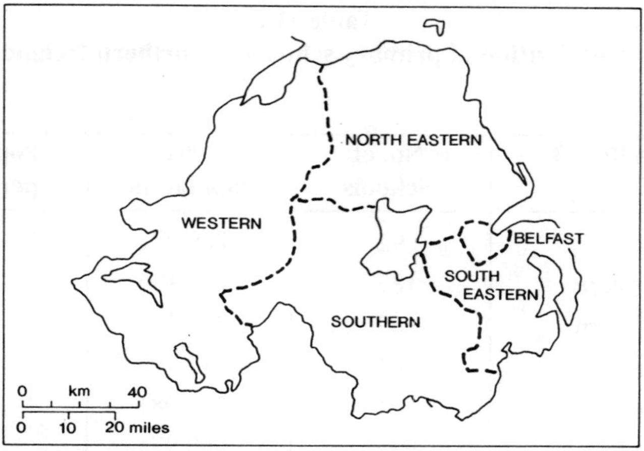


**Figure 11.1 Education and library board areas in Northern Ireland**

## Number, location and size

*(1) Geographical distribution*

As illustrated in Table 11.2 below the Belfast Education and Library Board area (Belfast District Council) has the smallest number of schools compared with more rural parts of Northern Ireland such as the Southern and Western Education and Library Board areas where the largest numbers are located. The resource implications of this rural provision are strongly suggested by data relating to population support per establishment. The more urbanised Belfast, North Eastern and South Eastern Education and Library Board areas have average support populations above the Northern Ireland average. In contrast, the Southern and Western Board areas are marked by a substantially lower average population support per primary school. Large tracts of the problem rural areas of Northern Ireland identified by Armstrong et al (1980) are served by such schools.

**Table 11.2**
**Distribution of primary schools in Northern Ireland**

| Area Board | No. of Schools | 1991 Population | Population per School |
|---|---|---|---|
| Belfast | 92 | 280,972 | 3054 |
| North Eastern | 187 | 361,136 | 1931 |
| South Eastern | 162 | 351,120 | 2167 |
| Southern | 263 | 317,309 | 1206 |
| Western | 201 | 258,981 | 1288 |
| Total | 905 | 1,569,971 | 1734 |

Source: Department of Education and Northern Ireland Census 1991 Preliminary Report

*(2) Enrolment*

When size of primary schools is considered Belfast has, not surprisingly, the largest mean enrolment of 328 pupils as opposed to a regional average of some 200 pupils. The Southern and Western areas have the smallest mean enrolments of 162 and 179 respectively.

**Table 11.3**
**Primary school enrolment in Northern Ireland**

| Area Board | School Enrolment Mean |
|---|---|
| Belfast | 328 |
| North Eastern | 197 |
| South Eastern | 218 |
| Southern | 162 |
| Western | 179 |
| Total | 198 |

*(3) Rural Primary Schools*

For the purpose of this chapter schools in local catchment areas of less than 5,000 people in the South Eastern, North Eastern, Southern and Western Area Boards are treated as rural. Using this criterion there are 506 rural primary schools (56 per cent) and 399 urban schools (44 per cent). The highest proportion of rural schools is in the Southern Board's area (Table 11.4)

**Table 11.4**
**Rural primary schools in Northern Ireland**

| Area Board | No. of Rural Schools |
|---|---|
| Belfast | - |
| North Eastern | 106 (21%) |
| South Eastern | 83 (17%) |
| Southern | 179 (35%) |
| Western | 138 (27%) |
| Total | 506 |

*(4) Rural primary schools and the enrolment baseline*

An enrolment of 100 pupils has been given by the Department of Education for Northern Ireland as a baseline figure for rural primary schools. The application of this criterion identifies a total of 308 rural primary schools in Northern Ireland with enrolments below the standard set (Table 11.5). The Southern and Western Board areas account for some 65 per cent of this total. If all schools whose enrolment is below the DENI baseline were closed such action would adversely affect the overall primary school stock in the region to such an extent that it would become so seriously depleted as to impair the delivery of primary education. Rationalisation of rural school places solely on the basis of enrolment numbers would pose a major policy challenge, especially in the Southern and Western rural periphery of Northern Ireland.

**Table 11.5**
**Number of rural schools with enrolments under 100 pupils**

| | ≤26 pupils | 27-56 pupils | 57-100 pupils | Total |
|---|---|---|---|---|
| Belfast | - | - | - | - |
| North Eastern | 4 | 25 | 30 | 59 |
| South Eastern | | 21 | 27 | 48 |
| Southern | 7 | 51 | 54 | 112 |
| Western | 4 | 43 | 42 | 89 |
| Total | 15 | 140 | 153 | 308 |

## The cost of rural education in Northern Ireland

Using Local Management of Schools (LMS) data for school budgets published in 1992 by each Education and Library Board it is estimated that the mean cost per pupil in all primary schools in Northern Ireland is £1,339. For schools defined in this chapter as rural the cost rises to £1,399 as against £1,262 for urban primary schools. But if schools are considered in terms of the size of their enrolments, educational provision in all schools of less than 26 pupils costs £2,776 (mean) as opposed to £2,567 per child in rural schools of this size. These figures are hardly significant since they only apply to 18 rural and urban schools in total. However, if consideration is given to 2 teacher schools (27-56 pupils) then the comparative costs are £1,584 for all schools and £1,576 for rural schools. For all 3 teacher schools (57-100 pupils) the corresponding figures are £1,388 as opposed to £1,325. Again the comparative differences may be small and not significant but at least these figures show that primary education is not necessarily more expensive in rural areas when compared to all primary schools.

**Table 11.6**
**Urban and rural primary school per capita expenditure in Northern Ireland**

| School Size | Urban | Rural |
|---|---|---|
| Fewer than 26 pupils | £3,892 | £2,567 |
| 27-56 pupils | £1,710 | £1,576 |
| 57-100 pupils | £1,418 | £1,325 |
| 101-150 pupils | £1,352 | £1,204 |
| 151-200 pupils | £1,275 | £1,152 |
| 201-500 pupils | £1,214 | £1,148 |
| 501-750 pupils | £1,124 | £1,147 |
| More than 750 pupils | £1,116 | - |

Source: LMS Data

Rural and urban school expenditure per pupil for the year 1992 by school size is set out in Table 11.6. While the number of schools in each group is unequal the data do show that in terms of school size rurally located schools are not more expensive to run than their urban counterparts. However, if Belfast is compared with other board areas a striking picture emerges of per capita pupil costs. In relation to all sizes of primary schools education in Belfast costs more per capita than in any other part of Northern Ireland (Table 11.7). Even schools with fewer than 100 pupils in the North Eastern, Southern and Western Boards are more economical to manage than primary schools with up to 200 pupils in Belfast.

**Table 11.7**
**Primary school per capita expenditure for area boards in Northern Ireland**

| School Size | Belfast | NEELB | SEELB | SELB | WELB |
|---|---|---|---|---|---|
| Fewer than 26 pupils | - | £2,869 | - | £2,504 | £3,063 |
| 27-56 pupils | - | £1,589 | £1,629 | £1,573 | £1,572 |
| 57-100 pupils | £1,719 | £1,360 | £1,285 | £1,354 | £1,307 |
| 101-150 pupils | £1,551 | £1,295 | £1,264 | £1,185 | £1,216 |
| 151-200 pupils | £1,425 | £1,219 | £1,236 | £1,156 | £1,174 |
| 201-500 pupils | £1,264 | £1,169 | £1,195 | £1,169 | £1,203 |
| 501-750 pupils | £1,061 | £1,114 | £1,151 | £1,117 | £1,108 |
| More than 750 pupils | - | - | £1,176 | £1,111 | £1.056 |

Source: LMS Data

**Educational outcomes in rural primary schools**

There has been no satisfactory conclusion to the search for differences in the educational attainment of rural and urban schools. The idea that rural children are slower than their urban counterparts is difficult to sustain on existing research evidence. Studies such as that of Bessant (1978) have found trivial differences in the abilities and attainments of rural and urban children. He argued that social class differences can be used to explain rural/urban discrepancies. However the problem is in comparing a rural area with an urban as if all rural areas are equal or all urban areas are equal. The significant differences are not between urban and rural areas *per se*, but between rich and poor people. Thus, for example, recent research reported by the Education Commission of the Conference of Major Religious Superiors[2] suggests that in Ireland the linked incidence of family poverty and educational failure is substantial. Serious literacy and numeracy problems have been found in areas where children are poor. It is also just as important to understand the specific disadvantages of rural poverty as it is to understand those of urban poverty. Thus families living at the end of a long lane, away from regular public transport may suffer from a degree of isolation not evident in urban locations. Research in the Welsh Valleys has shown that such isolation may be a significant factor in school failure (Bessant 1978).

The quality of the curriculum offered is a further issue. In a study of small schools (mainly those with a teaching principal and 1 other teacher) Caul and Harbison (1988) showed that small schools gave time to those subject areas that have been traditionally defined as deficient in the rural school, namely, music, craft, needlework and physical education. Schools in Scotland, however, benefited from a more supportive management policy in providing for those aspects of schooling often judged to be at risk in the small school. The development of cluster experiments among small schools in Scotland demonstrated the value of co-operation in freeing the teachers from a sense of vulnerability caused by isolation. The statements of school principals in Northern Ireland did seem to reflect such a feeling of isolation and a lack of support. Principals tended to argue that school management policy benefited large schools at the expense of smaller schools. Nevertheless principals did stress the advantages of the small school at every level from the individual attention given to the pupils to the coherence of the curriculum. The research provided information on the goals of the small school set in the context of the physical and academic resources provided. There were clear indications that not all the myths about small schools are true and that the advantages may not all be on the social and personal side at the expense of the educational and the purely academic. The study demonstrated that small rural schools did have a range of advantages not evident in larger primary schools, especially in their flexibility and management coherence.

## The future of small rural primary schools

The small rural primary school in Northern Ireland is typically a school with an average enrolment of 55 pupils. It is normally a 2 teacher school. About half of such schools receive additional supplements to help them deliver the Northern Ireland Curriculum. However, it would not seem to be a feasible proposition to close a significant proportion of these small rural primary schools. The overall infrastructure simply would not be able to sustain a reduction of the order suggested by DENI's policy in *Demographic trends* (1983). There is little available evidence to suggest that these schools are more expensive to manage per unit or that educational provision is as deficient as suggested by some commentators. Some of the most insightful and innovative educational work has historically occurred in this environment. Indeed the flexibility and opportunity afforded by its necessary classroom structure and curriculum coherence may have privileged the small school as a centre of learning. Nevertheless, the contemporary demands to deliver the Northern Ireland Curriculum, rapidly becoming a string of 9 specialist areas of knowledge, are creating many problems for all teachers and not least for those teachers who work in small schools.

The educational problems are often aggravated by a sense of isolation. This together with a relative under-resourcing does contribute to the difficulty of managing a large number of small schools. However, if as argued in this chapter small rural schools are not more expensive to run than their urban counterparts it should be possible to organise clusters of 4 or 5 establishments in a group to deliver the Northern Ireland Curriculum. This would mean that the same population would be served by the same number of schools but that the flexibility of a cluster could provide more expertise in some subjects and more efficient use of the available specialisms among school staffs. This could occur at a unit cost no higher than in an urban school, reduce feelings of isolation and improve the delivery of specialist staff and resources to the small rural school.

Consideration should be given to the use of computer networks to link and co-ordinate teaching, management and curriculum among the schools in a cluster. At relatively low cost, high grade curriculum materials, inter-active video and email links could provide schools with a range of specialist facilities and resources. The small rural school, once the poor relation of the education service, could become the pioneer of a new electronic revolution designed to service the more isolated and disadvantaged parts of Northern Ireland.

## Conclusion

The rural school is at the heart of the education system in Northern Ireland and has a long and distinguished history of serving rural communities. It has borne the brunt of attacks on its value and purpose for many years but this chapter has argued that the rural school is an indispensable part of the education system. More attention needs to be given to preserving its virtues as a flexible element in the delivery of education. New technologies offer opportunities to deliver a service to the many rural and more isolated parts of Northern Ireland. Clusters of small schools should be identified and supported in the redefinition of their collective potential contribution to the education of future generations.

## Notes

1. There are 2 principal categories of primary school in Northern Ireland : controlled and maintained. Schools provided by the 5 Education and Library Boards and managed by them are controlled schools. Most maintained schools are Catholic and are owned by church appointed trustees. The Education and Library Boards are required to ensure that there are sufficient schools of all kinds to meet the needs of their areas. However, the Education

Reform (NI) Order 1989 has established a statutory body with planning, advisory and management responsibilities for all Catholic maintained schools. This is known as the Catholic Council for Maintained Schools. It works closely with the Education and Library Boards and the Department of Education. The Department is responsible for overall policy, financial control, legislation, standards, programmes and priorities.

2. See *The Irish Times*, 25 February 1993, p.2.

## References


Addison, S. (1982) *Small rural schools project: 1964-1982.* Northamptonshire Education Authority.

Archibold, A. and Nisbet, J. (1977) Parents attitudes to the closure of small rural primary schools. *Scottish Educational Studies*, Vol. 9, No. 2, pp. 122-7.

Armstrong, J., McClelland, D. and O'Brien, T. (1980) *A policy for rural problem areas in Northern Ireland.* Working Research Paper Series, Vol. V, No. 1, School of Applied Economics, Ulster Polytechnic.

Aston University (1981) *The social effects of rural primary school reorganisation.* Final Report, University of Aston, Birmingham.

Bessant, B. (1978) Rural schooling and the rural myth in Australia. *Comparative Education,* Vol. 14, No. 2, pp. 121-151.

Board of Education (1937) *Handbook of suggestions for the consideration of teachers and others concerned in the work of public elementary schools.* HMSO, London.

Boyd, G. (1972) *Socio-economic and educational factors influencing the decline of the one-, two-, and three-teacher elementary schools in Northern Ireland since partition, with reference to the current trends in Great Britain and the Republic of Ireland.* Unpublished Ph.d, The Queen's University of Belfast.

Caul, L. and Harbison, J. (1988) *A comparative study of curriculum provision in small schools in Scotland and Northern Ireland.* NICER. Belfast.

Caul, L. (1990) *Schools under scrutiny: the case of Northern Ireland.* Macmillan Educational, London.

Claypole, J. (1990) *James Boyce is late.* Friar's Bush Press, Belfast.

Coatesworth, D. (1976) Is small still beautiful in rural Norfolk? *Education*, 10 October 1956, pp. 275-6.

Department of Education for Northern Ireland (1983) *Demographic trends.* Bangor.

DES (1977) *Falling numbers and school closures.* Circular 5/77, HMSO, London.

Dunne, E. (1977) Closing smallness: an examination of small school experience in rural America, in Sher, J. (ed) *Education in rural America*. Westview Press, Boulder, Colorado.

Finch, D. (1986) *A study of the social environment of small rural schools, with particular reference to the nature of inter-personal relationships*. Unpublished study, School of Education, University of East Anglia.

Forsythe, D. (ed) (1983) *The rural community and the small school*. Aberdeen University Press Aberdeen.

Gittins Report (1963) *Primary education in Wales*. HMSO, Cardiff.

Gregory, R. (1975) The education advantages of the small primary school. *Forum*, Summer, Vol. 17, No. 3, pp. 79-82.

Hadow Report (1926) *The education of the adolescent*. Report of the Consultative Committee of the Board of Education. HMSO, London.

Hadow Report (1931) *Report of the consultative committee on the primary school*. HMSO, London.

Hind, I.W. (1977) Estimates of cost functions for primary schools in rural areas. *Australian Journal of Agricultural Economics*, Vol. 21, No. 1, pp. 13-25.

Johnson, R. (1981) The survival of the small school, in Scottish Educational Department, *Off the Beaten Track*. HMSO, Edinburgh.

Lewes, G. (1980) The disadvantages and advantages of small rural schools in Watkins, R. (ed) *Educational disadvantage in rural areas*. Centre for Information and Advice on Educational Disadvantage.

Lloyd, G. (1978) *Deprivation and the bilingual child*. School Council Research Studies, Blackwell, Oxford.

Mackay, G.A. (1983) The economic context, in Forsythe, D. (ed) *The rural community and the small school*. Aberdeen University Press.

Ministry of Education (1959) *Primary education*. HMSO, London.

McKeown, P. and Connolly, M. (1992) Education reform in Northern Ireland: maintaining the distance. *Journal of Social Policy*, Vol. 21, No. 2, pp. 211-232.

McWilliam, E. (1978) *100 years of a village school: Bransombe School 1878-1978*. Private publication.

Marshall, D.G. (1985) Closing small schools or when is small too small? *Education Canada*, Fall, pp. 10-16.

Nash, R. (1977) *Conditions of learning in rural primary schools*. Report to the Social Science Research Committee, London.

National Association of Local Councils (1979) *Rural life, change or decay.*

Newsom Report (1963) *Half our future*. Report of the Central Advisory Council for Education. HMSO, London.

Nordic Council of Ministers (1977) *Pre-schools in sparsely populated areas: a report of recent and current experiments in Finland and Norway schools.*

Northern Ireland Council for Educational Development (1983) *The small rural school*. Belfast.

Owen, J.G. (1977) *The planning of alternative pre-school arrangements in an area where few pre-school establishments exist: Devon in the United Kingdom*. CCC, OECD. 44, Paris.

Pahl, R.E. (1965) *Urbs in rure: the metropolitan fringe in Hertfordshire*. London School of Economics, Geography papers No. 214, London.

Plowden Report (1967) *Children and their primary schools*. HMSO, London.

Rogers, R. (1977) Closing village schools: what the LEA are up to. *Where*, No. 133, November.

Rogers, R. (1979) *Schools under threat: a handbook on closures*. Advisory Centre for Education.

Russell, L.T. (1935) *The child and his pencil: adventures in a country school*. Allen and Unwin, London.

Shaw, M. (1976) Can we afford villages? *Built Environment Quarterly*, 17 June, pp. 135-75.

Sher, J.P. (1978) *Revitalizing rural education: a legislator's handbook*. National Conference of State Legislatures.

Sher, J.P. and Tomkins, R.V. (1977) Economy, efficiency and equality: the myths of rural school and district consolidation, in Sher, J.P. (ed) *Education in rural America: a reassessment of conventional wisdom*. Westview Press, Boulder, Colorado.

Sigworth, A. (1984) *Rural teachers' perceptions of their task*. Paper presented at the British Association for the Advancement of Science, University of East Anglia.

Simkin, T. (1980) The economics of smallness: the case of small primary schools. *Educational Studies*, Vol. 6, No. 1, pp. 79-91.

Solstad, K.J. (1981) Locally relevant curricula in rural Norway: the Lofoten Islands examples, in Sher J.P. (ed) *Rural education in urbanized nations*. OECD/CERI Report, Westview Press, Boulder, Colorado.

Standing Conference of Rural Community Councils (1978) *The decline of rural services*.

Strain, M. (1992) Education reform in Northern Ireland. *Local Government Studies*, Vol. 18, No. 2, pp. 9-17.

# 12 Health care provision in rural areas

*Mark Conway*

## Introduction

Any discussion of rural health care in Northern Ireland will rapidly find itself governed by the major generic issues facing rural service provision. The dilemmas of isolation and access, centralisation and decentralisation are just as potent in the health care area as they are elsewhere (see Kilmurray and Bradley 1989, McPeake and Murtagh 1991, and Quinn 1988). Before going on to consider these issues in more depth, it is essential to restate and re-emphasise the classic attributes of Northern Ireland's rural dwellers. Essentially they live in the open countryside, in dispersed, isolated and owner-occupied houses, exhibit an extremely strong attachment to place, frequently have some ties to the land and generally suffer from higher than average levels of social and economic deprivation. Caldwell and Greer's (1984, p.1) context-setting for the dilemmas that have emerged in rural land use planning is just as valid for other policy areas

> Northern Ireland remains essentially rural in character, its cultural and physical landscapes less influenced by the process of urbanisation which has had a major impact upon much of the remainder of the United Kingdom. More specifically, there are extensive areas of the Province where a dispersed settlement pattern, housing a closely knit conservative population, continues to personify a way of life suspicious of and resistant to change, the more so if the policies advocating change fail to recognise the complex values and traditions of this rural society.

This chapter will consider some of the main issues involved in developing a model for rural health care. It will begin by presenting an outline of the overall National Health Service (NHS) structures in Northern Ireland, summarise some of the traditional responses to the health care needs of rural areas, move on to consider the possible implications for rural dwellers of the NHS reforms and conclude by discussing the current and planned responses of one particular Unit of Management to the delivery of rural health care.

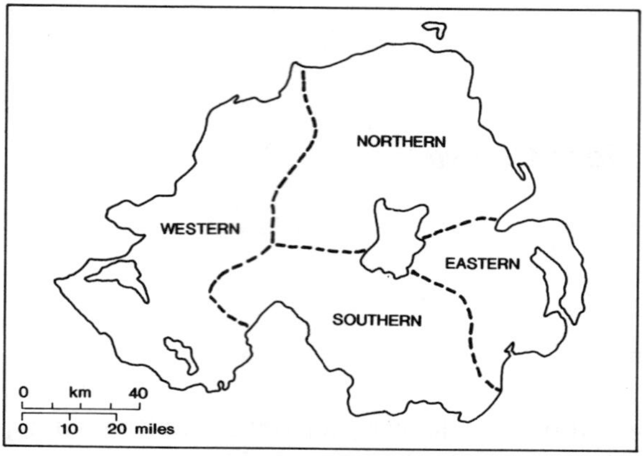


**Figure 12.1 Health and social services board areas in Northern Ireland**

## The health service in Northern Ireland

In strict terms the health service in Northern Ireland is not part of the NHS but exhibits management and organisational differences which reflect the region's unique political circumstances. One key feature of the local arrangements is their ability to deliver comprehensive, integrated health care including personal social services : instead of a National Health Service Northern Ireland thus has a Health & Personal Social Services (HPSS) structure. Overall policy is made by the Department of Health and Social Services but a separate Management Executive, established in 1990, is charged with ensuring that policy is implemented. The next tier down is occupied by four Health and Social Services Boards (Fig. 12.1) which, within the context of the NHS internal market, act as purchasers of health and social care. Essentially the Boards' role is to :

(1) assess the state of health and social welfare of their resident populations;

(2) identify their service requirements accordingly;

(3) plan and manage the purchase of services so that their populations have access to a comprehensive range of conveniently sited, high quality and value for money services.

The fourth and final tier of the local NHS is filled by 22 Units of Management. Again within the context of the NHS reforms these Units act as the providers of health care and will increasingly assume responsibility for delivering contracted services within the quantity and quality specifications laid down by the Boards. These (initially at least) directly-managed Units may in turn agree contracts with private and voluntary providers at the more local level for the delivery of specific health care services. The basic relationships involved would not change were individual Units to become self-governing Trusts.

Historically any consideration of specifically rural health care issues has achieved only a minor, and at times transient, ranking on the overall health policy agenda. In most cases, rural issues have emerged as a secondary finding following analyses which have focused on clear correlations between deprivation/disadvantage and poor physical/mental health. The use of Townsend Scores or Jarman Indices (for example see WHSSB 1988, Wilkinson 1992) to identify areas of disadvantage -and by inference populations at greater risk of poor health - readily highlights peripheral rural areas. But whilst the identification of existing and potential rural health problems may be quite sophisticated, what is still to be resolved is the sophistication and even the appropriateness of the actual responses to those problems.

In his seminal consideration of rural deprivation, Moseley (1980) argued that the real problem with rural deprivation was not that it differed generically from urban deprivation but rather that it was responded to in different ways. Too much rural deprivation research concentrated almost exclusively on the consumers of deprivation to the exclusion of the producers. The differences between rural and urban managerialism - i.e. how institutions allocate resources spatially - and society's overall economic and political treatments of rural and urban areas had simultaneously been ignored. Thus whilst the nature of rural and urban problems had much in common, the nature of the responses to them had not. Within this interpretation Friedmann's comment (1972, p.93) of two decades ago seems consistently valid :

> . . . peripheral regions are subsystems whose development path is determined chiefly by core region institutions with respect to which they stand in a relation of substantial dependency.

In any examination of the relevance of this thesis to rural health care the location of the vast majority of the regional health care specialities in and around the Belfast Urban Area could be taken as one clear indicator of a dependency relationship in Northern Ireland. Coyle (1990) has no doubt as to the validity of the premise and has commented that the effective result is an under provision of health care in rural areas. Notwithstanding these arguments and what might be termed the endemic centralisation of services generally in Northern Ireland over the past three decades, specific attempts have been made to reflect rural particularities in some aspects of health care. Three of these are considered briefly below :

*(1) Rural practice scheme*

This scheme was devised to compensate doctors for the additional expenses involved in visiting patients in rural areas. Any doctor with at least 10 per cent of patients living three miles or more from the surgery would qualify : in 1990, however, this criterion meant that 75 per cent of Northern Ireland's 933 GPs (including several in the Belfast Urban Area) qualified for the scheme. Clearly a more sophisticated measure of patient dispersion would be required were the resources allocated to the scheme to be better targeted to reflect the difficulties of delivering primary health care to truly rural populations.

*(2) Essential small pharmacy scheme*

Crude measures of dispersion and remoteness were again used to identify small pharmacies for financial assistance. Those pharmacies dispensing fewer than 1,300 prescriptions per month and located more than two miles from the next nearest pharmacy qualified. In 1990 these comprised just over 3 per cent (17 pharmacies) of Northern Ireland's 509 pharmacies. However while in global terms the numbers may have been small, in terms of safeguarding pharmacy provision at the margins, the scheme may have been quite significant.

*(3) Dispensing doctors scheme*

This scheme enables doctors to dispense drugs or appliances to any patient who, because of distance, poor communication or other reason, would have major difficulties in obtaining them. Again it should be most relevant to people living in remote rural areas and, in 1990, 63 doctors (just under 7 per cent of Northern Ireland's 933 GPs) serving 53,000 patients were classed as dispensing doctors.

Whilst these traditional responses to the perceived problems of rural areas have hardly been revolutionary in their impact the tantalising prospect now is that the current NHS reforms may help bring about a Health Service that better responds to the needs and aspirations of rural dwellers. Hambleton (1992) has developed a representation of trends in local government management (see Figure 12.2) which seems just as valid in the health care arena. Suggesting that the three broad (though not mutually exclusive) alternatives for the 1990s are the "dismantled state", the "decentralised state" and the "empowering state", Hambleton's primary message is that the "bureaucratic paternalism" of the first three post war decades is now consigned to history.

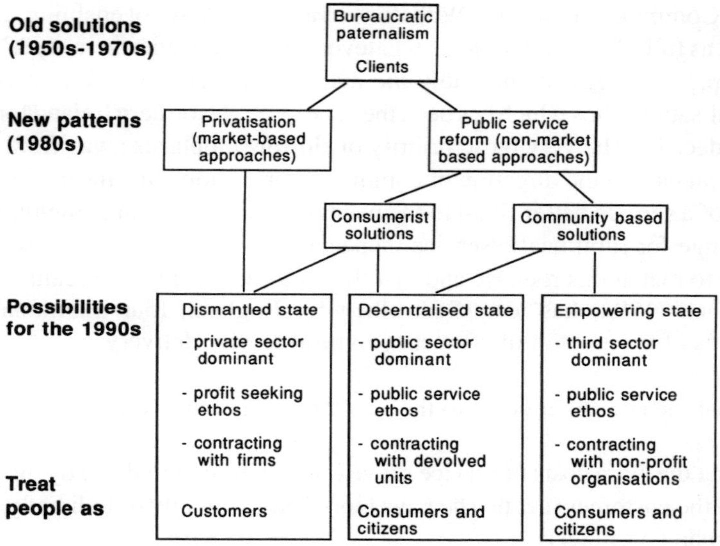


**Figure 12.2 Trends in local government management**

Source: Hambleton (1992)

Rural Northern Ireland has not prospered under bureaucratic paternalism, very largely because historically the bureaucratic paternalists have tended not to understand it. Hambleton's suggestions for the 1990s lay the emphasis on service recipients as customers, consumers and citizens. This status, and the power that goes with it, are matters to which Northern Ireland's rural dwellers have not been accustomed, but to which they have long aspired. It may thus be extremely fortunate that the current major reforms within the NHS have coincided with the unprecedented attention that is now being given to rural issues in Northern Ireland. Much of the publicity attached to the NHS reforms, and indeed many individuals' perceptions of them, have tended to be negative. Hospital closures, opting out, a relegation of clinicians' authority and an abdication of responsibilities to voluntary and private providers have become the accepted wisdom as to what the reforms are about. This is not the place to debate these many complex issues but it is an appropriate setting in which to touch on some of the very real opportunities that the reforms offer for moulding a health service much better fitted to rural Northern Ireland.

## NHS reforms : the opportunities for rural areas

The major opportunity now in front of the rural constituency must be the Care in the Community initiative. With its overriding objective of enabling "... people to live as full a life as possible, in whatever setting best suits their needs" (DHSS 1990 p.3) it represents probably *the* major about-turn by government on the centralisation ethos which has been the bane of rural Northern Ireland for the past three decades. Its very basic priority of shifting emphasis away from hospital inpatient care in the direction of community provision must mean the development of a service better fitted to the needs of dispersed rural communities. The challenge for rural health service managers is to ensure that the resources are found to match this rhetoric and that the rhetoric becomes the reality.

Fennell (1992) has identified, albeit for England, four traditional consequences of the pursuit of efficiency in rural service delivery :

(1) that the consumer come to the service (and not vice versa);

(2) that the extra costs of service provision may be externalised by the provider to the customer (i.e. he/she pays more, either directly or indirectly, than the urban consumer);

(3) that fragile rural services are often withdrawn first when budgets are stressed;

(4) that services are often enhanced by making use of voluntary organisations to help secure their delivery.

The first of these has been a major problem for Northern Ireland's rural dwellers. The sentiments of Care in the Community, however, mean that instead of people being obliged to come to the service, the emphasis will now be on bringing the service to people. Exactly the same principles are contained within the Housing Executive's recent rural housing policy review (see McPeake and Murtagh in this volume). A challenge for individuals, groups and/or communities in rural areas must now be to lobby and organise to ensure that opportunities for local service delivery are exploited.

A second major opportunity for rural areas lies in the reforms' renewed emphasis on integration in the planning and delivery of care. The virtual absence of integrated public sector plans and programmes has been a consistent and valid complaint from rural dwellers. The Rural Affairs Divison of the Department of Agriculture for Northern Ireland (DANI) has now acted upon these criticisms with its appointment of Area Co-ordinators, and the development of joint planning of health care can also address them. Joint planning may currently be little more than a gleam in the Health Boards' and the Housing Executive's eyes but it does offer a hitherto unavailable chance to make sure that rural health and rural housing policies are pulling in the same direction. When, as they surely must, DANI's Area Co-ordinators and the Rural Development Council (among others) are brought into the process, rural communities can only benefit.

A third opening lies in a phrase which usually arouses a great deal of suspicion, "the mixed economy of care". The notion of private individuals providing care services which traditionally have been the property of HPSS units is often anathema to many people. However, if the reality to date is considered in just one small segment of the mixed economy, i.e. the spread of independent nursing homes, the outcomes for rural areas can just as easily be seen as positive. In the rural areas served by the Western Health and Social Services Board for example, 16 such facilities offering some 350 places now exist. Thus not only are rural people now being cared for in their own environment and by people from that environment but many people who previously would have suffered great privation rather than leave their neighbourhood now receive the appropriate care. All the while, and of no little consequence, nursing homes bring valuable employment, particularly for women, into rural areas. Independent provision is still slanted towards the larger urban centres (in the Western Board area a further 31 facilities offering 950 places are available there) but the independent sector's ratio of a 2.7:1 urban/rural provision is markedly superior to the public sector's 11:1 urban/rural provision ratio. The independent sector's 350 rural places also contrast sharply with the public sector's mere 44 rural places.

The introduction of the NHS reforms would thus appear to offer an unprecedented opportunity for the emergence of a health service more responsive to the needs of rural communities. However contemporaneous with these new positive possibilities is a series of threats to the distribution of certain elements of acute hospital care. The tendency for Northern Ireland's regional specialities to be concentrated in and around the Belfast Urban Area has already been commented on. An extreme argument would be that Belfast hospitals could quite readily serve the entire needs of Northern Ireland for acute medical and surgical care, no part of the region being more than two hours by road from the city.

Hospital provision is not, however, something that is assessed on rational unemotional grounds by the majority of health service users. The current debate about the future of several acute hospitals in London (see Paton and Bach 1990, Benzeval et al 1991) is as indicative of the issues involved as are any of the debates about acute provision for Northern Ireland's rural dwellers. Hayes (1986, p.498) has described hospitals as the virility symbols for many urban centres and has further suggested that:

> . . . the mechanistic approach to health care which has characterised western medicine tends to put the emphasis on these facilities. People forget that the pattern of hospital provision and modern hospital care are comparatively recent developments. A measure of the shift is seen in the fact that at the inception of the NHS two-thirds of doctors worked in general practice and one-third in hospitals. That ratio has now been exactly reversed. Hospitalisation, particularly in an acute hospital, is for most people an episode in a life-time, and on any day the chances of any citizen in Northern Ireland being in hospital is less than 1 in over 2,000.

The rationality of Hayes's proposition is invariably lost on those for whom it simply represents a threat. In the rural context, the most immediate threat faces those maternity units which serve essentially rural populations. The DHSS (NI) recommendation that maternity units should have at least 2,000 - 2,500 deliveries per annum means that serious questions are currently being asked of each of the 13 non-metropolitan maternity units in Northern Ireland. Given that these units currently deliver in total some 10,000 babies per year, it is not unthinkable that rationalisation could result in the 13 units being reduced to 6 or fewer. Part of this process has already commenced with the decision by the Western Health and Social Services Board that the maternity unit in Omagh (circa 1,000 births per year) should close and that the hospital maternity needs of a population of 133,000 should be met centrally in the Erne Hospital, Enniskillen (currently circa 825 births per year).

The initial announcement that one or other of the Units was to close brought furious local reactions from citizens, interest groups and politicians alike. In the event, however, the issue turned into an unseemly squabble between the champions of the respective Units. Little emphasis was given to the much more significant underlying issues such as :

(1) the relevance of global norms in a particularly rural setting;

(2) the actual importance of the hospital maternity unit in the complete birth cycle and the question of what really is the proper balance between ante-natal, hospital and post-natal care for rural people.

An opportunity to replace a tug of war over a physical facility with a zero-based discussion on a new model for rural maternity care seems to have been lost. Even at this early stage it may well be that the extremely positive aspects of Care in the Community will tend to be overshadowed, and even supplanted, by the necessarily complementary negative impact on hospital provision. It is perhaps an indictment of the first forty years of the NHS that all too often the health service is seen as synonymous with a hospital service. This misunderstanding is - and has been -particularly perilous for rural areas since its consequence is a reliance by rural people on a number of centralised hospitals as the main means of delivering their health care. In virtually every other sector, centralisation and rural Northern Ireland have been uneasy, if not totally incompatible, bedfellows. It would be ironic were rural people to use centralist arguments to thwart the exciting possibilities that Care in the Community opens up.

**Towards a rural health care model**

The suggestion was made above that the Care in the Community initiative represents perhaps the greatest opportunity to date for a more rural-specific model of health care delivery to emerge. The remainder of the chapter thus attempts to describe some of the changes that have been wrought by one Unit of Management in the west of Northern Ireland. The Unit is a mental health unit and whilst that may seem to be a particularly narrowly-focused Unit on which to concentrate it is in fact in many ways ideal since it is one that has had and is continuing to wrestle with the difficulties of shifting from a service dominated by centralised hospital provision to one underpinned by decentralised community provision.

The Western Health and Social Services Board's Area Mental Health Unit was established on 1st April 1990 as one of four Units of Management within the Western Health and Social Services Board Area. It is the only Area-wide Unit and was structured deliberately so in order to best address the task of shifting from a primarily hospital-based to a more community-based model of service delivery. In covering the complete Western Board Area, the Unit caters for the mental health needs of Limavady, Derry, Strabane, Omagh and Fermanagh District Council Areas, with a combined population of some 260,000. For operational purposes the Unit Area is divided into Northern (Limavady, Derry and Strabane District Council Areas) and Southern (Omagh and Fermanagh District Council Areas) Sectors : Strabane, however, is not rigidly tied into the Northern Sector alone. Each Sector has traditionally had as its focus a large psychiatric hospital - Gransha in the Northern and the Tyrone and Fermanagh in the Southern. Crucially, the vast majority of the Unit's care resources (83 per cent of salaries and wages for example) is consumed by these two hospitals.

In terms of geographical spread, the Unit is the largest in Northern Ireland, covering as it does some 1900 square miles. It also incorporates in areas like the Sperrins, West Tyrone and South and West Fermanagh, some of the most remote and sparsely populated parts of Northern Ireland (see Fig. 12.3). The principle of delivering services to people thus involves much more than simply paying lip service to a concept: accessibility and transport issues are fundamental to much of the Unit's work. The social contexts of the Unit reflect the population distributions. In the rural areas traditional kinship ties remain strong, attachment-to-place is often paramount and independence is jealously guarded. The urban areas more closely reflect overall United Kingdom patterns with greater mobility, a weakening of traditional family and kinship structures and a greater awareness of/reliance on the provisions of the welfare state. Again, a key task is to develop services which reflect these contexts.

Mental health services locally have largely been perceived to be synonymous with the Area's two large psychiatric hospitals, Gransha and the Tyrone and Fermanagh. This ultra-centralised provision of care for the mentally ill in the west of what is now Northern Ireland was effectively the unquestioned status quo for a century and a half from the building of the original two asylums in the late 1820s. Whilst their building "can reasonably be regarded as the renaissance of the humane and enlightened care of the mentally ill in Ireland" (McClelland 1988) it is testament to the stigma attached to mental illness that such centrali-

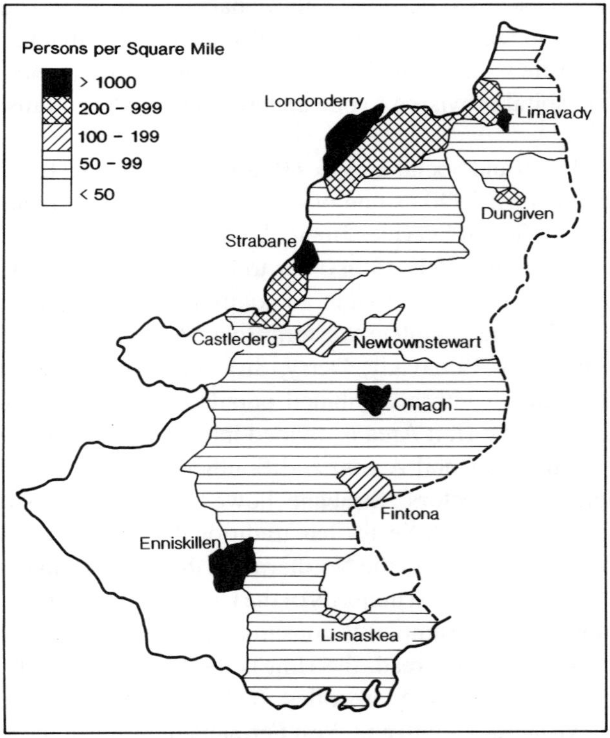


**Figure 12.3 Population density in Western Health and Social Services Board area, 1991**

sation lay virtually unchallenged in a region where the local siting and ownership of facilities is both jealously guarded and actively pursued - viz the Omagh/ Fermanagh maternity unit debate.

The centralisation of mental health services is not of course something unique to the rural west of Northern Ireland, Enoch Powell's classic description of the nineteenth century asylum and the realignment he felt was needed, being applicable throughout the UK and Ireland:

> There they stand, isolated, majestic, imperious, brooded over by the gigantic water-tower and chimney combined, rising unmistakable and daunting out of the countryside - the asylums which our forefathers built with such immense solidity to express the notions of their day. Do not for a moment underestimate their powers of resistance to our assault... The transformation of the mental hospitals is not only a matter of buildings, the change of a physical pattern, it is also the transformation of a whole branch of the profession of medicine, of hospital administration. Politics apart, let us admit that we all have a great deal of conservative in our make-up, and find it easier to envisage things going on much as at present, or with small or gradual modifications, than deliberately to choose and favour the unaccustomed, the drastic and voluntarily to bring about a pattern of organisation in which new tasks will be performed in a new and wider setting (Powell 1961).

Only in the early 1960s, after a century and a quarter of centralised provision, did the first stirrings of a move away from this model of care appear. King (1991) provides a graphic account of how this move was accelerated in the south west of England and describes a standard of service that most would envy. In the west of Northern Ireland it is perhaps ironic that the most recent major stimuli for decentralisation came from without in the form of DHSS targets. The Regional Strategy for the Health and Personal Social Services 1987-1992 demanded a 20 per cent reduction in psychiatric inpatient numbers whilst its successor, the Strategy for 1992-1997, has maintained the impetus with similar, though more detailed targets. The historic and planned impact on inpatient numbers in the Unit's two psychiatric hospitals is shown in Figure 12.4 which depicts a dramatic decline of some 67 per cent, from 1155 to circa 385 beds.

A range of community services has been simultaneously developed across the Unit area and some indication of the number and distribution of these is given in Figure 12.5. As Figure 12.6 shows, in volume terms the planned changes are no less dramatic, community-based residential places being increased fourfold to almost 300 and community-based day care places by 35 per cent to more than 500. Limavady and Fermanagh Districts were given priority in the development

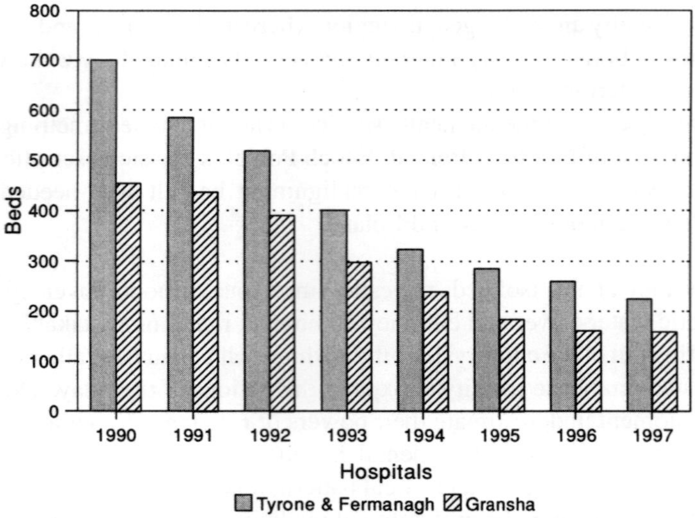


**Figure 12.4 Area mental health unit hospital bed reductions, 1990-1997**

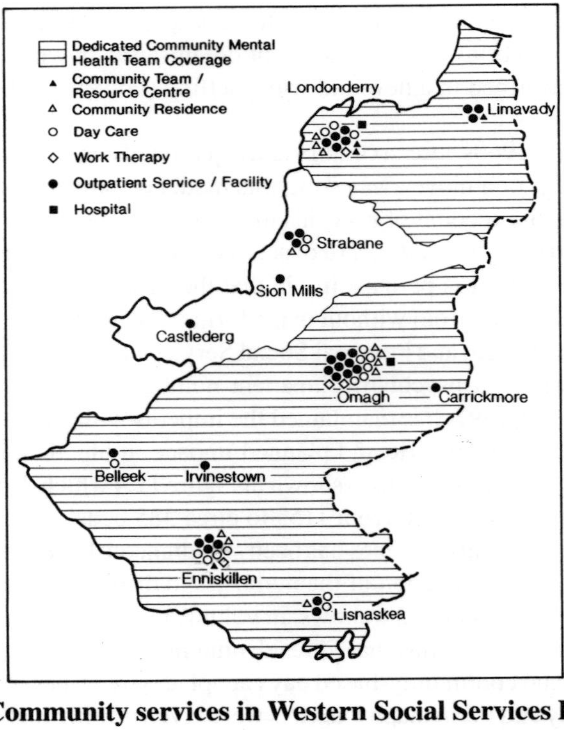


**Figure 12.5 Community services in Western Social Services Board area**

of community-based services and in both mental health services are now centred around multi-disciplinary teams working from a common base in the heart of the community which they serve. This is now widely accepted as the cornerstone of good community psychiatric services. The Limavady Team for instance now provides day care and day hospital services and has developed a whole network of relationships with the community and local voluntary groups. Not only is the feedback from general practitioners, consumers and carers very positive but the referral rate has tripled since the Team was established in 1990 and the admission rate to hospital has fallen. In essence what this means is that the 29,000 people who live in Limavady District - two thirds of whom are rural - now have the bulk of their mental health services decentralised to within their District. Historically the vast majority of provision was hospital-based and centralised in Gransha Hospital, Londonderry.

It is now perhaps useful to move on to consider in more detail how services are simultaneously being developed in Fermanagh, one of Northern Ireland's most rural Districts. Located in the extreme south-west of Northern Ireland, Fermanagh District (Fig. 12.7) has come to be accepted as perhaps the epitome of peripheral rurality in Northern Ireland. Two thirds of its population of almost 54,500 live outside the three main towns of Enniskillen, Lisnaskea and Irvinestown and overall the District is characterised by the main features of marginal rural living. Economically it is heavily reliant on a declining small-farm agriculture although tourism is increasingly economically significant. Communication problems (the District is effectively dissected by Upper and Lower Loughs Erne), poor housing (27 per cent of homes were statutorily unfit in 1984) and

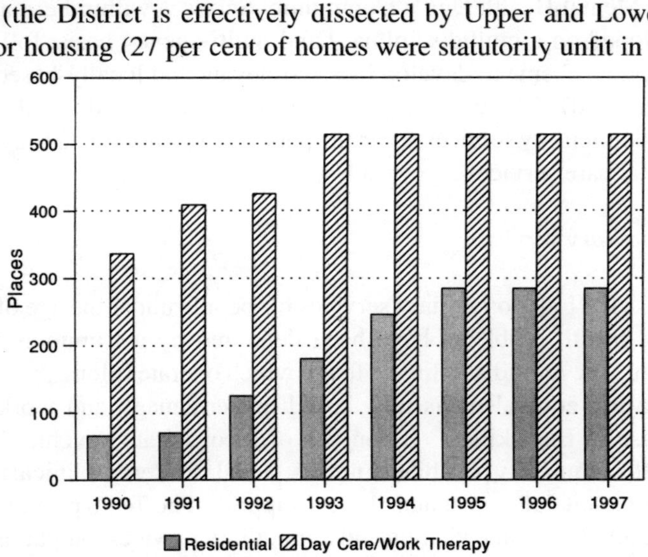


**Figure 12.6 Area mental health unit selected community provision, 1990-1997**

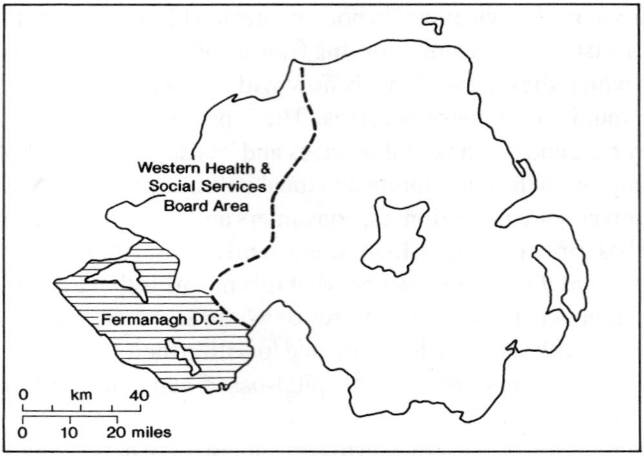


**Figure 12.7 Location of Fermanagh District Council area**

heavy emigration rates combine to make it a classic example of rural living on the locational and economic periphery In spite, or perhaps because of, these multiple disadvantages it has however begun to assemble a whole series of innovative, and largely community-based projects aimed at countering these difficulties (see McGinley in this volume).

The Area Mental Health Unit's Community Services within Fermanagh, are being developed on a multidisciplinary and multi-agency basis, following an innovative pilot scheme to develop locally-relevant and locally-based services that began in 1987. The current provision of care can be divided into three groups: (1) domiciliary services (i.e in the person's own home); (2) day services; (3) residential care services.

### *(1) Domiciliary services*

Since August 1991 all domiciliary services for people under the age of 65 years with mental health problems have been delivered by a Community Mental Health Team. The multidisciplinary Team, which operates along the same lines as its Limavady equivalent, is now based in Fermanagh and works from a common base in Enniskillen. It consists of a consultant psychiatrist, junior medical staff, community psychiatric nurses, social workers, a clinical psychologist, an occupational therapist and clerical support. The Team provides a range of services including home visiting and domiciliary services, outpatient clinics, one-off assessments and advice or support to any member of the public who calls to the centre. Staff also provide an assessment and counselling service to appropriate patients at the Erne (General) Hospital, Enniskillen. In addition to the services provided to people under 65, Community Services are also delivered to people over 65 who suffer from either a severe degree of dementia or other mental illness. A Community Alcohol Team offering addiction and substance abuse services on a multidisciplinary basis also operates within the Fermanagh area. Home-based services are provided in close liaison with general practitioners and the hospital and community staff of the Omagh and Fermanagh Hospital and Community Services Unit of Management.

*(2) Day care services*

In total Fermanagh now enjoys some 170 day care places where previously provision had been virtually zero. These services can be divided into the following three groups:

(a) *Structured day care.* Day care is now provided in four locations across the county, i.e. Enniskillen, Lisnaskea, Brookeborough and Belleek. The services concentrate on the development of social and life skills and are undertaken in conjunction with voluntary and community groups.

(b) *Industrial therapy.* Negotiations have been completed with the Industrial Therapy Organisation for the development of these services in Fermanagh. A 40 place workshop is now operational in Enniskillen and there are plans to develop a number of satellite work therapy centres across the county.

(c) *Informal day care.* The Unit, in conjunction with the Western Board, currently contracts with the Northern Ireland Association for Mental Health (NIAMH) to deliver a range of services (which include luncheon clubs, drop-in and social activities) in Enniskillen, Lisnaskea and Belleek.

*(3) Residential care services*

Residential care in Fermanagh is delivered in conjunction with other statutory, voluntary and private agencies - a classic example of the mixed economy of care. Some 30 places are now available and a joint scheme currently being progressed by Praxis and the Church of Ireland Housing Association in Lisnaskea should add a further eight. People from Fermanagh who require psychiatric inpatient care currently receive this service at the Tyrone and Fermanagh Hospital, Omagh. Hospital care is now just part of the service however, a marked contrast from the relatively recent past when it effectively was the service.

## Current issues

While the continuing decentralisation of services and facilities into and throughout Fermanagh represents significant progress towards a model rural mental health care provision, the successful implementation of such a model across all rural areas will hinge on the resolution of a number of broad issues. These are considered below.

*Housing*

It may be stating the obvious but the shift from a hospital to a community base can occur only if there is an adequate supply of appropriate housing in the community - and by this is meant the full range of options that is so heavily emphasised in *People first* (DHSS 1990). The Unit's experience to date has highlighted a number of points:

- the private sector can provide facilities on the ground very fast;
- the public and voluntary sectors (due to issues of accountability and probity) operate at a slower pace : the development of a mixed economy of provision is therefore proceeding at a dual pace;
- if care in the community is to be in the community then the fullest possible use must be made of existing NI Housing Executive stock : given however that some 4 per cent only of Fermanagh's NIHE stock is located in the truly rural areas, the implications for successful care in the rural community are obvious;
- the provision of suitable housing in the rural areas, and particularly in the more remote or peripheral communities, is likely to be problematic: the involvement of local community groups in this process is of fundamental importance.

Finally, while there may be an undersupply of suitable housing in the community, the legacy of this irrevocable shift has been an oversupply of accommodation in the hospital base, primarily the Tyrone and Fermanagh Hospital in Omagh. The Hospital's now empty main building and its 20,000 sq m of floorspace represent both a challenge and an opportunity for rural development in the widest sense in the west of Northern Ireland.

*Transport*

Given the nature of the Unit area, covering 1900 square miles and including some of Northern Ireland's most remote and sparsely populated areas, transport is a key consideration in implementing the new strategy. Bringing services to the people is neither cheap nor easy. Indeed not all services can, nor should be brought to people : very often it is more appropriate to bring people to the service. Again this is neither cheap nor easy, but any public service in the west of Northern Ireland which does not take on board issues of remoteness and accessibility will not be an effective service. Mohan (1992) has argued that access and transport considerations have largely been ignored in health care policy nationally : in the context of rural Northern Ireland they simply cannot be ignored.

Recent research (Transport Research Group 1992) has coincidentally highlighted the difficulty in travelling even relatively short distances by public transport to Omagh's Tyrone and Fermanagh Hospital. An example of the total logistics involved in attending a mid-morning appointment at the Hospital for a typical village resident was found to be as follows :

Appointment time : 1100 am
Origin village : Drumquin

| | | |
|---|---|---|
| Journey time : | | |
| Depart Drumquin by bus | : | 0822 |
| Arrive at Omagh bus station | : | 0855 |
| Depart Omagh bus station | : | 1025 |
| Arrive at hospital | : | 1035 |
| Appointment time | : | 1100 |
| **Total journey time** | **:** | **158 minutes** |

Return to Drumquin, after a 35 minute appointment

| | | |
|---|---|---|
| Depart hospital | : | 1135 |
| Arrive at Omagh bus station | : | 1140 |
| Depart Omagh bus station | : | 1315 |
| Arrive at Drumquin | : | 1340 |
| **Total journey time** | **:** | **125 minutes** |

Keeping a 35 minute appointment thus demands more than five hours of the individual's day. For those truly rural residents who may require additional transport to and from the village, the picture is even more bleak. These difficulties are not of course the specific preserve of rural areas. Pearson (1992) has highlighted similar problems experienced in actually getting to outpatient appointments in Merseyside. Access and transport are thus generic issues for health care provision : they are however much more acute issues for rural dwellers.

*Collaboration*

Since the Unit is moving into new territory, both literally and metaphorically, it is essential that it combines forces with those agencies already in place. The possibilities offered by the government's rural development initiative and the links which can be forged with District Councils are two of the more immediate possibilities. There is, however, a great deal more scope for collaboration with other agencies : one area that begs for such innovation is that of transport. The difficulties experienced by health care users who are reliant on public transport have already been highlighted. The paradox is that the Western Education and Library Board, whose area of operation is exactly coterminous with that of the Area Mental Health Unit controls a very large school bus fleet yet, because of legislative constraints, is unable to use this fleet for anything other than educational purposes. In the longer term collaboration and the resultant synergy may be most effectively achieved or facilitated through the contracting mechanisms now available. The Board and the Unit will as a result be able to direct resources to those third parties which can help achieve the strategic objectives for mental health.

## Conclusion

One of the biggest challenges facing the rural community in terms of health care is the need for that community to work out its own position as regards a rural-specific model of health care delivery. Critical questions concerning the historic reliance on, and popular affinity with, hospital-based care must be addressed. Rural communities must rid themselves of the belief that "It has been . . . therefore it ought to be". After two-to-three decades of bitter struggle against many government policies, the rural constituency has in the last year or two begun to see many of its arguments accepted. It has successfully opposed many policies that undermined or ran counter to the rural fabric. It would of course be naive to assume that the NHS reforms will unaided lead to the New Jerusalem in rural areas. But equally it would be foolhardly to ignore the opportunities that now lie ahead. In turn, however, there remains an even greater obligation on health policy makers and managers to look afresh at the health care needs of rural people. They in particular must also dispel the notion "it has been . . . therefore it ought to be", or, "It is somewhere else . . . therefore it ought to be here". They must honestly and openly evaluate the relevance of urban models and levels of provision in the rural setting and begin to examine the possibility of creating rural-specific models of care. Such a task should be part of the remit of the various Health and Social Services Boards as they begin to develop their needs assessment and purchaser roles. The new opportunities in health care, the flexibility offered by contracting, the obligations to undertake detailed needs assessments and the ever increasing focus on the needs of the service user could result in a health service more finely tuned to rural needs and aspirations. Whether they will remains to be seen.

## References


Benzeval, M., Judge, K. and New, B. (1991) Health and health care in London. *Public Money and Management*, Vol. 11, No. 1.

Caldwell, J. and Greer, J. (1984) *Physical planning in rural areas of Northern Ireland.* Occasional Paper No.5, Department of Town and Country Planning, Queens University, Belfast.

Coyle, A. (1990) *Rural poverty in Northern Ireland.* Rural Action Project, Derry.

DHSS (1990) *People first: community care in Northern Ireland for the 1990s.* HMSO, Belfast.

Fennell, J. (1992) *Health care in rural England.* ACRE, Cirencester.

Friedmann, J. (1972) A general theory of polarized development, in Hansen, N.M. (ed) *Growth centres in regional economic development*, The Free Press, New York.

Hambleton, R. (1992) Decentralisation and democracy in UK local government. *Public Money and Management*, Vol. 20, No. 6.

Hayes, M. (1986) Your good health: access to health and health care in Northern Ireland. *Regional Studies*, Vol. 20, No. 6.

Kilmurray, A. and Bradley, C. (1989) *Rural women in South Armagh: needs and aspirations.* Rural Action Project, Derry.

King, D. (1991) *Moving on from mental hospitals to community care: a case study of change in Exeter.* Nuffield Provincial Hospitals Trust, London.

McClelland, R.J. (1988) The madhouses and mad doctors of Ulster. *The Ulster Medical Journal*, Vol. 57, No. 2.

McPeake, J. and Murtagh, B. (1991) *Rural household survey 1991.* NI Housing Executive, Belfast.

Mohan, J. (1992) Who foots the bill? *Health Service Journal*, 27 August.

Moseley, M. (1980) Is rural deprivation really rural? *The Planner*, Vol. 66, No. 4.

Paton, C. and Bach, S. (1990) *Case studies in health policy and management.* Nuffield Provincial Hospitals Trust, London.

Pearson, M. (1992) Outpatients outclassed. *Health Service Journal*, 15 October.

Powell, E. (1961) Speech given at a conference held by the National Association for Mental Health, Church House, Westminster, London, 9 and 10 March.

Quinn, B. (1988) *Belcoo and District area plan: the community perspective.* Rural Action Project, Derry.
Transport Research Group (1992) *The transport needs and resources for groups in Northern Ireland.* University of Ulster, Jordanstown.
Wilkinson, J. (1992) Thursday's children. *Health Service Journal*, 2 April.

# Section 4
# ACTION AND CHANGE

# 13 Local government and community participation

*Aideen McGinley*

## Introduction

The Northern Ireland voluntary sector ranges widely across social, economic and cultural activities and has become increasingly vigorous during the past 20 years. In 1992 it comprised some 3000 groups, employed 25,000 people and generated the equivalent of 6 per cent of GDP in the region (NICVA 1992). Community based initiatives represent an important component of this sector. As noted in the report of the Community Development Review Group (1991) various types of activity are involved. These comprise community economic development, community relations, community care, community education and community service in both urban and rural locations. Inevitably central government support has been of crucial significance in nurturing the participation by community groups in these pursuits. Core funding has been provided for support organisations such as the Northern Ireland Voluntary Trust, the Northern Ireland Council for Voluntary Action, Community Technical Aid and the Rural Action Project. In February 1993 government published its *Strategy for the support of the voluntary sector and for community development.* The special role of the Department of Health and Social Services as the liaison between the voluntary sector and government departments is confirmed and the intention to recognise this co-ordinating role formally by establishing a Voluntary Activity Unit within that Department is expressed.

But at local government level it is the case that District Councils in Northern Ireland have adopted a varied and largely uncoordinated response to community development responsibilities. In 1975 the Moyle Report recommended that local authorities should be responsible for grant aid to community groups, for giving support and advice to these groups and for the employment of community services officers. For most District Councils, however, this has remained a low priority (Community Development Review Group 1991). Fermanagh District Council is a notable exception to this broad observation. This chapter identifies the level of community based activity taking place within Fermanagh District, located in the rural periphery of Northern Ireland. It sets out the strategic commitment of the local authority to the execution of its community services responsibilities and describes key initiatives undertaken with local communities on a partnership basis. It is argued that the participatory approach underpinning this work provides a useful example of the contribution which local government can make to rural development.

## Community based activity in Fermanagh District

In 1976 Fermanagh District Council became one of the first local authorities in Northern Ireland to undertake a community services function. At that time there were only 5 local groups within the district; no community centres had been established. In responding to this challenge the Council agreed an initial objective of actively encouraging, supporting, developing and sustaining community activity in its area. It became associated, for example, with the Community Worker Research Project which over the period 1978 to 1982 funded the employment of a full-time worker with a local community development association (Department of Education 1983). By 1992 there were 52 community based organisations within the district, each pursuing a development approach responsive to local needs and working closely with local government.
These groups can be divided into 3 broad categories:

(1) temporary, coalition or ad hoc groups which have formed in a reactive way in order to address a particular issue;

(2) single issue permanent groups which concentrate on a particular topic such as welfare or tenants' rights;

(3) multi-issue permanent groups such as community associations or townland groups which adopt a holistic approach to the problems in their local areas.

The varied focus of activity by groups in Fermanagh is summarized in Table 13.1 below. More particularly there are 22 village associations, 14 town based groups and 16 townland projects with 9 community centres and a further 3 on stream. In addition there are 6 Council community centres, 12 history societies, 5 women/community health groups, 25 playgroups and mother and toddler playgroups, 22 senior citizen clubs, 12 credit unions and 7 mummers groups.

**Table 13.1**
**Classification of community activity in Fermanagh District**

| Community Care | Issues | By Area |
|---|---|---|
| Old age pensioners | Rural Development | Community |
| Playgroups | Poverty | Townland |
| Vulnerable groups in society | Economic Development | Rural |
| Women's Groups | Training | Urban |
| Youth Clubs | Arts | County |
| Education/Schools | Culture | Networks |
| Mothers & Toddlers | History/Heritage | Cross Border |
| Uniform Groups | Crafts | UK |
| Community Health Groups | Tenants Rights | EC |
| Disabled People | Community Relations | |
| | Pressure Groups | |
| | Environmental Issues | |
| | Play facilities | |
| | Education | |
| | Services/Closures | |
| | Housing | |

The financial resources which these varied groups have been able to draw down have been quite substantial involving both statutory and voluntary sources. These commitments include:

- funding for 11 Action for Community Employment schemes;
- £25,000 annually from the Northern Ireland Voluntary Trust;
- £250,000 from the Cadbury Foundation since 1986;
- £373,000 from Children in Need since 1988;
- £100,000 from Central Community Relations Unit to Fermanagh District Council for community relations;
- £8,000,000 from the International Fund for Ireland for 5 village regeneration projects.

Clearly, community based activity in Fermanagh District is multi-faceted and is demanding of sustained and relatively high levels of funding.

## Local government strategy

This level of community investment has helped promote local confidence about and enthusiasm for rural development. Progress, however, has not been fast and has required some 15 years of effort. The District Council has contributed to this outcome. It is located between state institutions above and local people below and has endeavoured to forge working partnerships between all participants in the development process, including elected representatives. In order to execute this catalytic role more effectively the Community Services Department of the Council undertook a strategic review of its operations in late 1991. From this exercise a mission statement to cover the period to 1997 was agreed as follows:

> *Community Services in Fermanagh recognises and values the rich diversity of community life in the County. It is strategically placed to identify local needs and to promote an integrated approach to the effective targeting of resources from many sectors towards meeting those needs. The overall aim of the Department is the enhancement, preservation and improvement in the quality of life for all, socially, culturally, economically and intercommunally.*

In short the approach endorses the need for inter-agency action, recognises the importance of voluntary-statutory partnership and accepts the value of local ownership in meeting the rural development challenge. It is appropriate at this juncture to consider two examples of local government policy in action which have run contemporaneously with the review by the Community Services Department and the initial implementation of the mission statement objectives.

**Fermanagh rural community initiative**

The Fermanagh Rural Community Initiative commenced in 1989 as a partnership project initially between Fermanagh District Council, the Northern Ireland Housing Executive, Fermanagh Training Agency and Help the Aged. The aim is to tackle rural deprivation by using an integrated community development approach. A key problem in the district is the level of housing unfitness which, at 27 per cent of the housing stock, is the highest in Northern Ireland. Large numbers of elderly people live in these poor conditions. It was appreciated from the outset that there was a much deeper set of problems which had to be addressed if the whole cycle of deprivation was to be broken. Accordingly, the major priorities for the project were identified as providing:

- somewhere decent to live;
- an adequate income;
- access to education, employment, social services and transport;
- opportunities for social, community, economic and cultural development.

The project aims to refurbish and repair sub-standard housing for the elderly and other disadvantaged people by using trainees skilled in traditional crafts such as stonemasonry. At the same time the other social and community elements of transport and community care will be realised through an inter-agency approach involving voluntary and statutory partners. The refining of this project has generated tensions around issues such as the demarcation lines of responsibility drawn by statutory bodes. These have been eased somewhat by the new rural development structures set in place by government. A management board representative of the statutory and voluntary sectors has been formed and the appointment of a Chief Executive will allow the initiative to be taken forward with EC INTERREG and Cadbury Trust funding. The initiative as a whole offers a practical way of tackling problems of rural deprivation by securing an overall improvement in the quality of life of those who are most disadvantaged in Fermanagh District.

**Fermanagh model of consultation**

In Northern Ireland town and country planning is the responsibility of the Department of the Environment. Planning application decisions are taken not by local government elected representatives but by appointed civil service officials. The Department is also responsible for the preparation and review of development plans prepared usually but not necessarily on a district council area basis. As discussed by Milton in this volume, rural planning in Northern Ireland is contentious and frequently revolves around the key issue of new development in the open countryside being granted or refused planning permission. This debate is keenly rehearsed in County Fermanagh which, with its setting of mountain and lake, contains some of the most scenic landscapes in Ireland.

Accordingly, when the Department of the Environment decided in 1990 to appoint consultants to prepare a rural development strategy as part of the area plan review process, it was specifically requested that a broad based consultative process with local people should take place. Initially this was interpreted to mean the convening of two meetings concerned solely with economic development, oriented only to local groups, with no prior briefing being provided or outline proposals available for comment. Fermanagh District Council rejected this approach and in conjunction with the Rural Action Project and Community Technical Aid (with the subsequent blessing of the Department of the Environment) designed a more meaningful process of community consultation. This involved:

(1) a general public meeting explaining aims, objectives and methods of study;

(2) a widely circulated questionnaire outlining potential issues;

(3) the formation of a steering committee of local people and interest groups from County Fermanagh;

(4) the organizing of 6 local information days;

(5) the preparation of a report of findings by Community Technical Aid which was presented to the Department of the Environment and other relevant agencies.

A wide range of opinions on a variety of issues was obtained (Community Technical Aid 1990). Most importantly rural people themselves believed that the exercise was worthwhile. However, key questions remain regarding the extent to which policy formation can be strongly influenced by this type of input. It is interesting to note that this intensive process of consultation was subsequently used across Northern Ireland for a review of rural housing policy (Community Technical Aid 1991) and for a review of rural planning policy (Community Technical Aid 1992).

## Conclusion

Fermanagh District Council is committed to a community based approach which is practical and proactive. This chapter has sought to demonstrate how the Council is targeting all available resources at the needs of local communities and how by means of participatory processes it is involving these communities in articulating and meeting their aspirations. The guiding principle holds that the greatest gift that can be given to a community is the opportunity for it to protect, sustain, develop and create a place which embodies the richness of rural life.

## References

Community Development Review Group (1991) *Community development in Northern Ireland: perspectives for the future*. Community Development Review Group, Belfast.

Community Technical Aid (1990) *Fermanagh rural development strategy: a summary of strategic issues arising from the community consultation process in Fermanagh rural area undertaken by Community Technical Aid, Rural Action Project and Fermanagh District Council.* Community Technical Aid, Belfast.

Community Technical Aid (1991) *Rural housing policy review: leading the way -a community response prepared for Rural Action Project.* Community Technical Aid, Belfast.

Community Technical Aid (1992) *Rural planning strategy review: a community consultation response.* Rural Development Council, Cookstown.

Department of Education for Northern Ireland (1983) *The Community Worker Research Project 1978-1982 evaluation report.* Belfast.

Northern Ireland Council for Voluntary Action (1992) *Voluntary action pulling together: 1991-1992 Annual Report.* Belfast.

*Strategy for the support of the voluntary sector and for community development in Northern Ireland* (1993) Belfast.

# 14 County Development Teams and rural regeneration

*Vincent Reynolds*

## Introduction

The concept of adopting an integrated approach to the problem of rural regeneration in the Republic of Ireland was first accepted in the Second Programme for Economic Expansion published in July 1964. This followed a study by a select committee appointed to consider and report on measures to deal with the special problems of agriculture in the western part of the country, where small farms predominated (Government of Ireland 1965). The committee recommended that western development be approached on a broad multi-sectoral basis, embracing agriculture, industry, tourism, forestry, fisheries and services. As a consequence, County Development Teams, which had been initially established on an informal basis in 1963, were reconstituted in 1965 in counties Cavan, Clare, Donegal, Galway, Kerry, Leitrim, Longford, Mayo, Monaghan, Roscommon, Sligo and West Cork. West Limerick was added in December 1967 (Fig. 14.1). At the same time, a Central Development Committee (CDC), located in the Department of Finance, was established to foster economic development in the West and co-ordinate the activities of the County Development Teams.

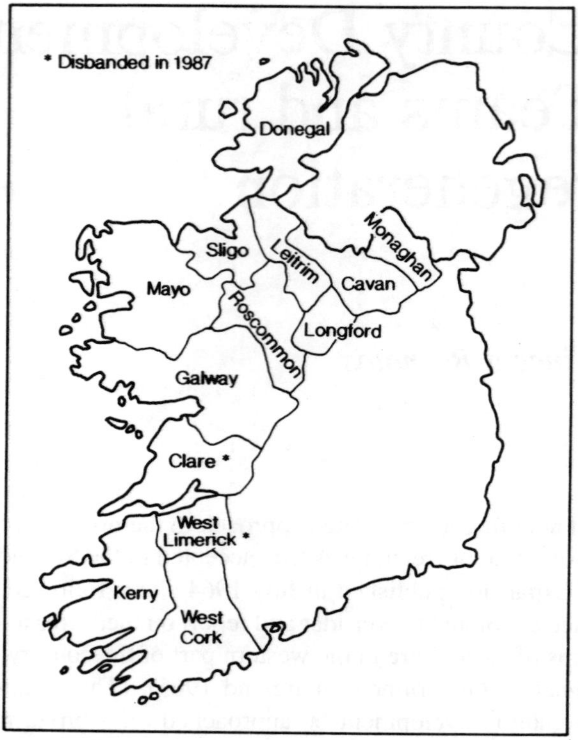


**Figure 14.1 County development teams in the Republic of Ireland**

## County Development Teams - membership, role and functions

A broad range of economic development interests are represented on County Development Teams. Their membership comprises:

- the County Manager who is Team Chairman;
- the Chairman of the County Council;
- the County Engineer;
- the Chief Agricultural Officer, Teagasc;
- the Chief Executive Officer of the Vocational Education Committee;
- a representative from the training agency (FAS);
- the Regional Manager of the Industrial Development Authority (IDA); and, as appropriate, representatives of Shannon Development and Roinn na Gaeltachta/Udaras na Gaeltachta.

The County Development Officer, a civil servant seconded from the Department of Finance, is Team Secretary. In most counties, an Assistant Team Secretary is in place, through the secondment of the officer from the host local authority. Secretarial services and office accommodation are also provided by the local authority. The role and functions of the Teams can be broadly seen as including:

- the promotion of economic activity in the county;
- increasing county income by, inter alia, ensuring that maximum economic advantage is secured for the county from EC/state grants and incentives;
- the creation of an environment in which industrial development can take place, through, for example, encouraging local authorities to provide and develop industrial sites at strategic locations; optimising the numbers availing of state support schemes in the areas of training, feasibility studies, product research and development and employment incentives; nurturing the development of small industries, in conjunction with the IDA, from the stage of stimulation of project proposals to the provision of formal review/after-care service on behalf of the IDA;
- securing maximum job creation, and retention of the rural population through the promotion of co-operative ventures and maximising opportunities for off-farm employment;
- identifying development possibilities and potential developers;
- community development;
- providing co-ordination at county level of all activities having a bearing on development, whether undertaken by state departments, state agencies, local authorities, voluntary bodies or local people, and acting as a catalyst in this context.

**Central Development Committee**

The functions of the Central Development Committee (CDC) are:

- to act as a co-ordinating agency in relation to development and implementation of official policies for the Western Designated Areas;
- to facilitate the work of the County Development Teams;
- to co-operate with other national agencies contributing to economic development;
- to examine proposals submitted for assistance from the Special Regional Development Fund (now the Western Development Fund).

Membership of the CDC consists of the Chairman, who is an officer of the Department of Finance; six County Managers from the Western counties (on a rotational basis); representatives from the IDA, from FAS, and from the

Departments of Industry and Commerce, Energy, Labour, Environment, Agriculture and Food, Tourism, Marine, Gaeltacht, Communications and Education. The CDC is serviced by a permanent Secretariat located in the Department of Finance. The main tasks of the Secretariat are:

- the examination of proposals for assistance from the Western Development Fund and the preparation of individual project reports for consideration by the CDC;
- monitoring the day-to-day co-ordination of the Teams and providing the County Development Officers with assistance necessary to carry out their tasks;
- providing the necessary administrative services for the CDC to function, undertaking special assignments on its behalf and handling the financial arrangements on projects once decisions have been ratified by the Minister for Finance.

A unique attribute of the CDC/County Development System is its multi-sectoral brief. It is, indeed, the only state institution which has a role in all economic sectors. In their operations, the Teams seek to maintain a close working relationship with all of the departments and agencies concerned with economic development. Through the CDC, direct links are forged via the departmental and agency representatives who make up the membership of the CDC. It was never intended that County Development Teams would be big budget organisations or be seen as major grant aiding institutions. Where possible the policy is to secure finance for projects from the line departments/agencies responsible for the various sectors. A major part of the Teams' role is to encourage promoters to come up with new ideas for development and to nurture those ideas to fruition, through encouragement, and the provision (through referral) of advice on all relevant aspects of any particular project. They maintain up-to-date banks of information relating to their particular counties and on the various support schemes in existence. The Teams also act as honest brokers between promoters and the line departments and agencies, so as to ensure, as far as possible, that no breakdown occurs in the support structures for emerging entrepreneurs.

**Support schemes for rural development**

A number of special support schemes for rural development in which the CDC/County Development Teams are involved will now be described.

*(1)    Western Development Fund*

The main objective of this Fund, which was established in 1967, is to provide a flexible means of assisting economic projects in the Western Designated Areas, which would otherwise not qualify for support from any existing scheme of state grants or incentives. Its purpose is to act as a safety net to ensure that worthwhile projects do not fail to establish for want of finance. The Fund is confined to aiding economic projects but is not limited to any particular economic sector. Activities eligible under an existing scheme of assistance or excluded under national sectoral policy criteria are ineligible for aid. Due to its flexibility, the fund has the ability to adapt quickly to changing situations. An interesting feature has been its pioneering role, through the provision of support, on a pilot basis, for new programmes/projects, many of which are subsequently extended nationwide and administered by the relevant agency or department. Two examples, i.e. a private bog development scheme and a programme to support timber harvesting contractors, were successfully initiated with assistance from the Fund. Both were subsequently expanded through the introduction of national schemes administered by Bord na Mona and the Department of Energy respectively.

Grants in excess of IR£5,000 (Main Grants) are subject to the approval of the Central Development Committee (CDC), while grants of up to IR£5,000 (Discretionary Grants) are approved by the County Development Teams in consultation with the CDC Secretariat. In order to ascertain how effective the Fund has been, its activities over the years 1981 to 1990 have been examined. A total of 2,366 projects received assistance over the ten year period. Grants to the value of IR£6.8m were paid out, contributing to the creation of 4,257 jobs, and resulting in a grant cost per job of IR£1,600 (gross IR£3,200). In considering the gross cost (i.e. including administrative expenses), it is important to note that the total operational costs of the County Development Teams and the CDC Chairman/Secretariat are included, whereas only a fraction of their time is devoted to Western Development Fund type grant work. Apart from directly creating significant employment in disadvantaged areas of the Republic of Ireland, the Fund provides seed capital for the initial development of projects, many of which, with further development, may subsequently qualify for assistance from other state agencies e.g. IDA and Bord Failte.

*(2)    Integrated Rural Development*

In the Republic of Ireland, a pilot two year integrated rural development programme was established in twelve selected areas in 1988. The aim of the programme was to mobilise local people to work for the economic, social and cultural development of their own areas, to decide on their own development priorities and to take initiatives to bring their aspirations to fruition. The process was intended to include new job creation and improvement of living standards. Following appraisal of the pilot phase (see O'Malley in this volume), and drawing on the experience gained during its operation, the government announced, in July 1991, new administrative structures to be responsible, at local level for the implementation of a nationwide programme of rural development. In the western designated counties, responsibility for administration of the programme was assigned to the County Development Officers/Teams. This was a decision which enabled the government to capitalise on existing expertise and resources. It has placed the County Development Officer/Team at the centre for the delivery, at local level, of future integrated rural development programmes. For the non-western areas of the country, the Department of Agriculture and Food is to appoint rural development co-ordinators to be based in a number of strategically located centres. To finance the programme, IR£7.6m has been provided (for the period to December 1993) from the Operational Programme for Rural Development (EC Structural Funds 1989-1993).

It is within this framework that a scheme of support for small and community enterprises has been introduced. The special emphasis of this scheme is to encourage and facilitate a bottom-up process, which will help to create a social and economic climate conducive to local enterprise. This focus on the bottom-up process has three elements:

(1) increasing awareness of the development potential of local resources and helping to identify suitable projects and opportunities;

(2) co-ordinating the activities of state agencies at local level;

(3) providing a flexible fund which can act as a safety net for viable projects.

The scheme gives support to individual, group or community projects in rural areas to provide products or services which have the capacity of achieving commercial viability. It also provides assistance for feasibility studies and business plans. For the purposes of administration "rural areas" means any place outside the Greater Dublin Area and the County Boroughs of Cork, Limerick, Galway and Waterford. To be eligible for assistance a project should be in the commercial sphere and be capable of attaining economic viability, without ongoing state or EC aid. It should also add value so as to generate income or supplement income for those involved and have the capacity to create new direct employment, either full-time or part-time/seasonal. At a minimum, it should contribute directly to the maintenance of employment in a rural area. The following grant levels apply:

- a maximum of 50 per cent of the cost of capital investment;
- a maximum of 75 per cent of the cost of obtaining technical asistance subject to an overall limit of IR £5,000 in the case of a single project.

*(3) County Enterprise Funds*

An initiative taken by the County Development Teams, following the establishment of the International Fund for Ireland (IFI), culminated in the setting up (in 1988) of County Enterprise Fund Companies in the six border counties, to administer revolving business development funds, assist the provision of workspace facilities and encourage community-based economic projects. Detailed local knowledge of the needs of community enterprise groups and small businesses generally provided the stimulus for this action. The companies have been funded by the IFI and local subscriptions. IFI support to-date has amounted to IR£591,000 per county (IR£3,546,000 in total) conditional on each company raising IR£92,500 locally (IR£555,000 in total).

The structure in each county is that of a company limited by guarantee, having charitable status for tax purposes, and managed by a Board of Directors representative of business, community and agency interests. The County Development Officer is a Director/Company Secretary and his office provides the day to day management/administration functions. Three schemes are operated by the companies:

(1) a Revolving Business Enterprise Fund which provides loans or investments up to IR£15,000 in new or developing manufacturing or service projects;

(2) a Workspace Scheme which provides assistance up to IR£25,000 or 50 per cent, whichever is the lesser, towards the provision of premises for suitable projects;

(3) a Community Based Economic Projects Scheme which provides assistance up to IR£20,000 to local enterprise groups engaging in economic projects.

By 1992, the six companies had provided support to 324 projects, resulting in the creation of 1159 full-time and 276 part-time jobs.

*(2) EC INTERREG Programme*

The purpose of this special EC initiative is to assist border areas in Ireland to overcome the development problems arising from their relative isolation, within the two national economies and the European Community as a whole, and to promote the creation and development of networks of cross-border co-operation. In 1983 the Economic and Social Committee of the European Community described this sub-region as amongst the least developed in Europe with the additional handicap of being cut in half by a frontier that hampers normal economic development. County Development Teams and the Central Development Committee have been assigned responsibility in the Republic of Ireland for the evaluation and recommendation of projects submitted for support under the Community Development Measure of Sub-Programme 5 (Regional Development). The measure will be implemented by:

(1) promoting the development of community associations throughout the INTERREG area and encouraging them to engage in collaborative development, particularly on a cross-border basis;

(2) providing assistance for these organisations to prepare area-based and multi-sectoral development plans;

(3) advising the promoters of these development plans where aid may be available from national or EC sources or providing limited grant aid where appropriate and where this would not be available otherwise.

The total financial provision for this measure up to the end of 1993 is 6.113m ECUs (i.e. for both Northern Ireland and the Republic of Ireland) with a maximum aid rate of 75 per cent.

*(5) EC LEADER Programme*

This pilot EC initiative aims to encourage and assist rural communities to develop their own areas, in accordance with their own priorities. The now popularised bottom-up approach is being adopted, with financial assistance being made available by the EC and the state towards the cost of implementing multi-sectoral business plans drawn up by the rural groups themselves. In the Republic of Ireland, some seventeen groups have been approved for funding involving a total investment of approximately IR£70m. The EC is contributing about IR£21m with a further IR£14m coming from the Republic of Ireland Exchequer. The rate of aid to individual projects will not normally exceed fifty per cent. Activities to be supported will include vocational training, assistance for the relief of unemployment, rural tourism, development of small firms and craft enterprises and the marketing of local produce. The County Development

Teams have had considerable involvement in the preparation and submission of business plans for their areas. In addition, some are directly involved in the administration of individual approved programmes.

## Conclusion

This chapter has endeavoured, to chart the origin, evolution, role and functions of the County Development Team system in the Western Designated Areas of the Republic of Ireland. It has also attempted to describe the various funding programmes relevant to rural development in which the Teams are involved. The operation of these programmes represents only part of the work of Teams in the area of rural development. Much of their time is spent on the provision of encouragement, guidance and support to emerging entrepreneurs and community organisations. Teams have never been big budget organisations. In the main, apart from administration of the schemes described, they operate as mediators between individuals and grant-giving agencies, between non-statutory groups and public authorities, and they provide essential liaison between county and central departments. They provide inputs to both the decision-making about and implementation of local development projects. The government has decided to convey to County Development Teams responsibility for implementation (in the Western Areas) of the national rural development programme. Given the current problems in the rural economy, the challenge to arrest population decline and stimulate the required level of economic activity in rural areas, is, indeed, daunting. No single agency possesses the capacity to provide the entire policy response. However, given their pivotal position, the County Development Teams do have the capacity to make a significant contribution to the process of change.

## References


Economic and Social Committee of the European Communities (1983) *Irish border areas - information report.* ESC-84-002EN, Brussels.

Government of Ireland (1965) *Report of the inter-departmental committee on problem of small western farms.* Stationery Office, Dublin.

Lynch, C.P. and Boylan, T.A. (1991) The contribution of community development teams to rural and regional development: the implications of recent changes in industrial policy, in Varley, T., Boylan, T.A. and Cuddy, M.P. (eds) *Rural crisis: perspectives on Irish rural development*, Ch. 7, pp. 142-155, Centre for Development Studies, University College, Galway.

# 15 The pilot programme for Integrated Rural Development 1988–1990

*Eoin O'Malley*

## Introduction

The pilot programme for integrated rural development (IRD) in the Republic of Ireland operated during the two-year period October 1988 to October 1990. It was stated at the time of the launching of the pilot programme that the intention was to gain the experience necessary before considering whether to launch a nationwide IRD programme. Subsequently, it was in fact decided to proceed with a nationwide initiative. This chapter gives an account of the experience of the pilot phase; a more detailed account of that experience can be found in O'Malley (1992).

## The meaning of Integrated Rural Development

"Integrated Rural Development", or IRD, was the name given to the particular pilot programme which was operated in the Republic of Ireland in 1988-1990. However, the term "integrated rural development" has also been in use in Ireland and in other countries, for some time past, to refer to a general concept or set of concepts. However, while the term IRD has been commonly used, it does not have a single universally accepted meaning; it means somewhat different things to different people (Murray 1989). As Varley (1988, p.29) observes, integrated rural development "can be variously interpreted to mean a multi-sectoral, co-ordinated approach to development, the pursuit of growth-with-equity objectives, participative development or even environmental protectionism". More specifically, Commins (1991) and Greer and Murray (1991) present lists of the various prescriptions or elements which could be included as part of the IRD approach. These include:

- IRD should link together various projects into an integrated programme.
- IRD should involve a multi-sectoral approach to development, promoting, e.g., tourism, forestry and industry in addition to agriculture, preferably in a mutually supportive manner.
- IRD should be planned and implemented on a geographical basis.
- An IRD programme should link activities across several years (multi-annual planning).
- IRD should enhance the collaboration of statutory agencies and non-statutory organisations in development efforts.
- In the IRD approach, local people should become actively involved in identifying needs and opportunities for development in their areas, and in the implementation of projects. To this end IRD should give attention to the promotion, training and mobilisation of local leadership and initiative.
- IRD should involve a degree of devolution of powers from the central to the regional and local levels of administration.
- IRD should concentrate efforts on aiding poor areas and, more specifically, the poorer people living in such areas.

In practice, various efforts at what has been termed integrated rural development have incorporated different combinations of elements such as these. The Irish pilot IRD programme of 1988-90 involved most of these elements (with more emphasis on some than on others), but not all of them. Thus it did aim to link and promote multi-sectoral projects. It operated on a geographical basis and looked ahead over a number of years. It also sought to mobilise local leadership and initiative in order to identify and implement projects, and to encourage non-statutory or voluntary local organisations to avail of the assistance available from statutory agencies. However, the pilot programme did not involve substantial devolution of formal administrative powers. Nor did it involve an explicit concentration on the poorest areas of the country or on the needs of the poorest people in the areas where it operated, although a particular focus on the needs of such people in the areas concerned was not ruled out.

**Design and structure of the programme**

The general objective of the pilot IRD programme was to improve the employment opportunities, earning potential, quality of life and sense of community identity among people in rural areas. It aimed to achieve this by mobilising local people to work for the economic, social and cultural development of their own area, to decide on their own development priorities, and to take the initiative in bringing their own aspirations to reality. The emphasis was on fostering viable private and community enterprise, based on full utilisation of the abilities and talents of local people. Thus, the pilot programme did not aim to impose rural development from the top-down, but rather it sought to stimulate and encourage development initiatives coming from the bottom-up.

The pilot programme operated in twelve selected rural areas, which are shown in Figure 15.1. Most of these areas have a population of between 6,000 and 15,000 people, although the population of Inishowen is larger at almost 30,000 while the population of each of the two groups of islands is less than 2,000. In choosing the pilot areas, it was intended to select a variety of areas which would be broadly representative of the variety of rural districts in the country, with a good geographical spread. In practice, the twelve areas selected were somewhat more representative of the western than the eastern half of the country.

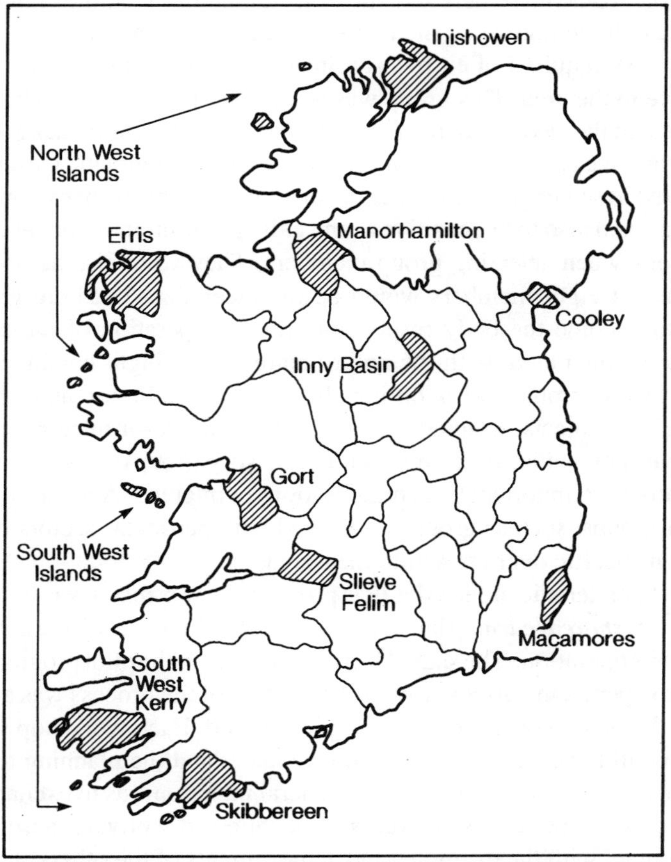


**Figure 15.1 Location of Integrated Rural Development pilot areas in the Republic of Ireland**

The overall design and subsequent management of the pilot programme, and the training of the full-time staff engaged in it, were entrusted to consultants from outside the civil service. These consultants, together with senior civil servants from the Department of Agriculture and Food, constituted a "planning team". This planning team held regular meetings during the course of the programme to review progress and to resolve any operational problems arising. The programme design allowed for a full-time rural development co-ordinator to be appointed to each pilot area. The task of the co-ordinators was to stimulate their local communities to consider new activities and developments, to encourage them to come up with new initiatives, to give practical assistance in implementing such initiatives, and to liaise with existing advisory and developmental agencies and with local voluntary organisations. It was not intended that the co-ordinators would be leaders and initiators; rather they would stimulate, assist and facilitate the initiatives of members of the local community.

The first task required of each co-ordinator was to organise a core group of local people in the area. This group was to consist of individuals with a strong commitment to the development of the area and a willingness to make the effort, on a voluntary basis, necessary to bring about such development. Co-ordinators were advised to select group members with a variety of relevant experience and competence, and also to be sensitive to any existing community or development organisations when selecting group members. They were also advised that a group of about eight members would be the ideal size. The core group was intended to become the body responsible for the operation of the pilot programme in its own area, with the co-ordinator increasingly handing over the initiative to the group and adopting the role of facilitator and adviser in implementing projects selected by the group. The co-ordinators were also advised that they could, if desired, set up advisory groups in order to involve representatives of important local organisations or interests. And they could also set up sub-groups, such as groups concerned with particular sectors or groups focusing on specific districts within their areas.

A basic characteristic of the pilot IRD programme was that it was built around the concept of *shared learning* between all the individuals and all the core groups engaged in its operation. The shared learning process in the pilot programme was designed to operate in various ways. A key aspect of the process was a series of four workshops held over the two-year pilot period. Each workshop was to be attended by all the core groups, the co-ordinators and the planning team. The agenda for each workshop varied, but a general intention was to exchange ideas and to report on experiences, as well as to inspire and motivate those involved through contact with the examples and achievements of the others. The timing and agendas of the workshops were also intended to set a quite ambitious pace for achieving results, and to communicate a work ethic and seriousness of purpose. The shared learning process was also intended to operate by individual core group members benefiting from interaction with their fellow members. In addition, the co-ordinators were to meet each month, together with members of the planning team, to share experiences, discuss progress and problems, and to receive further training and guidance.

Finally, each pilot area was to be twinned with another, and the co-ordinators and core groups from the two areas were to visit each other at regular intervals to compare problems, discuss solutions, exchange ideas and assess progress and aspirations. In the second half of the pilot programme, the twinning system was revised and became a more flexible networking arrangement. This allowed core groups, or some members of them, to visit other areas in which they had a special interest related to their own development projects.

It was intended from the start that little additional funding would be made available to finance projects emerging as a result of the pilot programme. Rather, it was aimed to ensure that effective use would be made of existing financial resources, as well as the services, expertise and financial assistance available from state development agencies. The only finance made available under the pilot programme itself to help get potential projects started was a small technical assistance fund. Aid was made available from this fund to meet part of the cost of obtaining professional advice or assistance required to advance projects which were identified by the core groups. The total amount available for such technical assistance was IR£126,000 over the two-year pilot period and the total cost of the pilot programme was IR£1.5 million, most of which was contributed by the EC.

A basic feature of the programme was that each core group was encouraged to identify the needs and potential of its own area, and to pursue its chosen objectives in a manner which it judged most appropriate. No restriction was placed on the type of project, or the sectors or range of activities which might be pursued. The only requirement was that actions undertaken should be aimed at the development of the area, in accordance with the wishes of the local community. Thus, there were no very precise expectations about what sort of initiatives would emerge from the pilot programme, although it was envisaged that the core groups might aim to foster small or medium-size enterprises, agricultural diversification, rural tourism and amenity and social improvements.

## The operation of the pilot programme

In general, the programme of training for the co-ordinators, the workshops, the monthly meetings of the co-ordinators and members of the planning team, and the other formal events and activities which were intended to be held under the pilot programme, operated as planned. The first training session for co-ordinators was held at the start of the pilot period and subsequent training sessions were held during the course of the programme. The core groups were largely formed in the first two months, in time for the first introductory workshop in November 1988, and there was a good attendance at that workshop. The core groups generally met regularly and they had provisional lists of projects or types of projects, which they would aim to foster, ready for presentation at the second workshop in March 1989. Twinning and networking visits between core groups took place during the programme, as intended. The core groups also set up a number of sub-groups for specific purposes. At the third and fourth workshops, held in November 1989 and May 1990, the core groups reported on progress on their selected projects and these two events were well attended.

The formal events and activities held under the IRD pilot programme can be summarised statistically as follows:

| | |
|---|---|
| Number of Workshops | 4 |
| Number of Co-ordinators' Meetings/Training Sessions | 22 |
| Number of Core Group Meetings | 274 |
| Number of Sub-group Meetings | More than 380 |
| Number of Twinning Meetings | 17 |
| Number of Networking Visits | 34 |
| Number of Public Meetings | 156 |

## Getting the pilot programme established

In getting the pilot programme established, the co-ordinators had to familiarise themselves with their pilot areas and select a core group. Together with their core groups, they then prepared profiles of their areas for presentation to all the other core groups at the first workshop. The co-ordinators generally began by making contact with bodies such as existing community councils and development associations, state development agencies, local authorities, sporting organisations, the Irish Countrywomen's Association, co-operatives and farmers' organisations, as well as local councillors, clergy and business people. By such meetings and contacts, the co-ordinators were able to reach decisions about who to invite to participate in the core groups.

Most of the core groups ended up being a little larger than the originally envisaged eight members. Relative to the pilot areas' population as a whole, the core group members included a high proportion of managers, business people and professional people; between them, these categories accounted for 57 per cent of the core group members. There was also a relatively high proportion of public administration employees, many of them involved in development activities. Farming was also quite well represented. Other occupations had a very limited presence in the core groups. As was intended, most of the core group members had a record of voluntary involvement in local organisations and development activities and indeed many of them were active in more than one such organisation. Thus, once the core groups were established, contacts with local community organisations were thereby consolidated.

## Project activity in the pilot programme

During the course of the pilot programme, each core group identified and selected a number of ideas for projects which it aimed to advance for the purpose of furthering the economic and social development of the area concerned. The groups' activity was then largely focused on furthering the implementation of their agreed priority projects. The twelve core groups combined settled on a total of 397 priority projects. These projects, however, were not all fully implemented by the end of the two years of the pilot programme, since many of them were then still in the planning stage or the early stages of implementation. The priority projects covered a very diverse range of activities. Classified by sector, they were distributed as shown in Table 15.1. While close to one-fifth of the projects were concerned with community development or social and cultural objectives, the large majority of them were overtly productive in character, aiming to make a contribution to the local economy, whether by giving employment or by generating additional incomes.

**Table 15.1**
**Distribution of projects by sector**

| Sector | Number of projects | Percentage of projects |
|---|---|---|
| Primary agriculture | 25 | 6.3 |
| Alternative farm enterprise | 38 | 9.6 |
| Tourism | 111 | 28.0 |
| Heritage | 24 | 6.0 |
| Social/cultural | 33 | 8.3 |
| Community development | 36 | 9.1 |
| Small and medium-size enterprise: | | |
| - Manufacturing | 17 | 4.3 |
| - Processing | 9 | 2.3 |
| - Services | 8 | 2.0 |
| Infrastructure | 24 | 6.0 |
| Aquaculture/mariculture | 29 | 7.3 |
| Other* | 43 | 10.8 |
| Total | 397 | 100.0 |

* *Note:* The "Other" category includes some multi-sectoral projects as well as environmental projects, among others.

The core groups' priority projects included some which were completely new and were initiated during the pilot IRD programme, while others involved giving impetus to existing initiatives. About two-thirds of the priority projects were in the first category while the remainder related to existing initiatives. To understand the role of the core groups in developing their projects, it is necessary to bear in mind that the core groups, by design, did not constitute companies or business entities. Consequently, the core groups were not in a position to undertake directly the implementation of most of their priority projects, so that they needed to work with some sort of project promoter on most of them. The core groups worked with various types of promoters on different projects. Almost half of the projects were promoted by local community groups or development associations, a further 11 per cent were promoted by co-operatives, and 30 per cent were promoted by private companies or individual entrepreneurs.

Basically, the role of the core groups and co-ordinators was to act as catalysts, in a manner that was additional and complementary to the activities of local groups and associations, State development agencies, local authorities and private enterprises. The core groups generated or identified ideas for projects, they sought out suitable promoters, and with the full-time assistance of the co-ordinators they identified sources of funding, organised various forms of assistance for promoters, and frequently brought together and co-ordinated numbers of people or organisations as required for individual projects.

## Views of the co-ordinators

At the end of the pilot programme, most of the co-ordinators were distinctly positive in their overall assessment of it. In a written report, they considered it a "privilege" to have participated in it and they felt that the programme was "unique and refreshing in its approach and progressive in its outlook". They also concluded that the design of the programme was effective in mobilising local human resources and providing a structured approach to community-based development. They considered, too, that the IRD pilot programme, in a relatively short period of time, brought about real beneficial change in the pilot areas. On the basis of their experiences, therefore, they recommended retaining in any future programme the key elements of the programme design, including core groups, workshops, networking, technical assistance funding, state-paid co-ordinators, professional consultants and a planning team and monthly co-ordinator meetings. Against this background of overall satisfaction with the pilot programme, however, the co-ordinators were also somewhat critical of certain aspects, and they made a number of recommendations for changes in any future programme.

## Views of the core groups

At the end of the pilot programme, each of the core groups prepared a report on their own experiences and views. Like the co-ordinators, the core groups were generally positive in their overall assessment of the pilot programme. They mostly approved of its general approach and most of the principal elements of the programme design, and they wanted to see it continue, although with various suggested modifications. Against this background of prevailing overall approval, most of the core groups had some criticisms and recommendations for changes or modifications in a follow-up programme, but there was little agreement between them on these. The core groups were asked to recommend in their reports which elements of the pilot programme should be retained and which should be changed or modified in a future programme. Nearly all of the core groups recommended retaining co-ordinators, core groups, workshops, twinning/networking (with rather more specific mention of networking than twinning) and technical assistance funding. There was also much support for retaining the bottom-up approach and the planning team. As regards changes or modifications, the only recommendation which was put forward by a majority of the groups was to provide more financial assistance, including more technical assistance funding and/or more broadly applied funding for purposes such as feasibility studies and seed capital.

## Impact of the pilot programme

In considering whether the pilot programme was a success, it is significant that the prevailing overall view among the co-ordinators and the core group members was that it was very worthwhile. In particular, in the case of the core group members, it should be borne in mind that their participation in the pilot programme was entirely voluntary and unpaid. There was no very strong incentive for them to stay with it (as nearly all of them did), or to pronounce it an overall success and to recommend its continuation, unless they really felt that it was achieving worthwhile results for their area.

While the main participants in the pilot programme mostly regarded it as successful and worthwhile, it is rather difficult to assess its impact objectively in quantitative terms. This is so for a number of reasons. First, two years is too short a period of time for a programme aiming to foster economic and social development to be able to demonstrate its impact fully. Many of the projects selected were still in the planning stage or at the very early stages of implementation when the pilot period concluded, and consequently they had yet to deliver the full expected results. A second difficulty in measuring the effects of the programme is that much of what was undertaken in it involved making some contribution to projects rather than taking sole responsibility for implementing them. Core groups and co-ordinators initiated and assisted many projects and in some cases helped to build on existing projects, but in most cases external promoters did much of the work, often with the assistance of public bodies and agencies. Thus, quite frequently, the IRD participants could not be fully credited with all the results since others also made major contributions. This naturally creates a basic conceptual difficulty in measuring the impact of the IRD programme *per se*. A third difficulty in measuring the effects of the pilot programme is that a significant minority of the projects undertaken had inherently non-quantifiable social objectives.

Despite these problems in assessing the full results of the pilot programme in a quantitative manner, it is at least possible to say that the projects undertaken had already generated significant employment and incomes by the end of the pilot period. If the full expected results were to be eventually attained, or even mostly attained, the outcome would be impressive. While it would be too much to claim, certainly after just two years' experience, that the approach of the pilot IRD programme could substantially transform rural areas, it did look likely that it could make a distinctly useful contribution to economic and social development.

The method of operation of the pilot programme meant that, for relatively small expenditures on employing paid staff, the voluntary efforts of much larger numbers of people were mobilised. With twelve full-time paid co-ordinators together with quite intensive management and guidance as well as administrative back-up, the programme secured the involvement of about 125-130 core group members (the precise number varied). It also involved a larger number of sub-group members, and stimulated new efforts by many members of other local organisations and other project promoters. Given this high level of voluntary work (or at least unpaid by the state) in relation to the numbers of paid staff, the programme probably gave good value for money.

## Conclusion

The pilot programme sought to bring to rural development policy a programme with an IRD approach. The term "IRD", however, does not have a single generally accepted meaning. In the case of the Irish pilot programme, it meant a programme aiming to link and promote multi-sectoral projects, on an area basis, over a number of years. It also meant aiming to mobilise local leadership and initiative, and to encourage non-statutory or voluntary organisations to foster development projects while availing of the assistance available from statutory agencies. A further point of considerable importance was that it incorporated the notion that systematic learning and sharing of ideas, experience and information can be beneficial in a process of participative change and development. The pilot programme demonstrated that the approach adopted is capable of stimulating considerable voluntary efforts by local people to promote economic and social development in their own areas. It was clear, too, that those involved generally found the experience worthwhile and looked forward to continuation of the programme in some form. In terms of what it aimed to achieve, the programme could be regarded as successful, providing good grounds for continuing with this approach, with appropriate modifications.

While the pilot programme stimulated and encouraged initiatives coming from local communities themselves, it needs to be recognised that this was not spontaneous and that the programme worked through a focused, directed and quite conscious process. The initiatives taken on projects were genuinely local, but there was systematic central guidance of the overall process. Establishing and guiding the process took considerable care, and attention.

The pilot IRD programme itself offered little in the way of new direct financial assistance for development projects, although it did facilitate people in drawing on financial assistance from existing development agencies and other sources. Apart from this, what it did as a means of promoting development efforts was to stimulate new thinking and initiatives, promote the exchange of ideas and information, and co-ordinate and harness the available resources and efforts of many people. Thus, what it offered as a means of promoting development was partly stimulation and support of enterprise, in the broadest sense. But more than this, it became evident from many of the projects which emerged that, quite apart from the quality or spirit of enterprise of individuals, there are certain types of project activity which can be initiated and developed more effectively through the process of co-ordinating and linking people. This made it possible for some things to be done which would have been unlikely or much slower to happen simply by relying on enterprising individuals in isolation.

## References


Commins, P. (1991) *Rural change and development in the Republic of Ireland: global forces and local responses*. Paper to the Annual Conference of the Sociological Association of Ireland, Termonfeckin.

Greer, J.V. and Murray, M.R. (1991) *Rural development in Northern Ireland: connecting the bottom up and top down approaches*. Paper to the Annual Conference of the Sociological Association of Ireland, Termonfeckin.

Murray, P. (1989) *The use of social indicators to identify areas of particular disadvantage within Ireland*. Combat Poverty Agency, Dublin.

O'Malley, E. (1992) *The pilot programme for integrated rural development 1988-90*. Broadsheet Series Paper No. 27, The Economic and Social Research Institute, Dublin.

Varley, T. (1988) *Rural development and combating poverty*. Social Sciences Research Centre, University College Galway.

# 16 Rural development and paradigm change

*Michael Murray and John Greer*

## Introduction

Rural areas in Ireland face an uncertain future. Contributions in this book have provided many insights into the contemporary limitations of orthodox policy responses to rural problems. The underlying argument is that the traditional paradigm for development is redundant and deserves to be replaced by a more appropriate set of ideas and shared beliefs for shaping rural society, economy and land use. However, the paradigm substitution process is as yet unfinished. If the integrated rural development approach espoused in Chapter 1 is to become more deeply embedded in the policy frameworks for both Northern Ireland and the Republic of Ireland there must be a significant realignment of the agenda for action and change. Accordingly, this chapter reviews briefly the theoretical provenance of paradigms and paradigm change. It then considers some of the key characteristics of the dominant paradigm for rural areas in Ireland and identifies important symptoms of crisis which are contributing to its breakdown. The final section of this chapter sets out a suite of important issues for debate and resolution among those interested in the theory and practice of rural development.

## Paradigms and paradigm change

A useful starting point in an appreciation of the theoretical foundation for policy revision is provided by Kuhn (1970) in his essay *The structure of scientific revolutions*, published originally in 1962. This work was initially addressed to physical scientists but during the interim has received a sympathetic hearing from social scientists. An important feature of this contribution to theory is the emphasis placed on the revolutionary character of scientific progress, whereby a revolution involves the abandonment of one theoretical structure and its replacement by another incompatible one. The driving force for change, it is argued, comprises the members of a scientific community whose work is structured within and directed by a distinctive intellectual framework. Kuhn labels this a "paradigm" which more specifically is defined as a:

> disciplinary matrix of theory, shared beliefs and values, and a common repertoire of problem solutions that link a scientific or professional community. (Kuhn 1970, pp. 181-182)

The hallmark of a paradigm is thus a strong technical consensus within a scientific community whose professional calling is underpinned by deep commitment to the continuation of a particular research tradition. However, Kuhn's analysis does not seek to represent a static view of scientific endeavour and in discussion of the way a science progresses, three crucial stages are identified:

(1) the appearance of anomaly: the initial paradigm is demonstrated as broadly adequate for dealing with problems; difficulties in the form of unsolved puzzles are to be expected but eventually these may be assimilated into an adjusted paradigm.

(2) the development of crisis: an anomaly will be regarded as particularly serious if it is perceived as striking at the very core of a paradigm and yet resists attempts by members of the relevant scientific community to remove it. Persistence over time combined with an increase in the number of serious anomalies promotes the development of crisis. Decreasing utility is accompanied by pronounced professional insecurity and while the initial paradigm may still survive, eventually few practitioners will remain in complete agreement about its viability. The crisis becomes real when standard solutions deemed to have resolved former problems are called into question.

(3) scientific revolution: finally the scientific community recognises that an existing paradigm has now ceased to function adequately in the exploration of an aspect of nature to which that paradigm had itself previously led the way. The paradigm is redundant and is replaced in whole or in part by an incompatible new one. Its proponents claim that the problem which initially promoted crisis can now be solved although its critics will point to other problems that remain outstanding.

Inevitably there is an iterative dimension to this process of paradigm change. But of particular importance in the context of this chapter is Kuhn's emphasis on an increasing shift in the distribution of professional allegiances as a new paradigm supplants its predecessor. The intellectual transformation is not just about the revised form of substantive theory but is akin to a spiritual conversion which subscribes at the outset to the triumph of faith over experience. Followers believe that the new paradigm will be successful notwithstanding the many large problems confronting it and the failure of the previous paradigm with only a few such limitations. The application of this perspective to the domain of public policy would suggest that a paradigm which informs policy formulation and implementation can not only become obsolete but can also be dismissed as unhelpful by the relevant policy community. The first step involves a limited number of supporters who over time can develop the paradigm to a point where robust arguments can be produced and multiplied. This book on rural development in Ireland fits well with these concerns by seeking to offer a contribution to the debate on policy succession.

## The dominant paradigm and crisis

Policy for rural areas in Ireland has long mirrored the post war policies introduced in Great Britain and designed to produce more and cheaper food, to protect against the loss of agricultural land and, especially in Northern Ireland, to retain the natural character of the countryside. As Curry notes in Chapter 2 one effect of this dominant approach has been that town and country are seen as opposites. The imperative for urban areas is land development with that for the countryside being resource conservation. This position demonstrates little affinity with a rural society more complex than perceived. Indeed a misplaced paternalistic view has held sway that rural people can and want to avail of better social and economic opportunity in urban areas and therefore want to live in that environment. Marsden et al (1992) suggest that there is much evidence to dispel the myth that high levels of mobility, related to either residence or work, tend to reduce an individual's commitment to the relevance and distinctiveness of rural places. Those who live in rural areas invariably seek a rurality apart from the urban existence and assume that public policy can help to deliver this. Chapters 10, 11 and 12 dealing with rural housing, rural primary schools and rural health care demonstrate well the need for a new sensitivity to the preferences and expectations of rural people. Inevitably a more complete transformation of the policy framework, traditionally associated with geographical concentration, requires new ways of thinking about resource efficiency and the social obligation of equity.

A second feature of the dominant paradigm for rural areas in Ireland has been the view that effective landscape protection is dependent upon rural planning control. In Chapter 9 Milton's analysis of pre and post Cockcroft policy in Northern Ireland encapsulates the debate on how the countryside should look. Comparable concerns about landscape amenity and the need for more restrictive development control to ward off excessive "bungalow blitz" have been voiced in the Republic of Ireland (see McDonald 1987). However, recognition that the countryside is itself a managed resource whose quality depends upon the underlying characteristics of the rural economy and society has featured little in the advocacy of greater restraint. Strict controls on development are valid within the environs of urban areas (Murray 1991) but the application of a policy norm which places landscape before people and community across the whole of rural Ireland has little merit. Thus Moss and Chilton's review of the operation of the Mourne and Slieve Croob Environmentally Sensitive Area Scheme in Chapter 5 provides a timely argument for integrating farm practices more closely with environmental management concepts and fits well with the wider re-formulation of productionist agricultural policies. A lived-in landscape is an essential part of this adaptation.

A related issue is that those rural areas of scenic beauty, perhaps designated as National Parks (in the Republic of Ireland) or Areas of Outstanding Natural Beauty (in Northern Ireland), have traditionally been perceived as places for recreation and tourism. In Chapter 9 Milton suggests that with an ever increasing number of facilities and higher participation levels it may well be the case that the landscape lobby will find itself opposing the recreational use of the countryside in order to protect its interests. Those rural communities which look to tourism for local economic regeneration, as illustrated by Keane in Chapter 8, may well become embroiled in this difference of perceptions. Already the conflict between amenity protection and local development has surfaced in Ireland in regard to the siting of interpretative centres in heritage landscapes (see Colleran 1992). These tensions are perhaps symptomatic of a deeper dichotomy between the perceived responsibilities of planning control and opportunities afforded by environmental management.

A third longstanding characteristic of the dominant paradigm for rural Ireland is the absence, until lately, of any profiled response by governments to the plight of disadvantaged areas. As noted in Chapter 3 by Commins and Chapter 4 by Murray and Greer the contribution of external stimuli has been important in bringing rural development on to the policy agenda. The influence of the European Commission has been especially significant over a period when it has been grappling with the need for reform of support measures. One consequence of this adjustment has been the launching of a large number of programmes, often with pilot status. It may well be questioned whether such initiatives, which within a global budgetary context command modest resources, really do represent an optimum commitment to addressing the specific problems of rural economy and society. Employment and wealth creation remain key objectives in rural areas and while the chapters by Ní Dhubháin on forestry, Hart on enterprise and Keane on tourism point to potential opportunities, the overarching conclusion must be that progress on these fronts will be modest in the short run *vis a vis* the scale of the unemployment and underemployment problems.

A final consideration in regard to the dominant paradigm for rural areas and its contemporary breakdown is the relationship between state and community. Government in both Northern Ireland and the Republic of Ireland is highly centralized and is organised across a series of departments; bureaucratic arrangements have traditionally been aligned vertically within individual departments rather than horizontally across several departments and downwards to local areas. In the Republic of Ireland one response to the difficulties of targeting policy has been the establishment of County Development Teams which, as Reynolds notes in Chapter 14, have forged some useful links between local initiative and government agencies. In February 1993 the Irish Government detailed its commitment to the establishment of County Enterprise Partnership Boards. A key feature of their role is responsibility for promoting and assisting integrated local development plans in consultation with community organisations, employers, trade unions and the public sector at local level. In Northern Ireland the stunted responsiveness of centralised government to local circumstances has long been exacerbated by the limited developmental responsibilities of district councils following their reorganisation in the 1970s. The newly established structures for rural development described in Chapter 4 demonstrate recognition of policy omission in the past. However, it remains questionable whether there still is an optimum targeting of public sector resources on disadvantaged rural areas.

The significance of these adjustments lies with the weight now given to the involvement of the rural constituency in thinking more about the future and putting into practice its ideas for securing that future. In Chapter 13 McGinley's account of the ways in which one District Council in Northern Ireland is working with rural people by providing scope for inputs into strategic policy making captures one aspect of this participation. O'Malley's analysis of the integrated development programme in the Republic of Ireland in Chapter 15 confirms the energy of human capital required by and available from rural communities. Across Ireland as a whole there is a new urgency attached to action and change. Rural society now holds an important enabling and facilitating role in the development process and thus needs stronger bonds with government agencies. Nowhere, perhaps, is this being put to the test more aggressively than in the West of Ireland where a new regional initiative "Developing the West Together" is seeking to challenge traditional policy responses to acute disadvantage. A major study of this area, funded by the European Commission is due to report in 1993. Its guiding vision is the empowerment of local communities which, as McInerney (1993) suggests, requires strategic direction, adequate resources and technical assistance. However, the paradigm substitution process which can nurture this bottom-up capacity is far from complete. Varley (1991) provides a salutary reminder of the fact that the basic parameters of rural development programmes, comprising content guidelines, localities to be included, the role of partners, the money to be spent or levered in and the timetables, are all decided in advance by the state perhaps in partnership with the European Commission. Community groups are not yet equal members of the policy community.

**Realigning the policy agenda**

The rural development challenge in Ireland shares many of the difficulties, influences and opportunities faced by other late 20th century advanced capitalist economies on the periphery of Europe. The future of rural areas remains inextricably linked to the outcome of the reform of the Common Agricultural Policy, the resolution of negotiations on the General Agreement on Tariffs and Trade and the effect of market penetration by farm products from central and eastern Europe. The single market programme will intensify the process of industrial restructuring by which, for example, agribusiness will not remain unaffected. In short, peripheral regions can be expected to face continuing handicaps *vis a vis* core areas in Europe in regard to economic development. These circumstances dictate that endogenous regional development must be central to the future policy agenda. Stöhr (1985) has detailed this approach as follows:

(1) the use of development strategies which are widely differentiated with respect to the historical, cultural, institutional and physical conditions existing in different areas and which seek to mobilize the broadest range of local and regional resources;

(2) the deployment of initiatives which give priority to the production of goods and services considered to be socially valuable in regions and which are not sufficiently taken care of by the market mechanism;

(3) participation which is organised on an enterprise related, sector related, or primarily territorial basis; this is viewed as a necessary but not sufficient pre-condition for development;

(4) initiatives which aim at more diversified and multi-sectoral economies with greater interaction between activities within individual regions;

(5) the promotion of regional economic and financial circuits which can facilitate the retention of a higher share of added value within individual regions, can safeguard regional investment requirements, can increase innovative capacity and can create a greater resilience against global economic shocks;

(6) innovation in the organisational and institutional spheres, such as in forms of decision making and co-operation;

(7) promotion of territorial identity to assist the process of collaboration among diverse interest groups;

(8) greater integration at the regional level of decision making structures with economic activities and local populations;

(9) the promotion by central governments of trans-regional linkages for co-operation.

This prescriptive inventory has important implications for Ireland and, if nothing else, makes the case that the future for rural areas must be closely linked to regional policy. As Cuddy (1991) remarks:

> The economic and social future of rural Ireland cannot be distinguished from the future of Ireland and its regions. The future of both depends on the capacity to formulate and implement development policies within Ireland and on the evolving relationship between Ireland and the European Community.

It is now appropriate, therefore, to identify a number of pressing issues for consideration by the rural policy community. The matters raised are crucial to the establishment of a new paradigm for integrated rural development in Ireland.

*(1) Policy vision*

At present neither the Republic of Ireland nor Northern Ireland appear to have a guiding vision for the future of rural society, economy and environment. One result of this shortcoming is a lack of co-ordination between government departments, agencies, interest groups and local communities which are involved in rural development. In the Republic, for instance, it is questionable whether there is a coherent rural policy even though a plethora of rural measures and schemes have been advanced. Rural development really is in urgent need of a guiding philosophy to inform policy formulation and delivery. As a first step, greater visibility, clarity and certainty for rural objectives could be introduced into the corporate plans of public agencies on both sides of the border. Moreover, an integrated approach should influence policy for rural communities, the key principles of which should be similar to those set out at the start of this section.

*(2) Structures for policy delivery*

Rural development currently places much emphasis on collaboration between local communities, private enterprise and statutory agencies as well as multi-dimensional programmes instead of single projects. The capacity for integrated action is set against strong traditions of administrative territoriality which can impair commitment to joint and collaborative schemes. Rural development requires close links between central government agencies and local implementation so that policy bottlenecks and obstacles can be addressed quickly. It is, perhaps, paradoxical that it is Northern Ireland, coming from an urban policy tradition, and not the Republic of Ireland with its longer association with rural issues, that has established an apparatus for policy delivery that comes closest to this requirement. Particularly important is the bridge between top-down and bottom-up approaches provided by the Rural Development Council. Monitoring and evaluation of the different structures for policy delivery in Ireland must be a priority. Moreover, it is important that findings are disseminated among those with an interest in rural development in order to build up the necessary intellectual support for shared learning and policy succession.

*(3) Regional planning*

Regional planning in Ireland has traditionally had an urban bias with public and private sector capital investment being targeted at a select number of centres. Notwithstanding the passive role ascribed to rural hinterlands within this planning context, it is the case that a constellation of economically vibrant towns can have a positive impact not only at a regional scale but also on local rural communities. It is important that this contribution by urban areas should continue to be recognised by policy makers but in a manner which is supportive of the need for greater interdependence between country and town. Armstrong (1992) has succinctly summarized this relationship in respect of Northern Ireland:

While we have certainly come to question whether the growth centre concept can or should be used as a solution for rural disadvantage, this does not deny the importance of the social, administrative, and economic links between the district towns and their surrounding rural hinterland. It is important, therefore, that the coherence of the urban region approach is retained in any new physical planning strategy.

There is also a wider dimension to regional planning that should be noted. The peripherality of the island of Ireland within the European Community demands that full use is made of its locational advantages if it is effectively to combat an ever greater concentration of investment in core regions during the 1990s and beyond. A key issue here is how to effect a shift towards closer economic partnership between Northern Ireland and the Republic of Ireland so as to give Ireland a new competitive edge as a single economic entity. At present Ireland is included in the EC Border Areas Programme (INTERREG) and investment plans relating to transport and communications, tourism, environmental protection and waste disposal have been prepared. Co-operation, however, is still regarded as being inter-state rather than truly inter-regional and while structures for cross-border discussion and information exchange are quite well developed there is, as suggested by the Commission of the European Communities (1991), a need to move towards a more committed expression of regional and sectoral planning which can generate integrated cross-border action programmes.

### *(4) Sustaining community involvement*

With an ever increasing number of local groups seeking to become involved in the process of rural regeneration, a key challenge facing policy makers must be sustaining community involvement. The investment of human capital is high in terms of the sheer number of people participating and the time allocated by individuals, often voluntarily. The preparation of project submissions makes imperative the collection, analysis and presentation of data on a host of subjects. It is often the case that data are not available from published sources, due to the fine grain of the material involved and thus local surveys are considered necessary to legitimise the process of needs identification. Acquisition of such data is both difficult and expensive. Moreover local communities, even when they have the services of a full-time project officer, must consult and negotiate with a very wide spectrum of agencies in order to advance any development proposal. This is again time consuming and often exasperating because while government departments and agencies have time and resources on their side, local communities do not. Delays in the progress of processing proposals can cause disillusionment in communities and entropy can all too easily occur, making the job of a project officer even more difficult, coming as it does on top of other problems of animating the community and ironing out differences of opinion and attitude. There is, therefore, a clear need for mutual support by rural development groups which combines the sharing of experiences, the gathering of information and the pursuit of joint ventures. A key issue must be how to best achieve this networking activity.

An allied issue in regard to community involvement in rural development is the apparent under-representation of women in local initiatives. Byrne et al (1993) have identified that the literature on women's experience and perception of rural living is scant. However, research on women in the rural world has now commenced in both the Republic of Ireland and Northern Ireland. It is designed to establish the extent to which women feel that their needs are reflected in the work of local development groups, how accessible local development groups are to women and what factors contribute to female participation in development groups (Hobson and Clarke 1993).

### *(5) Environment*

A longstanding tension in rural areas of Northern Ireland is between development and landscape protection interests, a concern echoed more recently within the Republic of Ireland in regard to rural housing and tourism infrastructure. Frequently the pursuit of landscape protection is incompatible with measures intended to strengthen local rural economies. As a result, it is important that the environment is inserted into the development process (Mack 1991). In this respect the concept of sustainable development which allows for present needs to be met without compromising the ability of future generations to meet their own needs is appropriate (Brundtland 1987). This concept seems especially relevant when dealing with recreation and tourism pressures in areas with landscapes of scenic importance. Indeed many of the tourism development projects advanced by rural community groups and local authorities could fit within this framework.

### *(6) Education and training*

If rural development in Ireland is to be a success there is a need to build up professional skill and confidence. Towards this end rural development must cease being viewed as a geographical or conceptual dimension of other kinds of economic or social activity. There is a tendency for education and training to be strongly sectoral extending across agriculture and forestry, through craft industry, business management, leisure and tourism, to environmental conservation, town and country planning and community development. However, the very essence of rural development is that it is integrative in nature and should be acknowledged as such in curriculum planning and provision. Progress on this front is encouraging: within the Republic of Ireland a suite of courses relating to rural development are offered at University College Galway (since 1985) and University College Dublin (from 1992). Experience suggests that a successful programme not only requires inputs from a wide range of academic disciplines but also depends upon contributions from policy makers and practitioners. In Northern Ireland the long overdue provision of training and education in this field presents an opportunity for collaboration between the two universities in the region with institutions in the Republic. Reaching out to the rural constituency itself through the provision of extra mural teaching programmes is a further issue to be addressed. All in all, a failure to invest in human capital will create an impenetrable barrier to the achievement of a deep and sustained rural consciousness.

*(7) Capacity building*

In simple terms, capacity building can be defined as "increasing the ability of people and institutions to do what is required of them" (Newland 1981). It necessitates the forging of new skills within rural communities related to leadership, mediation and conflict resolution, group processes, understanding the business of government organisations, and the articulation and achievement of community visions. The goal is to secure the empowerment of rural people to better manage their own affairs, thus reducing dependency on state intervention. The concept looks to positive attitudes and constructive approaches for the promotion of change. The benefits of capacity building processes have been succinctly summarised by Luther and Wall (1989):

- evidence of strategic thinking by community leaders, which draws upon historical strengths and an appreciation of new opportunities;
- the presence of an entrepreneurial spirit, which is prepared to be creative in community problem solving;
- an orientation towards positive attitudes and action, based on a confidence that local people can make a better future for themselves;
- evidence of a planned programme for community improvement, which may include responding to the challenge of economic development through organised action;
- a thoughtful approach to the future, which is concerned with wider quality of life issues in the local community.

Arriving at this outcome requires time and commitment by a range of participants. Outside involvement by community animateurs, whose brief is wider than group formation, would seem a necessary prerequisite. But as suggested by Brown and Glasgow (1991), the emphasis on capacity building is to lessen dependency on outside experts and institutionalise capacity into a local community's permanent structure. In short the contribution made by the process of capacity building to rural development in Ireland is as important as product investment.

*(8) Research*

This is not the place to construct detailed research agendas but nevertheless it would seem de rigueur to identify some important directions for future work. More baseline studies on the condition of the rural constituency are needed in order to ground policy more deeply in the physical, sociological and economic milieu of rural living. At the same time the commitment of the policy community to the challenges of rural regeneration deserves close scrutiny. The critical requirement here is for effective delivery mechanisms which in turn points to the importance of early and sustained monitoring research embracing the methodology and content, advocacy and receptiveness, implementation and impact of local development programmes and the performance of different actors in the development process. But this essentially indigenous activity must also be complemented by wider comparative research in the reasonable supposition that an understanding of rural development based on the intensive study of different socio-economic, cultural and political contexts can help widen a parochial perspective. One of the problems which bedevils research on rural development in Ireland is the geographical spread and often isolation of committed individuals. Operationalizing the concept of the "invisible college" would in the first instance provide a useful forum for regular debate and exchange of ideas among those whose common interest is rural development and whose shared commitment is to paradigm redundancy and substitution.

## Conclusion

Within Ireland rural development is now a matter of some consequence. This book has reviewed key initiatives taken to date and has concluded by devising an agenda of issues for future policy formulation and implementation. A particular concern has been to dispel the popular view among policy makers (and some academics) that rural development is a subset of agriculture. Rather, rural development has an integrity of its own. Within the theoretical framework of paradigm change it is suggested that there are sufficient serious anomalies in the dominant intellectual model to warrant recognition of a crisis condition. In

Kuhn's words this could pave the way for a subsequent scientific revolution. While political and bureaucratic pragmatism in the formation and delivery of rural policies will play a major part in conditioning the outcome it is argued here that only a strong commitment to the prescription offered above by the rural policy community within the island of Ireland, in partnership with the European Commission, will provide the necessary transformation.

**References**


Armstrong, J. (1992) *Rural development in Northern Ireland - an overview.* Paper presented at the Annual Conference of the Irish Planning Institute, 30 April - 1 May, Newcastle.

Brown, D.L. and Glasgow, N.A. (1991) Capacity building and rural government adaptation to population change, in Flora, C. and Christensen, J.A. (eds) *Rural policies for the 1990s.* Ch. 16, pp. 194-208, Westview Press, Boulder.

Brundtland, G.H. (1987) *Our common future.* The World Commission on Environment and Development, Oxford University Press, Oxford.

Byrne, A., Lymer, B. and Owens, M. (1993) *Women in the rural world : the rural women's research project.* Paper presented at ESRC Workshop on Agriculture and Rural Development, 3 February, The Queen's University of Belfast.

Colleran, E. (1992) Interpretative centres, tourism and the environment in Ireland, in Feehan, J. (ed) *Environment and development in Ireland.* pp. 583-587, The Environmental Institute, University College Dublin.

Commission of the European Communities (1991) *Europe 2000.* Brussels.

Cuddy, M. (1991) *What future for rural Ireland? Rural development in a market economy.* The R.T.E. Open-Mind Annual Lecture, November 28, Dublin.

Hobson, T. and Clarke, P. (1993) *Rural Development Council for Northern Ireland primary research programme on women in rural development.* Paper presented at ESRC Workshop on Agriculture and Rural Development, 3 February, The Queen's University of Belfast.

Kuhn, T.S. (1970) *The structure of scientific revolutions.* International Encyclopedia of Unified Science, Vol. 2, No. 2, The University of Chicago Press, Chicago.

Luther, V. and Wall, M. (1989) *The entrepreneurial community : a strategic leadership approach to community survival.* Heartland Center for Leadership Development, Nebraska.

Mack, N. (1991) *Rurality on the periphery : the environment and the concept of rural development.* Paper presented at the Sociological Association of Ireland Annual Conference, Termonfeckin.

Marsden, T.K., Murdoch, J. and Lingham, V. (1992) Planning for social limits to growth. *Journal of the Royal Town Planning Institute*, Vol. 78, No. 4, pp. 6-7.

McDonald, F. (1987) Bungalow blitz. *Irish Times*, 12 September, 14 September and 15 September.

McInerney, C. (1993) Developing the West together : a regional initiative. *Irish Reporter*, Vol. 9, No. 1, pp. 27-28.

Murray, M. (1991) *The politics and pragmatism of urban containment: Belfast since 1940*. Avebury, Aldershot.

Newland, V. and Wall, M. (1989) Local government capacity building. *Urban Affairs Papers*, Vol. 3, No. 1.

Stöhr, W. (1985) Changing external conditions and a paradigm shift in regional development strategies?, in Musto, S.A. and Pinkele, C.F. (eds) *Europe at the crossroads : agendas of the crisis*. Ch. 15, pp. 283-307, Praeger, New York.

Varley, T. (1991) Power to the people? Community groups and rural revival in Ireland, in Reynolds, B. and Healy, S. (eds) *Rural development policy: what future for rural Ireland?* Ch. 4, pp. 83-110, Conference of Major Religious Superiors (Ireland), Dublin.